PRESIDENTS AND POLITICS
The Limits of Power

CHARLES FUNDERBURK
Wright State University

BROOKS/COLE PUBLISHING COMPANY
Monterey, California

Brooks/Cole Publishing Company
A Division of Wadsworth, Inc.

Printed in the United States of America

10 9 8 7 6 5 4 3 2 1

Library of Congress Cataloging in Publication Data

Funderburk, Charles, 1943–
        Presidents and politics.

        Includes index.
        1. Presidents—United States. I. Title.
JK516.F86   353.03'1   81-15444
ISBN 0-534-01086-5   AACR2

Subject Editor: Judy Joseph

Produced by Ex Libris   Julie Kranhold
Manuscript Editor: Martha Ortlieb
Interior Design: Meryl Levavi
Cover Design: Sara Hunsaker
Illustrations: Vantage Art Studio
Typesetting: Vantage Art Studio
Cover Photo: S.M. Wakefield

Preface

The Presidency is perceived as perhaps the most powerful political office in the Western world. The high visibility of the office and the mystique surrounding it contribute to that impression. Recent events, however, illustrate that it is easy to overestimate the power of the Presidency. A realistic analysis of the Presidency encompasses the numerous constraints on the institution and the limitations on Presidential power. My objective in writing this book is to delineate and elaborate this theme in a readable and comprehensive fashion. My analysis assumes little formal experience in political science on the part of the reader.

No single framework can suffice for analyzing an institution as complex as the modern Presidency. In putting together *Presidents and Politics,* I synthesize diverse material from a wide variety of sources. In addition to research by political scientists and historians, I rely on reports by journalists and political practitioners.

The book is divided into two parts. Part One, The President and the Public, draws extensively on investigations of American political behavior to deal with the changing relationship between the President and the public. Emphasis is on the impact of changes in the Presidential selections process, as well as some difficulties Presidents face in translating public support into political power. Part Two, The Presidency, analyzes the institution of the Presidency. Specific ideas developed include: the increasing importance of the White House staff (Chapter 6), tools for managing the executive bureaucracy and the budget (Chapter 7), legislative-executive relations (Chapter 8), and the paramount importance of the President in national security policy (Chapter 9), and the importance of personality in understanding the performance of the individual in office (Chapter 10). The book concludes with a discussion of the potential for Presidential leadership in contemporary society.

In addition to the numerous scholars and commentators whose research and insights help us to understand Presidential politics, I would specifically like to acknowledge the help and support of my colleagues Robert Thobaben and James Jacob. In addition to providing comments on sections of the manuscript, their support and encouragement was indispensable. Congratulations to Mike Peters of the Dayton Daily News for winning the Pulitzer prize. Permission to reprint his cartoons is gratefully acknowledged. I would also like to express my appreciation to MacAlister Brown of Williams College, Larry Elowitz of Georgia College; Michael Menzy of DePaul University; H.L. Neiburg of State University of New York, Binghampton; Steven B. Wood of University of Rhode Island; and Margaret S. Wyzomirski of Rutgers, State University of New Jersey for reviewing the manuscript.

My personal thanks to Sandee Sherritt and Martha Jo Trent for their tireless work in typing the manuscript, and to Joyce and Scott Donald for bearing with me throughout this venture.

Charles Funderburk
July 1981

Contents

Chapter 1

The Modern Presidency

The modern Presidency is an institution of limited power and capabilities, which has become the focus of complex demands and unrealistic expectations. The American Presidency has traditionally operated within the constraints of a fragmented governmental structure and constitutional limitations on executive power. Increasing centralization of governmental authority and the primacy of the President in national security matters have converged since the Great Depression of the 1930's to promote a period of unparalleled Presidential activism. This period of intense activity by the national executive has not produced satisfactory Presidential leadership, judging by the public's evaluations of activist Presidents during the modern era.

Since the Great Depression, only three Presidents (Franklin D. Roosevelt, Dwight D. Eisenhower, and John F. Kennedy) have been able to maintain reasonably high levels of popularity during their terms of office. This may be partly attributable to the paradoxical and inconsistent nature of public expectations about the Presidency. Inflated public expectations are one consequence of an increasing emphasis on Presidential activism. There is little doubt, however, that the quality of the performance of Presidents in office during the last 20 years has contributed to widespread public dissatisfaction with political leadership. Declining public confidence in the Presidency,

1

as well as increasing cynicism about politics in general, are closely associated with the Vietnam War and the Watergate scandals.

The modern period of Presidential activism has also been characterized by considerable conflict between the Presidency and other institutions of government, particularly the Congress. Given the adversary nature of the relationship between the President and Congress, which is inherent in the American constitutional system, some degree of conflict is inevitable and may be attributed to political bickering. Of the eight Presidents since World War II, five (including Truman, Eisenhower, Nixon, Ford, and Reagan) have faced a situation of divided government in which at least one house of Congress was controlled by the opposition party. Presidents Nixon and Ford did not enjoy a partisan majority in either house of Congress. Only Kennedy, Johnson, and Carter served their terms of office with partisan majorities in both houses of Congress.

On occasion, during the period of postwar Presidential activism, conflicts between the President and Congress have transcended the bounds of routine partisan skirmishes, assuming the dimensions of a constitutional confrontation. Struggles over the limitations of executive power and privilege, the direction of national security policy, and Presidential war-making resulted in the retirement from politics of President Lyndon B. Johnson, and the resignation and near-impeachment of President Richard Nixon. This is ironic in that both Johnson and Nixon had been reelected by electoral majorities of landslide proportions. Growing popular discontent with Presidential performance was reflected in the subsequent defeat of two successive incumbent Presidents in the 1976 and 1980 elections.

The modern Presidency has undergone some fundamental transformations as an institution. Procedures for selecting Presidential candidates have been modified extensively, adding an element of unpredictability to the Presidential nominating process. Because of the proliferation of Presidential primary elections resulting from reforms in the nominating process, a key criterion in Presidential selection has become the candidate's ability to win a series of multi-candidate elections. There is growing concern among analysts that this system, which emphasizes campaign and organizational skills, may not adequately test the nominee's political and leadership abilities. In particular, the interpersonal skills of bargaining and persuasion, necessary to effective Presidential leadership, have become a secondary consideration in the nominating process. The new nominating system has enhanced prospects for little-known

(Photo by Bill Fitz-Patrick)

candidates and Washington outsiders to launch long-shot Presidential candidacies. The politics of nominating Presidents has, to a significant degree, become disconnected from politics in Washington. The process of selecting a President has become separated from the process of governing the nation.

The Presidency has expanded in size, as well as scope, assuming, in the process, some of the characteristics of a bureaucracy. Although various approaches to organizing the Presidency have been attempted, it is by now apparent that the growth of the White House organization has contributed to some of the difficulties besetting the modern Presidency. At the very least, the growth of the Presidency as an institution has contributed to a significant increase in the importance of members of the White House staff as Presidential advisers. This shift of power to the White House has accompanied a decline in influence of the Cabinet. Modern Presidents depend on the White House staff not only for advice, but increasingly for policy formulation as well. The expansion of the institutional component of the Presidency has increased the temptation for Presidents to confine their decision making to a highly cohesive and insulated group of White House loyalists.

Despite considerable institutional expansion, the Presidency retains a very personal dimension. In order to comprehend the behavior of modern Presidents, some consideration of the personalities of the individual officeholders is essential. Particularly important is the interaction between the President's personality and the institutional apparatus. The modern Presidency has exhibited a high level of potential for reflecting, or, perhaps, magnifying, the personal insecurities of its occupants.

The modern Presidency is a traditional institution which is evolving in an attempt to meet demands for political leadership in a complex modern society. In part, the dynamics of the modern Presidency reflect the tension between an activist orientation and traditional constraints imposed on executive power by other political institutions in the constitutional system. Developments since World War II suggest, however, that some of the popular dissatisfaction with Presidential leadership is related to the institution of the Presidency and the personalities of some of its occupants.

PRESIDENTIAL ACTIVISM

"The executive power shall be vested in a President of the United States of America."

Deceptive in its simplicity, elegant in its vagueness, the United States Constitution (Article II, section 1) declares the President to be the chief executive. But what does this declaration mean, and what powers does it confer? Is the President simply head of the executive branch, possessing the traditional powers of veto and appointment and removal of executive officials, or does this clause confer a constitutional *grant* of power, with limits not clearly specified? This latter interpretation (known as "inherent powers") assumes that, as chief executive, the President possesses powers that are neither expressly stated in the Constitution, nor specifically granted by the Congress.

Unquestionably, the more generous interpretation of executive power has dominated the Presidency in this century. Nonetheless, critics of the strong Presidency are inclined to inquire about the source of these powers. Inevitably, the reply is that they are "inherent" in the office, being *implied* by the executive-power clause. Since the inherent powers are nowhere clearly defined and specified, they are potentially expandable. This assumption underlies much of the expansion of Presidential power in the 20th century, and highlights an issue that has been debated by politicians, scholars, and Presidents since the origin of the Constitution. The nature and extent of Presidential power is a matter of interpretation, contingent upon a conception of the Presidential role in American politics. Presidents opt to follow paths of restraint or activism, depending on how far they are willing to push their inherent powers as chief executive and Commander in Chief.

The essence of Presidential restraint is a conservative interpretation of executive power. Specifically, executive power is construed to encompass only authority explicitly granted by the constitutional system. Exercise of executive authority must rest on a specific grant of power found in the Constitution, or an act of Congress, or be reasonably implied by such a grant as necessary to its exercise.[1] The President's primary responsibilities include dignified conduct as chief of state, efficient management of executive agencies and their budgets, veto of legislation considered to be unwise or unconstitutional, and restrained use of the powers of Commander in Chief. There are no undefined, or inherent, powers which may be exercised simply because it seems to the President to be in the public interest. With the exception of the administrations of Theodore Roosevelt and Woodrow Wilson, this interpretation dominated the 20th century Presidency until the Great Depression and the increasing importance of international affairs converged to promote a more activist role.

Presidents of the modern era have, of necessity, adopted a broader definition of executive authority. The concept of inherent powers permits the President to exercise powers other than those specifically granted by the Constitution or the Congress. Under this interpretation of executive authority, the President becomes, in the words of Theodore Roosevelt, the "steward of the people," bound to do all he can to advance the public interest. The only limits on executive power are specific restrictions in the Constitution and laws.[2] While Presidential restraint dictates that Presidents do only what they are

1. See President Taft's classic statement in *Our Chief Magistrate and His Powers.* New York: Columbia University Press, 1916, pp. 14–145.

2. See, for example, Theodore Roosevelt, "The Stewardship Theory of the Presidency" in *The Dynamics of the American Presidency,* edited by Donald B. Johnson and Jack L. Walker. New York: John Wiley and Sons, 1964, p. 136.

expressly *permitted* to do, activism encourages them to do whatever they are not legally *prohibited* from doing. This interpretation mandates strong executive leadership as a means of solving problems and managing crises. Activist Presidents are not content to be efficient managers; they seek to take the lead in shaping national priorities by initiating programs to deal with complex social and economic problems. Utilizing whatever resources are available, they bargain with Congress and the bureaucracy for their programs and the money needed to pay for them. Relying on energy, resourcefulness, and persuasion, as well as formal powers, they seek to make the Presidency a focus of public aspirations and the center of governmental activity.

The activist interpretation rests on two assumptions. The first is the claim to inherent executive powers, meaning that the only practical limits on executive power are legal prohibitions and political realities. Additionally, there is the assumption that the President's position in the political structure is unique. Being the only elected United States government official (other than the Vice President) with a nationwide constituency, the President can claim a mandate from the people. From the standpoint of democratic theory, this may be a questionable assumption, since America is approaching the point where a majority of eligible voters do not vote in Presidential elections. Be that as it may, the President frequently claims to be the "voice of the people" and, consequently, cannot be content to be merely a clerk. Activist Presidents strive to be leaders of Congress and the public because expectations about Presidential leadership in these areas have become institutionalized.

The activist Presidency has become a routine part of American politics. Demands for a more activist executive role have developed rapidly with the increasing complexity of an urban industrial society. A series of crises, including mobilization for two world wars, and the near collapse of the nation's economy during the Great Depression, have led inevitably to increasing centralization of America's economic and political affairs. The depression, in particular, led to significant modifications in American expectations about the relationship between government and the economy. With the advent of the so-called positive state, the Federal Government, and the President in particular, is now expected to provide leadership in developing policies to cope with national social and economic problems. The President is, in fact, legally required to initiate proposals dealing with unemployment, major economic dislocations and business cycles, as well as the national budget. As new programs are enacted, the size and scope of the executive branch increase, along with the President's responsibilities for oversight and management.

These factors—the increasing centralization of responsibilities for economic and political decisions in national institutions, the development of the positive state-mandating government action in economic and social matters, and the expansion of the regulatory and welfare bureaucracy it requires—have combined with the conception of inherent executive power to promote an activist role for modern-day Presidents. While modern social and political forces push Presidents in an activist direction, extensive legal and political constraints define the nature and limits of power available to activist Presidents.

PRESIDENTIAL POWER

The American President has been given an impressive array of titles and duties. It is important, however, not to confuse titles and responsibilities with *power.* The President's powers are seldom as impressive as his responsibilities, and, frequently, much less than his various titles would suggest. Clinton Rossiter's classic list of presidential roles serves to illustrate this point. The President is described as:

Chief of State
Chief Executive
Chief Diplomat
Commander in Chief
Chief Legislator
Chief of Party
Voice of the People
Protector of the Peace
Manager of Prosperity
Leader of the Free World[3]

All that is missing is Mover of Mountains and Raiser of the Dead. Such titles, or similar ones, are routinely heaped upon the President with little regard to constitutional and statutory powers, or political realities. Of this impressive list, only Commander in Chief is a title

3. Clinton Rossiter, *The American Presidency.* New York: Harcourt, Brace and Co., 1956, pp. 3–24.

bestowed by the United States Constitution. While the Constitution declares that that executive power is vested in the President, Rossiter is the first to acknowledge that, as chief executive, the President's powers are not equal to his responsibilities. This is true of all these roles except Commander in Chief, chief diplomat, and chief of state, which is largely a ceremonial and symbolic role.

Table 1.1 summarizes the relationship between formal and informal powers and constraints associated with various Presidential roles. This schematic matches the powers of the Presidency with their corresponding legal and political constraints and emphasizes the limits, as well as the powers, of the modern Presidency. In every area except military policy, each power assigned to the President by the constitutional system is carefully matched by powers given to other institutions, especially the Congress. Fundamental constitutional principles, such as separation of powers and checks and balances, shape the context in which national politics take place. The Congress cuts budgets and may override vetoes, and powerful Congressional committees routinely modify Presidential proposals. The Supreme Court can review Presidential decisions and define the limits of executive power and privilege. The concept of limited institutions sharing power continues to be the basic operating principle of American government.

The President's relationship to party and public is even more tentative, given his absence of control in these areas. Patronage, organization, and discipline are the essence of party control in government, but tight discipline has seldom been characteristic of American parties at the national level. The parochial orientation of Congress (emphasizing state and local concerns), combined with the factional nature of American parties, has made it difficult for Presidents to use party discipline effectively in their legislative struggles.

While Woodrow Wilson and Franklin D. Roosevelt were reasonably successful party chiefs in this century, they are the exceptions that prove the rule. The more typical pattern is one of party splits and infighting as developed in the Taft, Truman, Johnson, Ford, and Carter Presidencies. Taft, thanks largely to a split in the Republican party caused by Theodore Roosevelt's candidacy in 1912, bears the indignity of being the only incumbent President in this century to finish behind a third-party candidate in the popular vote and in Electoral College balloting. President Truman had to battle two other Democrats, as well as Republican Thomas Dewey, for reelection. Because of his war policies, President Lyndon B. Johnson

Table 1.1 Presidential Roles: Duties, Powers, and Constraints

Presidential Roles	Duties	Presidential Powers		Constraints
		Formal	Informal	
Head of State	Represent the United States and its government	1. Ceremony, protocol 2. Legitimacy	1. Visibility, publicity 2. Popular symbol of United States Government	1. Mostly ceremonial role 2. Decreasing public confidence in the presidency
Executive	1. Enforce laws 2. Manage crises	1. Coercion 2. Emergency powers 3. Amnesty, pardons 4. Appoint and remove executive officials	Discretion (selective enforcement)	1. Oversight by the Congress, courts, and press 2. Power of the Congress to define, delegate, and change the President's emergency powers 3. Power to appoint executive officials is shared with the Senate 4. Impeachment

Table 1.1 **Presidential Roles: Duties, Powers, and Constraints** *(continued)*

Presidential Role	Duties	Powers		Constraints
		Formal	*Informal*	
Administrative	1. Manage Federal Government bureaucracy 2. Set governmental priorities	1. Initiate Federal budget 2. Propose cuts or new programs 3. Appoint and remove top-level policy-makers 4. Impound funds	1. Administrative discretion 2. Bargain with bureaucracy over specifics of budget 3. Persuasion	1. Budgetary power is shared with the Congress 2. Legislative oversight and vetoes 3. Bureaucratic momentum: —prior commitments to existing programs —routine —civil service 4. Impoundments are subject to Congressional approval
Legislative	Propose legislative solutions for social and political problems	1. Initiative 2. Central clearance 3. Veto	1. Public and Congressional expectations 2. Visibility 3. Persuasion	1. Inaction by the Congress 2. Modification of President's program by the Congress 3. Power of the Congress to fund programs

Table 1.1 Presidential Roles: Duties, Powers, and Constraints *(continued)*

Presidential Role	Duties	Powers		Constraints
		Formal	*Informal*	
				4. Power of the Congress to override Presidential vetoes by vote of two-thirds of members
Diplomatic	1. Determine American foreign policy 2. Conduct United States foreign relations	1. Recognize foreign governments 2. Appoint ambassadors and foreign policy-makers 3. Negotiate treaties and executive agreements	High visibility and legitimacy in this sphere	1. Appointment power shared with Senate 2. Most funds for foreign aid are subject to Congressional approval 3. Treaty power shared with Senate 4. Executive agreements may require Congressional action to implement
Military	1. Protect United States national security 2. Plan United States defense strategy	1. Supreme military commander 2. Dispatch American combat forces	1. Very high visibility 2. Capacity to initiate war 3. Superiority of information and intelligence sources	1. War Powers Bill 2. Congress monitors defense budget

was challenged for renomination by two Democratic Senators and eventually decided not to seek reelection. These events, along with the experiences of Presidents Ford and Carter in being challenged by members of their own party for renomination, portray the President less like the commander of a disciplined crew, and more like the leader of a wolf pack struggling to maintain control. It is not unusual for Presidents to come to be regarded as much a liability as an asset by significant factions of their own party.

Party organizations are undergoing significant changes in this country. Neither patronage, nor the organizations it supports, can deliver the influence they once did. Under pressure of the direct primary, the organization's role in the nominating process has diminished. As the party has become less dependable, Presidents have chosen to rely more on personal organizations they can trust, and on hired services of advertising agencies, to conduct their election campaigns. The decentralized nature of American parties, combined with the increasing independence of voters, means that the President's tentative position as chief of party can be of only limited utility in bringing unity and coherence to national politics and policy.

It would seem that neither constitutional and formal powers, nor party and public support, are sufficient to insure successful Presidential leadership. A realistic appraisal of the nature and limits of Presidential power requires consideration of a third and key element—*persuasion.* This is the acid test for any President, requiring an astute and subtle combination of formal powers, status, informal influence, personal skills, and judgment applied in both public and private. In the public arena, the President's best resources are inspirational oratory, charisma and timing, combined with unlimited access to mass media. In more intimate small group settings, success at persuasion requires a feel for bargaining and compromise: What political commitments to make, which resources to spend, whose debts to call due, and which tactics are appropriate in different situations.

Richard Neustadt's classic book, *Presidential Power,* is the definitive statement of this thesis.[4] This well-known analysis has stood the test of time. Professor Neustadt concludes that Presidential power is essentially the power to persuade. This is so, he argues, because of basic realities of American politics. First, the government consists of separate institutions sharing powers, a point already made

4.   Richard E. Neustadt, *Presidential Power: The Politics of Leadership.* New York: John Wiley and Sons, Inc., 1960. See, especially, pp. 1–107.

but worth repeating. Second, many objectives of government policy can be achieved only through voluntary actions by powerful private institutions. Successful governmental administration requires cooperation with, and compliance by, large institutions, including business corporations and labor unions. Even the august title of Chief Executive does not spare the President the necessity of bargaining with his subordinates over budgets and programs. As economic manager, the President finds monetary policy (interest rates) largely in the hands of the Federal Reserve System. Fiscal policy (taxes and spending) is shared with the Congress, as is the power needed to create job programs and impose wage and price controls.

The inescapable conclusion is that the President's dealings with other powerful political actors are essentially relationships of mutual dependence. In situations where the President must persuade because he cannot command, the test of leadership becomes his personal capacity to influence others. He is dependent on those he would persuade for compliance and cooperation, because, in varying amounts, they, too, possess status, independent authority, and secure political bases.

It is a well-worn adage that, in the American governmental system, many of the advantages are on the side of those seeking to prevent, or modify, proposals for change. From this perspective the powers of the Presidency seem formidable indeed. Acts of Congress may be vetoed, funds impounded (subject to Congressional approval), and program budgets modified. Few major programs can become law without the President's approval. Presidents content to be guardians of existing programs face a different political configuration than those who are committed to innovation and change. Innovators encounter the planned obstructions of the system of checks and balances, and any significant Presidential proposal carries with it the liability of justification. Formal powers alone will seldom suffice to move the bureaucracy in a new direction, or blast a stalled proposal out of a Congressional committee. Here skilled leadership is required to arrange the compromises and concessions needed to dilute opposition and overcome the inertia built into the system.

The irony is that while many constitutional and legal advantages rest with passive, or obstructionist, Presidents, contemporary political and economic forces have tended to produce activist Presidents. Popular expectations surrounding the office, and the demands made of it by the Congress, the public, and the media converge to support an activist Presidency. These expectations, combined with skillful use of political resources and a little luck, enable an activist President to modify the nation's governmental priorities and affect the direction and pace of social change. This places a premium on the persuasive dimension of the office. In a position of unparalleled visibility at the center of the political, budgetary, and communications networks, activist Presidents are given the chance for leadership with no guaranty of success.

CONCLUSION

It is the destiny of activist Presidents to be frustrated. They are besieged by demands and expectations that far and away exceed the capacity of the Presidency to meet them. Difficulties in the exercise of Presidential leadership are not a new development, but the situation has been aggravated by two shattering events (Vietnam and Watergate) that have undermined public confidence in governmental institutions. Recent Presidents share the dubious distinction of having earned the lowest popularity ratings in the history of polling. Rocked by revelations of abuses of power, shady deals, and incompetence in high places, the government muddles along, seemingly unable to deal with crucial problems. Perhaps most telling of all, no President has completed two full terms in office since Eisenhower, who was first elected 30 years ago. While some recent Presidents have proven to be their own worst enemies, much of the problem goes beyond quirks of personality. The difficulties all Presidents encounter are rooted partly in the political and constitutional system and partly in the complexities of the Presidential institution itself.

FURTHER READING

Heineman, Ben W., Jr., and Hessler, Curtis A. *Memorandum for the President: A Strategic Approach to Domestic Affairs in the 1980's.* New York: Random House, 1980. Two Executive officials from the Carter administration discuss the power and limitations of the modern Presidency and suggest a Presidential strategy for the 1980's.

Hoy, John C., and Bernstein, Melvin H. (eds.). *The Effective President.* Pacific Palisades, Ca.: Palisades Publishers, 1976. A symposium of scholars, journalists, and politicians analyze the state of the American Presidency.

Newstadt, Richard E. *Presidential Power: the Politics of Leadership from FDR to Carter.* New York: John Wiley and Sons, 1980. Professor Neustadt updates his discussion of the role of persuasion in Presidential politics.

(Photo by S. M. Wakefield)

Part One

The President and the Public

Chapter 2

Many Are Called But Few Are Chosen: The Politics of Presidential Nominations

Changes in the American political party system have fundamentally transformed the manner in which Presidential candidates are nominated. In 1968, Vice President Hubert H. Humphrey was nominated as the Democratic candidate for President without having entered a single primary election. In 1976, Governor Jimmy Carter entered 26 Democratic primaries and won 18 of them en route to his party's Presidential nomination. Within a few years, the Presidential nominating process has been transformed so that it is unlikely that a Presidential aspirant could be nominated without a strong showing in the primaries.

Political scientists, politicians, and legislators have devoted considerable time and effort to defining what constitutes a political party. Using William Chambers' conception, a political party is defined here as a relatively durable social formation that seeks office, or power, in government and exhibits a structure, or organization, that links leaders at the center of government to a significant popular following by generating symbols of identification and loyalty.[1]

---

1. William N. Chambers, "Party Development and the American Mainstream," in William N. Chambers and Walter D. Burnam (eds.), *The American Party System: Stages of Political Development*. New York: Oxford University Press, 1967, p. 5.

That American political parties are durable is indicated by the fact that two major parties have dominated Presidential and Congressional politics since the Civil War. One of these parties, the Democratic, is generally regarded as the oldest active party in the world. During the course of American history, the party system has undergone several realignments and may be on the verge of another. The structure of American parties, and the relationship between party leaders and followers, has undergone significant changes affecting the Presidential nominating process.

THE PARTY SYSTEM IN TRANSITION

Three relatively autonomous components of the party are involved in the Presidential nominating process, although the relative influence of each has changed dramatically during the course of American history.

The Party in Government

The most visible component of a political party is comprised of public officials who have captured office through the symbols of the party and who generate much of the public record of the party.[2]   The chief executives and legislative parties of the nation and states, as well as prominent local officials, constitute the relatively small pool of government officials who are potentially influential in nominating candidates for the Presidency.[3]

Early in the history of the Republic, the party in government dominated Presidential nominations by means of the Congressional caucus.   Shortly after the advent of American political parties, Republican (Jeffersonian) and Federalist members of Congress began

2. Frank J. Sorauf, *Party Politics in America* (2nd ed.). Boston: Little, Brown and Company, 1972, p. 10. The organization of this discussion of the three components of political parties follows the tripartite conception developed by Sorauf.

3. Estimates are that not more than 2% of the public has ever run for public office. See Lester W. Milbrath and M. L. Goel, *Political Participation: How and Why Do People Get Involved in Politics* (2nd ed.).   Chicago: Rand McNally, 1977, p. 22, Table 1–2. The minority of successful candidatesdates, attaining sufficient prominence to be influential in the parties' Presidential nomination processes are likely to constitute considerably less than 1%.

meeting together regularly in caucuses to discuss issues and develop legislative strategy. By 1800, both parties were using their Congressional caucuses to nominate candidates for the Presidency.[4] This method of nomination survived until 1824, when extensive factions developed in the dominant Democratic–Republican party, resulting in four different candidates running under that label. Andrew Jackson, nominated by the Tennessee legislature, received the most popular votes and the most electoral votes (but not a majority). Jackson saw the Presidency slip away when the House of Representatives chose second-place finisher John Quincy Adams as President.

"King Caucus," denounced from many sides, was abandoned as a Presidential nominating device and was eventually replaced in 1832 by national nominating conventions. These were regarded as more representative, as well as more capable, of uniting diverse party factions behind a single nationally selected candidate. Until recently, the national nominating conventions permitted a considerable role for the party in government. Prominent national and state officials attended the conventions, with the most influential among them serving as power brokers and favorite sons. As leaders of large state delegations, they participated in convention bargaining, delivering substantial blocs of delegates in exchange for commitments made by Presidential aspirants. By pledging their votes to a prominent public official as a favorite son, state delegations were able to enhance their bargaining positions at the convention by remaining uncommitted. This arrangement also assured that influential government and party officials would be afforded an opportunity to scrutinize prospective Presidential nominees during the course of pre-convention negotiations and convention bargaining. The eventual nominee was assured of partisan support among an important Presidential constituency— prominent national and state public officials.

Modifications in party rules for delegate selection, and the increasing separation of public officials from the party organization, have worked to diminish the impact that the party in government has on Presidential nominations. Under current party rules, neither the organization nor the party in government can control the selection, or behavior, of state delegations to the party's national nominating convention. Selection of a substantial majority of delegates by primary elections makes certain that a few prominent state of-

4. Austin Ranney, *Curing the Mischiefs of Faction: Party Reform in America.* Berkeley: University of California Press, 1974, pp. 58–74.

ficials cannot handpick the delegations. Widespread reliance by both parties on primary elections also reduces the likelihood of a state's delegation being pledged to a favorite son. Most delegates now arrive at the convention publicly committed to one of the major contenders on the first ballot. The 1980 Democratic convention sanctified this principle by adopting a convention rule requiring delegates to vote according to the results of primaries in their states. These developments have affected not only the bargaining position of state delegations (reducing their room for maneuvering by committing them on the first ballot), but have, in addition, diminished the influence of elected public officials by largely eliminating their roles as power brokers and favorite sons. The most important decisions ("who gets the delegates") are made before the convention meets.

Table 2.1   Elected Officials at Democratic Conventions, 1956–1976[a]

Year	United States Senators (%)	United States Representatives (%)	Governors (%)
1956	90	33	100
1960	68	45	85
1964	72	46	61
1968	68	39	83
1972	36	15	80
1976	18	15	47

[a]The figures indicate the percentage of each group who were voting delegates or alternates. Source: Stephen J. Wayne, *The Road to the White House,* New York: St. Martin's Press, 1980. p. 92. Used with permission of the publisher.

The diminishing role of the party in government in nominating Presidents can be seen in Table 2.1, which documents the decline in the percentage of United State Senators, Representatives, and Governors attending Democratic conventions as delegates or alternates from 1956 to 1976. Many of the most influential government officials in the party are no longer involved in the convention nominating the party's candidates for President and Vice President.

In summary, the historical development of the Presidential nominating process has moved in the direction of decreasing influence for the party in government. In the days of the Congressional caucus, prominent government officials selected the party's Presidential nominee. The nomination of Presidents by national party conventions permitted government officials, especially those with strong organization support, to exercise considerable influence as leaders of state delegations. The impact of public officials on Presidential nominations has diminished as both parties have reformed the delegate-selection process. Nomination of Presidential candidates by brokered conventions has been replaced by an elaborate system of primary elections which usually determines the outcome of the nomination contest prior to the convention. With the national conventions reduced largely to the role of ratification of decisions made in primary elections, the focus of the struggle for the party's nomination has shifted to pre-convention activity. The extent of a government official's influence in a primary election depends upon whether that official's endorsement translates into organizational, financial, or voter, support for a particular Presidential candidate.

These developments have done little to assure support of government officials for the Presidential nominee or platform of their party. Campaign promises by Presidential nominees, and pledges written into the party platform, are disassociated from the government officials who will be asked to implement them.

The Party Organization

This component of the party includes those holding elective, or appointive, offices within the party (the formal organization) and the activists who do volunteer work for the party. The formal organization includes the national committeemen and women from each state and the state and local party officials. There are likely to be party officials at various levels, including state, congressional district, county, city, and ward committees—depending on the organization of the party in each state. Below the level of the ward committeemen and women are precinct workers, including volunteers loyal to the party—the activists who give their time, money, and skills to the party.[5] Membership in the party organization, including party officeholders and those activists belonging to political clubs, does not exceed 4% of the United States population. About 10% of the population contributes money to parties, or candidates, and an

---

5. Sorauf, *Party Politics in America*, pp. 9-10.

equal number have done volunteer work for a party, or candidate, at one time or another.[6]

The changing role of the activist in the party organization has implications for the Presidential nominating process. At the risk of some oversimplification, Table 2.2 portrays some distinctions between organizational activists in two different models of party organization. The old-style professional organization flourished prior to World War II and then began to decline. As described by Robert H. Salisbury, this type of party organization was made up mostly of male politicians, often first- or second-generation Americans, motivated by career opportunities in local or state government, or government-related jobs or contracts. The organizational activist was likely to be of a somewhat higher status than the voters he sought

Table 2.2   Characteristics of Organizational Activists in Two Models of Party Organization

	OLD STYLE *Party Professional Model*	NEW STYLE *Amateur Model*
Geographic locus	Urban	Suburban
Social status	Modest	Upper middle-class Professional
Motivation	Instrumental Oriented to party as a career for personal gain	Programmatic Oriented to candidates, issues, and policies
Loyalty to party organization	Strong Based on patronage, social network, and traditional ties	Conditional Based on support for issues and candidates
Politics	Pragmatic Oriented to victory in elections as a means of organizational maintenance	Ideological Concerned with policy issues along liberal–conservative lines

6. William H. Flanigan and Nancy H. Zingale, *Political Behavior of the American Electorate* (4th ed.). Boston: Allyn and Bacon, 1979, p. 163. See Table 7.1.

to deliver at the polls, but, generally, in education, occupation, and life style he remained reasonably close to his people.[7]

Most of the old-style urban organizations have withered away, due partly to the decreasing availability and importance of patronage jobs and partly to population changes. The public is now better educated and less interested in patronage jobs, and the central city is less important politically. The migration of millions of Americans to the suburbs and to smaller cities has produced a different type of party organization. The new-style amateur organization is almost totally dependent upon volunteer workers, and it tends to be dominated by upper middle-class activists—lawyers, doctors, teachers, and executives—who have little interest in patronage jobs. They participate in party politics out of concern about policy issues, ideological or reform goals, or loyalty to a particular candidate.[8] Bringing only conditional loyalty to the party, many of them are so concerned with ideological purity, or reform goals, that winning elections may become a secondary consideration. Because of the growing dependence of American parties on volunteer activists, it is now possible for the organization of either party to be penetrated by persons without reliable ties to the party. The proliferation of primaries and candidate-based organizations has provided activists with an opportunity to increase their influence in party affairs.[9]

The steady rise to power of the new-class activists has resulted in a growing gap between the elite of both parties and their mass followings. The decision-making structures of both parties, including the institutions that nominate Presidents, are now disproportionately influenced by well-educated, upper middle-class activists with pronounced ideological predispositions. These individuals have political opinions and values considerably different from the parties' regular voters. One consequence of party organizations becoming

7. Robert H. Salisbury, "The Urban Party Organization Member," in David W. Abbott and Edward T. Rogowsky (eds.), *Political Parties: Leadership, Organization, Linkage.* Chicago: Rand McNally, 1971, pp. 48–49. See, also, James Q. Wilson, *The Amateur Democrat.* Chicago: University of Chicago Press, 1962.

8. *Ibid*, pp. 48–61.

9. Jeane J. Kirkpatrick, "Dismantling the Parties: Reflections on Party Reform," in James I. Lengle and Byron E. Shafer (eds.), *Presidential Politics: Readings on Nominations and Elections,* New York: St. Martin's Press, 1980, p. 22.

more open is that party activists are much more ideologically polarized than are party voters. Activist Democrats are noticeably more liberal, and activist Republicans are more conservative, than the mass of party voters. The growing influence of liberal activists in the Democratic party has resulted in an especially pronounced discrepancy between the party elite and voters. As described by Everett C. Ladd, this split involves "nothing less than two world views, partly generational in origin, partly relating to different class experiences."[10]

. In summary, a combination of factors, including the nation's increasing suburbanization, growing party activism among middle and upper middle-class volunteers, and party reforms have transformed the organizations of both parties. Party organizations no longer command legions of loyal and disciplined workers sufficient to dominate state and local governments. The parties are increasingly dependent upon, and responsive to, the new class of volunteer activists who are ideologically oriented and offer their services out of concern for particular issues and candidates. The new party activists are not especially representative of party voters in terms of social backgrounds or political beliefs, but they are playing an increasingly important role in nominating Presidential candidates.

An excellent illustration of the extent of these changes in party politics was the clash between Senators Edmund Muskie and George McGovern for the Democratic nomination in 1972. Muskie had been designated as the Democratic front-runner, having been the party's nominee for Vice President in 1968, as well as the leader in the pre-primary polls in 1972. At the start of the campaign, McGovern had little popular support (being preferred by only 3% of the Democratic voters), but he had established an elaborate organization based on volunteer activists. After a year and a half of diligent labor, McGovern's personal organization was in place and functioning. The organization, directed by Gary Hart, consisted of a field organizer who directed local organizers in each primary state. The local organizations, using volunteer activists consisting mostly of housewives, peaceniks, and students, contacted other citizens. McGovern's organization expanded its base by using the peace issue to energize volunteers to activism.

After running an unexpectedly close second to Muskie in the New Hampshire primary, McGovern's forces organized for a knock-

10. Everett Carll Ladd, Jr., *Where Have All the Voters Gone: The Fracturing of America's Political Parties.* New York: W.W. Norton and Company, 1978, p. 39.

(Photo by S. M. Wakefield)

out in Wisconsin. By the time of the Democratic primary, every county in Wisconsin had been organized by McGovern activists. "McGovern's Army," as it came to be known, consisted mostly of amateur activists committed to the idea that politics could bring peace and justice. By primary day in Wisconsin, they numbered upwards of 10,000 volunteers.

Muskie, on the other hand, had organized from the top down—the traditional way—relying on the regular party organization. He had sought and obtained the endorsements of most county chairmen, executive committeemen, and state legislators. But he had few troops at the grass-roots level, and this showed in the election results. McGovern won all of the at-large delegates and most of the districts, and he established himself as a credible candidate. With a follow-up win in Massachusetts, he was on his way to front-runner status. Muskie eventually withdrew as a candidate after the Pennsylvania primary. The old politics had clashed with the new activism and had been found wanting.[11] Emerging victorious from this conflict was the prototype of the candidate-oriented volunteer organization—an army of activists—components of which could be moved from state

11. Theodore H. White, *The Making of the President–1972*. New York: Bantam Books, Inc., 1973, pp. 96–143.

to state to win primaries one at a time. This new nomination strategy
was refined and perfected by Governor Jimmy Carter and his fabled
Peanut Brigade in 1976.

Party Rank and File

The Democratic and Republican rank and file constitute the mass
base of support for the parties. American political parties do not rest
upon a base of formal mass membership consisting of dedicated,
dues-paying members. Rather, the rank and file of both parties
consists of, in Frank Sorauf's words, the party's fellow travelers—
the men and women who affiliate casually with the party, identify
with it, and vote habitually for it. They do not participate in the
party organization, nor interact regularly with its leaders and activists.[12] They are, in effect, spectators in the political process, participating vicariously, except at election time, when they constitute a
fairly dependable core upon which electoral majorities may be
mobilized.

  Voter affiliation with the parties is informal, manifesting itself
mainly as a personal preference or subjective identification, based
primarily on social and economic considerations and family traditions. Extensive research on voters' partisan preferences indicates
that party identification is partly hereditary, being shaped by family
socialization processes. Party attachments are learned fairly early,
so that by the fifth or sixth grade about half of school-age children
express a preference for one party or the other. For reasons of
parental identification and social class, this preference is likely to
be the same as that of their parents, especially if both parents share
the same party preference.[13]

  For the party professional and activist, the party is an organization. For the party voter, the party is a label which simplifies choices
and provides cues as to how to vote. The identification of voters
with a party is a link between candidates and voters, which structures
the vote by simplifying alternatives. A development of considerable
importance for the parties is the growing preference among citizens
for political independence. The size and commitment of the mass
base of both parties is shrinking, as illustrated in Table 2.3. For

12. Sorauf, *Party Politics in America*, pp. 10–11.

13. See, among others, David Easton and Jack Dennis, *Children and the Political
    System: Origins of Political Legitimacy*. New York: McGraw-Hill, 1969;
    Robert D. Hess and Judith V. Torney, *The Development of Political
    Attitudes in Children*. Garden City, N.Y.: Doubleday & Co., 1968.

Table 2.3 The Distribution of Party Identification in the United States, 1952–1978

Party	Percent	1952	1956	1960	1964	1968	1972	1976	1978
Strong Democrats		22	21	21	26	20	15	15	15
Weak Democrats		25	23	25	25	25	25	25	24
Independents		22	24	23	23	30	34	36	37
Weak Republicans		14	14	13	13	14	13	14	13
Strong Republicans		13	15	14	11	10	10	9	8
Apolitical/ Don't Know		4	3	4	2	1	3	1	3
Total Percent		100	100	100	100	100	100	100	100

Source: SRC/CPS Election Surveys reported in Herbert B. Asher, *Presidential Elections and American Politics: Voters, Candidates and Campaigns Since 1952* (revised ed.). Homewood, Ill.: Dorsey, 1980, p. 35. Used with permission of University of Michigan.

years, the Center for Political Studies at the University of Michigan has assessed the partisan preferences of the public by asking national samples the same question: "Generally speaking, do you think of yourself as a Republican, a Democrat, an Independent, or what?" Those classifying themselves as Republicans or Democrats are then asked to indicate how strong their party preference is. The results of these surveys are displayed in Table 2.3, which shows the distribution of party identification in the United States from 1952 to 1978.

Democrats have consistently outnumbered Republicans since the party realignment that occurred during the 1930's as a result of the Great Depression. Of more immediate interest is the long-term trend eroding the popular base of support for both parties. Although it has become customary to refer to the Democrats as the majority party, and Republicans as the minority, the fact is that *neither* party has the support of a majority of the public. Diminishing public attachment to the parties has been manifested by growing numbers of Independents, and by decreases in the intensity of partisan commitment. In 1952 strong partisans constituted more than one-third (35%) of the public, but by 1978, they were less than one-fourth (23%). This has been accompanied by a surge towards independence, especially among the younger voters. In 1952, Republicans outnumbered Independents 27% to 22%, but, by 1978, the number of Independents (37%) nearly equaled the Democrats (39%). The causes of this development are complex. The most readily apparent explanation of declining partisanship is the pronounced generational differences among voters. Surveys since 1972 show that a majority of the voters under 30 years of age identify themselves as Independents, and there is little evidence that their independence decreases with age.[14]

Party voters are playing an increasingly prominent role in Presidential nominations through the vehicle of the primary election. The importance of primaries has been growing since 1952 when the Eisenhower campaign used Republican primaries to demonstrate to party leaders the General's public popularity. After defeating Robert Taft's conservatives in New Hampshire, Eisenhower ran second to Minnesota's Harold Stassen, the favorite son, by an aston-

14. Paul R. Abramson, *Generational Change in American Politics.* Lexington, Ma.: D.C. Heath, 1975, pp. 56–70. See, also, Norman H. Nie, Sidney Verba, and John Petrocik, *The Changing American Voter* (enlarged ed.). Cambridge, Ma.: Harvard University Press, 1979, pp. 62–67. See, especially, Figure 4.8, p. 63.

ishing write-in vote of more than 100,000 in that state.[15] Through
his primary successes, Eisenhower established his ability to pull
votes, proved that his background as a military officer was not a
handicap, and achieved a political momentum that carried him to
the Republican nomination.

Primaries were pivotal in the contest for the Democratic nomination in 1960. For John F. Kennedy, there was no other route to
the nomination. By the standards of party leaders he was too young,
too inexperienced and, most damaging, Catholic. Without a dem-
onstration of strong voter appeal, it is unlikely that Kennedy would
have been nominated. By overwhelming Hubert Humphrey with
superior organization and finances in Wisconsin and West Virginia,
Kennedy proved he could win in the Midwest against a favorite son,
and that he could win in a state that was 95% Protestant.[16] By
winning 7 out of 7 primaries, he established himself as the pre-
convention favorite and was successful in fending off challenges by
Adlai Stevenson and Lyndon Johnson at the convention.

Prior to 1972, primaries were used mainly to demonstrate a
candidate's ability to pull votes from various constituencies. Prospective nominees, particularly front-runners, could use primaries
selectively, entering those most likely to enhance their prospects.
Support of party leaders at the convention was the most crucial
determinant of the nomination contest, and a strong showing in
primaries was one way to generate party support. Subsequent
changes in party rules for selection of convention delegates have
made primaries the most important aspect of the Presidential nominating process.

In summary, as with other components of the party, the rank
and file are in transition. A smaller percentage of the public now
identifies with the major parties than at any time since the Great
Depression. At the same time, changes in party rules permit the
rank and file to play an increasingly important role in Presidential
nominations. A large majority of delegates to the national conventions of both parties is now selected in primary elections, often by a
relatively small fraction of the voters.

The relationship between components of the party has been substantially altered. The party's elected officials, once a significant

15. White, *The Making of the President–1972*, p. 91.

16. Theodore H. White, *The Making of the President–1960*. New York: Pocket
    Books, 1961, pp. 93–137.

force in nominating Presidents, have been relegated to a secondary role. The party organization has proved vulnerable to take-over by activists of various ideological persuasions with tenuous commitment to the party. Modifications of party rules have assigned greater importance to party voters and activists in selecting delegates to the national nominating conventions. These developments have made Presidential nominations into a decentralized, and relatively open, process.

THE DELEGATE–SELECTION PROCESS

Presidential candidates of both major parties are formally nominated by national conventions composed of delegates representing the various state parties. To say that the process of delegate selection has undergone major changes would be an understatement. The turmoil surrounding the selection and composition of state delegations to national party conventions began amidst the shambles of the badly divided 1968 Democratic convention when, without entering any primaries, and over the vociferous objections of the party's anti-war faction, Vice President Hubert Humphrey was nominated for President. Delegates loyal to Senators Eugene McCarthy and Robert Kennedy did win one victory in Chicago. The convention leadership, apparently caught by surprise, was unable to defeat a resolution by the Ad Hoc Commission on the Democratic Selection of Presidential Nominees, thus setting in motion a thorough review of national convention nominating processes.[17] Humphrey and the party regulars had won the battle but lost the war.

Party Reform

The resolution passed by the 1968 Democratic convention in Chicago set in motion a wide-ranging series of modifications in the nominating process. The vehicle for these changes was a series of commissions which reviewed party delegate selection procedures and recommended changes, most of which were adopted by the Democratic National Committee. These rules changes have affected the procedures by which convention delegates are selected and the composition

17. Robert J. Huckshorn, *Political Parties in America*. North Scituate, Ma.: Duxbury Press, 1980, p. 127.

of state delegations. Two of the most influential of these commissions were the McGovern–Fraser Commission and the Mikulski Commission.[18]

The McGovern–Fraser Commission, chaired initially by Senator George McGovern, and later by Representative Donald Fraser, recommended revision of state party rules and laws governing selection of delegates to the national convention. The commission's recommendations were adopted by the Democratic National Committee and implemented at the 1972 convention. The goal of the commission was to promote internal party democracy, which was defined in terms of opening up the nominating process to greater participation by the rank and file.[19] The procedures adopted were aimed at:

> Assuring adequate public notice of party meetings
> Monitoring delegate selection by requiring written rules
> Limiting control by the state central committee to 10% of the delegates
> Requiring at least three-fourths of the delegates to be selected at the level of Congressional district or lower: all delegates to be selected within the same calendar year as the election
> Forbidding proxy voting and the unit rule; limiting fees to a maximum of $10.00
> Prohibiting the system in which party and public officials automatically become delegates
> Permitting all persons 18 or older to participate in party affairs

Equally important, and more controversial, were the commission's proposals to regulate the composition of state delegations by encouraging representation of minorities, women, and youths under 30 in "reasonable relationship to their presence in the state's popula-

18. In addition to the Democratic party commissions discussed, there were two others:
   (1) The O'Hara Commission dealing with changes in procedures at the convention; and
   (2) The Sanford Commission which drafted a charter for the party. Summaries of the accomplishments of these commissions can be found in Huckshorn, *Political Parties in America*, pp. 127–135.

19. Ladd, *Where Have All the Voters Gone?* p. 53.

tion."[20]   However intended, this was construed as a *de facto* quota system for state delegations to the national convention.

Ironically, after these rules were in place, they contributed significantly to the nomination in 1972 of Senator George McGovern, one of their principal architects.   After McGovern's disastrous defeat by President Nixon, discontent with some of the provisions (particularly the quota system) resulted in some modifications, but the procedures remained basically intact.   Another Commission on Delegate Selection, headed by Barbara Mikulski, made recommendations that essentially upheld the McGovern–Fraser guidelines, but with some important modifications and additions:[21]

> Rigid quotas were replaced with more flexible affirmative-action plans to encourage participation of minorities, women, and youth.
> Winner-take-all primaries were replaced by a system of proportional representation.
> Candidates for delegate to the Democratic convention were made subject to approval of the Presidential candidate with whom they were affiliated.

In addition, attempts were made to limit participation in the delegate selection process to members of the party. In theory, this should outlaw open primaries, but the party has encountered resistance from state legislatures on this matter. A number of exceptions were granted by the party for state primaries in 1976. By 1980, most Democratic states had closed their primaries to Republicans, although Independents were permitted to vote in several states. In other states, such as Michigan, where the legislature refused to close the primary, the selection of delegates was separated from the primary and transferred to the party caucus.[22]

In 1978, yet another commission, this one chaired by Michigan Democrat Morley Winograd, again tinkered with the party's rules. Two notable provisions were enacted. One expanded the size of state delegations by 10% to permit more attendance at the convention by state party and elected officials (who were finding them-

20. This summary of the McGovern–Fraser rules is based on Robert Huckshorn's more extensive discussion in *Political Parties in America*, pp. 127–135.

21. *Ibid*, p. 131.

22. *Congressional Quarterly Weekly Report,* April 19, 1980, p. 1207.

selves excluded under the new rules). The other again insisted that participation in the delegate selection process should be limited to Democrats.

Although they did not institute a quota system the Republicans adopted similar provisions for opening up the nominating process to greater participation. They were motivated partly by the desire to appear sympathetic to party democracy, and partly by the reality that numerous Democratic-dominated state legislatures had enacted reform provisions into law.[23]

Three immediate effects of these changes in party procedures were:

> Alterations in the composition of state delegations to national party conventions
> Greater reliance on primary elections to select delegates
> Increased importance of news media in the nominating process

Convention Delegations

Prior to 1972, delegates to national conventions included a substantial number of public and party officials, loyal organization workers, and large financial contributors. Consequently, the delegates were disproportionately white, male, and over 30. Specifically, Democratic conventions prior to 1972 included only about 5% minority delegates, 15% women, and a handful of individuals under 30. After the rules changed, delegations to the 1972 and 1976 conventions of both parties included significantly greater numbers of female, minority, and young delegates. In the 1972 Democratic convention, 40% of the delegates were women, 15% minority, 22% under 30. For the 1976 convention, the percentages were 33%, 11%, and 15% respectively. Similar, if less dramatic, changes occurred at the Republican conventions.[24]

23. The Republican commissions were the Delegates and Organizations Committee, and the Rule 29 Committee. Both are discussed in detail in Huckshorn, *Political Parties in America,* pp. 133–136.

24. *Commission on Presidential Nomination and Party Structure, Openness, Participation, and Party Building: Reforms for a Stronger Democratic Party.* Washington, D.C.: Democratic National Committee, 1978, p. 19. For figures on the 1968 and 1972 Republican convention, see Huckshorn, *Political Parties in America,* p. 135. For figures on both parties' conventions from 1892 to 1956, see Paul T. David, Ralph M. Goldman, and Richard C. Bain, *The Politics of National Party Conventions.* Washington, D.C.: The Brookings Institution, 1960, pp. 325–354.

Clearly, the rules were effective in altering the makeup of national party conventions. Despite these changes in the composition of state delegations, the social backgrounds, policy attitudes, and ideologies of the convention delegates are not representative of party voters, the public, or the subgroups for whom the affirmative action quotas were intended. The delegates, including women, minorities, and youth, are disproportionately well educated, of higher status and income, and more ideologically oriented than the people they represent. While seeking to become more representative of the rank and file, the parties have initiated procedural changes which have funtioned to increase the influence of atypical and polarized cadres of activists. Through adoption of rules rewarding activism, persuasive skills, and ideological motivation, while down-playing traditional assets, such as local ties and organizational loyalty, the activists have succeeded, under the guise of democratic reforms, in altering the rules of the game to their advantage. After analyzing the impact of the reform rules on the 1972 Democratic convention, Jeanne Kirkpatrick concluded that party reform essentially advanced the class interests of the reformers by rewarding persons with the skills and values of the reformers.[25]

Research by Everett C. Ladd on the 1976 Democratic convention reinforces this conclusion. Distinguishing between New-Class Democrats (individuals under 40, college-educated, and in professional and managerial jobs) and Old-Class Democrats (those over 50, without a college education, and in blue-collar occupations), Ladd documented sharp differences in political attitudes and policy preferences within the party. Ladd's findings are reproduced in Table 2.4, which indicates that policy attitudes of the convention delegates more closely approximate the values of the New-Class Democrats than the party rank and file. Differences between the party elite and voters were even greater in the 1972 Democratic convention.[26]

A fundamental difficulty now apparent in these attempts at party reform is that they incorporate contradictory goals into the nominating process. The traditional political goals of the nominating process (party unity, avoidance of divisive issues, nomination of electable candidates) are not totally compatible with the representational goals of the reform procedures. By assuming the paramount

---

25. Kirkpatrick, "Dismantling the Parties: Reflections on Party Reforms," p. 24.

26. Jeane J. Kirkpatrick, *The New Presidential Elite*. New York: Russell Sage Foundation, 1976, pp. 281 ff.

importance of representation of diverse interests and subgroups, the reform procedures may be counterproductive to electoral campaign goals. By handing over the national party's nomination machinery to the new-class activists, the reforms have increased the likelihood of conflicts between party professionals and amateurs. In 1972, for example, there was a substantial reduction in the number of delegates who were party or public officials and three-fourths of the delegates of both parties were attending their first national convention.[27]

Table 2.4   Attitudes of Democratic Nominating-Convention Delegates and Rank and File—1976

	1976 Democratic Convention Delegates	Rank and File Democrats	Old-Class Democrats	New-Class Democrats
Percentage who favor busing for school integration	50	24	23	33
Percentage who feel the United States is spending too much on defense	60	30	21	59
Percentage who favor right to abortion without restriction	83	42	34	72
Percentage who favor death penalty	54	76	83	54
Percentage who feel too much attention is being paid to minorities	14	42	44	32
Percentage who describe themselves as politically "conservative"	8	36	45	14

Source: Everett C. Ladd, *Where Have All the Voters Gone?* New York: W.W. Norton & Co., 1978, p. 65.

27. Stephen J. Wayne. *The Road to the White House: The Politics of Presidential Elections.* New York: St. Martin's Press, 1970, p. 92.

Illustrative of the tension between electorally oriented pragmatists and amateur purists was the refusal by the McGovern forces at the 1972 Democratic convention to seat the regular Democratic delegation from Chicago. This incident was a confrontation between party professionals, organizational loyalists, and elected officials and amateur activists and reformers. On another plane, it was a clash between the politics of realism and the politics of purity. Mayor Richard Daley of Chicago was unquestionably one of the most influential officials in the Democratic party for two decades. Frequently described as a Kingmaker by journalists, he was courted by Democratic Presidential candidates because of his ability to deliver convention delegates and because the Cook County Democratic organization could reliably turn out hundreds of thousands of Democratic voters on election day. In 1972, Mayor Daley was rebuffed by the new activists of his party. Specifically, the delegation from Cook County was challenged in the Credentials Committee. The delegation of 59 members, handpicked by Mayor Daley, was approved overwhelmingly by the Democratic voters of Cook County. In addition to containing too few women and minority delegates, the delegation was challenged because of the manner in which it was selected. It had been slated privately by Mayor Daley's machine prior to the election. Appeals to reason and compromise failed, and, in a bitter credentials fight, the elected delegates of the nation's second largest city were thrown out of their seats and replaced with a reform slate, some of whose members had been explicitly rejected by the voters of Cook County. McGovern organizer Frank Mankiewicz observed, with classic understatement, "I think we may have lost Illinois tonight."[28]

The penchant for electoral suicide is not confined to Democratic purists. A survey of Reagan delegates at the 1976 Republican convention showed that more than half of them preferred nomination of a conservative Presidential candidate over victory in the November election.[29]

Voter Participation in the Process

A major thrust of party reform in the 1970's was to open up participation in party affairs to the rank and file, and to strip the party

28. White, *The Making of the President—1972*, p. 219. This discussion of the 1972 credentials fight is based on White's analysis, pp. 217–219.

29. Kirkpatrick, "Dismantling the Parties: Reflections on Party Reforms," p. 22.

organization and public officials of special advantages. The practice
of selecting state convention delegations by the party's central committee, or by a handful of state government officials, has been cur-
tailed. A large majority of delegates are now selected either in
multistage state party conventions, or most often by a system of
primary elections.

Multistage Conventions This process begins with local party
caucuses, and proceeds through district and, finally, state conventions, which choose the state party's delegation to the national convention. Prior to the 1970's reforms, participation in party caucuses
was usually confined to members of the party organization (precinct
and ward committeemen and women) meeting locally to select
delegates to higher-level party conventions in the state. Consequently, the state party's delegation to the national convention
reflected the preferences of state and local party organization members. The result of opening up this process to party activists has
been to change the caucuses from intimate meetings of organization
regulars into larger participatory conventions.

The bottom level (still called the caucus) is open to any party
member—or, in some cases, anyone claiming to be a member. The
Republican party still permits caucuses to be confined to members
of the formal organization, and some states (Arkansas, for example)
have elected to do that. The Democrats require caucuses to be open
to party members, but permit states to define membership. Estimates
are that in 21 states using this system of delegate selection in 1976,
about 2% of the voting-age population participated in the first
stage.[30] Participation in caucuses fluctuates considerably, depending
on how open they are. Estimates are that in the 1980 Iowa caucuses,
about 14% of the state's Democrats and Republicans participated.
Michigan Democrats, however, closed their caucuses to all but those
officially enrolled in the Democratic party, with the result that
Michigan's delegation to the national convention was chosen by
15,360 of the state's 5.2 million eligible voters. This also had the
effect of reducing the state's preference primary to a beauty contest.[31]

---

30. Austin Ranney, "Participation in American Presidential Nominations," in
    Lengle and Shafer (eds.), *Presidential Politics*, p. 241.

31. *Congressional Quarterly Weekly Report,* April 19, 1980, p. 1207.

Opening the caucuses has made them vulnerable to manipulation by candidate- and issue-enthusiasts, with the result that party activists have considerable impact in shaping the composition of convention delegations. Like the proliferation of primaries, this development works to the advantage of Presidential candidates able to generate a relatively small, but enthusiastic, personal organization capable of turning out supporters. By producing good showings in the early caucuses, candidates can expect disproportionate media attention, an important consideration in generating momentum for the long nominating campaign. The caucus victories of George McGovern in 1972, and Jimmy Carter in 1976, were basic to their nomination strategies and were attributable largely to the efforts of their personal organizations. Neither candidate had significant support from party organization leaders at the time.

Presidential Primaries Perhaps the most significant recent development in Presidential nominations has been the steady increase in the number of primaries and the proportion of convention delegates selected by them. The number of state parties using primary elections (including the District of Columbia) increased from 15 in 1968 to 34 in 1980. In 1972, for the first time, a majority of delegates to the national conventions of both parties were selected by primary elections. In 1980, three-quarters of the Democratic delegates, and nearly as many Republicans, were either selected by, or bound by, the results of Presidential primaries.[32]

Types of Primaries

There are a variety of Presidential primaries, some more directly connected with delegate selection than others. Depending on state law and party rules, primaries may be binding or advisory. Binding primaries obligate the delegates to follow the results of the state's primary election for a specified number of ballots at the national convention. Advisory primaries permit the voters of a state to express their preferences among Presidential candidates, but do not bind the delegates. Slates of delegates may be elected directly by primary voters, or the delegates may be selected outside the primary by party caucuses or committees, usually with the candidate's approval. Table 2.5 is a classification of both parties' primaries in 1980

32. *Congressional Quarterly Weekly Report,* February 2, 1980, p. 281.

Table 2.5   Types of Primaries and Delegate-Selection Systems
             in Use in 1980

Method of	*Type of Primary*		
Delegate Selection	*Binding*	*Advisory*	*Total*
Delegates selected outside	I	III	
(by party or candidate committee)	23 Democratic	3 Democratic	26 Democratic
	21 Republican	2 Republican	23 Republican
Delegates elected by primary	II	IV	
	6 Democratic	2 Democratic	8 Democratic
	5 Republican	5 Republican	10 Republican
Totals	29 Democratic	5 Democratic	34 Democratic
	26 Republican	7 Republican	33 Republican

Source: Compiled from data in *Congressional Quarterly Weekly Report*, February 2, 1980,
        p. 284. Used with permission of the publisher.

on the basis of whether they were advisory or binding, with delegates elected directly by the primary, or selected outside of it by the party. The entries in each cell of the table are the number of state parties using each type of primary.

By far the most popular method was Type I, which combines a binding primary vote with selection of delegates outside of the primary by the party. This method attempts to ensure that the results of the primary will be followed by permitting the party to screen the delegates. Type II primaries are binding but elect the slates of delegates directly. Type III primaries are beauty contests which are not binding, and do not elect delegates. In addition to these four types, three Republican state parties use an unusual type of primary in which convention delegates are directly elected, but there is no preference vote among Presidential candidates.

The primary process is complicated further by the question of how delegates are to be allocated. There are essentially two methods—proportional representation or winner-take-all (or some modified version of winner-take-all). By the 1980 primary season, all but two Democratic primary states allocated delegates to candidates on the basis of proportional representation, as required by party rules. (West Virginia and Illinois were granted exceptions.) All told, nearly all the Democratic delegates (91%) but less than half of the Republicans (37%), were awarded in proportion to candidates' percentages of the votes.[33]

Under the system of proportional representation, candidates pick up delegates even when they lose primaries. Conversely, the winner of a primary cannot capture all of the state's delegates simply by finishing a few percentage points ahead of other candidates. For example, in 1976, in the Texas Democratic primary, Jimmy Carter finished first (with less than 50% of the votes), but was awarded 92 of 98 delegates; and in the California Republican primary, President Ford, with 35% of the votes got no delegates, while Ronald Reagan won all the delegates with only 65% of the primary votes. Thanks largely to the Republican winner-take-all system, in 1980 Ronald Reagan captured three-quarters of the Republican delegates with only 60% of the primary votes.[34] The elimination of winner-take-all primaries by the Democrats seems to have aided President Carter's renomination bid in 1980. By winning the early primaries in the South and Midwest, Carter built up a lead, and he then continued to pick up substantial minorities of delegates while losing to Senator Edward Kennedy in Massachusetts, Rhode Island, Connecticut, New York, New Jersey, Pennsylvania, California, South Dakota, New Mexico, and the District of Columbia.

Turnout in Primaries

The number of voters participating has increased steadily as primaries have proliferated. Turnout in 1980 primaries exceeded 32 million, compared with 26 million in 1976, 22 million in 1972, and 12 million in 1968.[35] This increase in primary turnout has resulted from the increasing number of primary elections, not from higher rates of voter participation. Measured as a percentage of voting-age population, the 1980 turnout rate of 24% indicates that the trend of declining citizen participation in primaries has not been reversed. Political scientist Austin Ranney, in an analysis of competitive (closely contested) primaries from 1948 to 1968, found that 39% of the voting-age population participated, compared with 28% in

33. *Ibid*, p. 286.

34. *Ibid*, p. 284.

35. The 1976 and 1980 figures are from *Congressional Quarterly Weekly Report,* July 15, 1980, p. 1875. The 1968 and 1972 figures are Austin Ranney's, cited in Wayne, *The Road to the White House,* p. 90.

1976.[36]   Decline in the rate of voter participation in primaries has been greater than the decline in turnout in Presidential elections.

The unrepresentative nature of voter participation in Presidential primaries is by now well documented. The general thrust of much research is that voters who participate in primaries of either party are more likely to be better educated, more interested, older, of higher social status, and more issue-oriented than non-participants.[37] The growing number of candidates entering Presidential primaries (partly as a result of public funding for campaigns) decreases the likelihood of anyone winning a majority of the vote, and increases the possibility that a small minority of voters can have considerable impact on the outcome.   This, along with the relative ease with which a well organized minority can manipulate the caucus system, has led to speculation that the growth of the primary system will promote the nomination of fringe candidates not acceptable to the majority of party rank and file. The success of the McGovern forces in 1972, as well as the strong showing by Senator Eugene McCarthy in 1968, and Governor Ronald Reagan in 1976 (when President Ford was the clear preference of Republican rank and file), lend some support to this contention.[38]   However, the nomination of Senator Barry Goldwater in 1964, who had only minority support among Republican rank and file, was attributable less to primary elections than to manipulation of the caucus system by Goldwater activists.

While it may, or may not, enhance the prospects of fringe candidates, the primary system has improved the chances for Washington outsiders to be nominated. From 1948 until 1972, only two Presidential candidates (Thomas Dewey and Dwight Eisenhower) who were not members or former members, of the United States Senate, were nominated by the major parties. (See Table 2.6.) The pre-

36. Ranney, "Participation in American Presidential Nominations," p. 244.

37. *Ibid.* See, also, Ladd, *Where Have All the Voters Gone?*, pp. 61–62; James I. Lengle, "Demographic Representation in California's 1972 and 1968 Democratic Presidential Primaries," in Lengle and Shafer (eds.), *Presidential Politics*, pp. 201–217; and Austin Ranney, "The Representativeness of Primary Electorates," *Midwest Journal of Political Science*, 12. May, 1968. pp. 224–238.

38. A Gallup opinion survey before the 1980 primaries showed that former President Ford, although not an active candidate, was preferred over Reagan by a margin of 56% to 40% among Republicans. Reagan was the leader among the active candidates, however. See *The Gallup Opinion Index*, 175. February, 1980. p. 21.

Table 2.6   Major Party Presidential Nominees: 1948–1980

Year	Democrats	Republicans
1948	President Harry S Truman (former Vice President and Senator)	Thomas E. Dewey Governor of New York
1952	Senator Adlai E. Stevenson	General Dwight D. Eisenhower
1956	Same as 1952	Same as 1952
1960	Senator John F. Kennedy	Vice President Richard M. Nixon (former Senator)
1964	President Lyndon B. Johnson (former Vice President and Senator)	Senator Barry Goldwater
1968	Vice President Hubert H. Humphrey (former Senator)	Richard M. Nixon (former Vice President and Senator)
1972	Senator George McGovern	President Richard M. Nixon
1976	Jimmy Carter (former Governor)	President Gerald Ford (former Vice President and Congressman)
1980	President Jimmy Carter	Ronald Reagan (former Governor)

dominance of the Senate as a source of Presidential candidates occurred simultaneously with the nationalization of politics in Washington. Increasing concern about international relations, vastly expanded Federal budgets, and increasing attention paid to Washington politics by the national news media made the Senate an ideal launching pad for a Presidential candidacy.

In 1976, Jimmy Carter became the first nonmember of Congress to be nominated since Eisenhower, and the first governor since Thomas Dewey in 1948. In the 1980 election, two former governors opposed each other for the first time since 1944. The dominance of the United States Senate as the route to the Presidency has been broken, thanks largely to the emergence of the primary system which permits little-known politicians, without a national following, to launch a serious Presidential candidacy. What is required is a tight-knit personal following, and some seed money to get the ball rolling.

With a good showing in the early primaries, the news media and public financing can do the rest.

Media, Primaries, and Nominations

National news media interpret the meaning of primary results and, in so doing, influence the outcome of Presidential nominating contests. The proliferation of primary elections has created an ambiguous situtation. In the early primaries, there are likely to be at least half a dozen candidates running in each party, with winners and losers being separated by only a few percentage points. The multitude of different types of primaries and caucuses is, to say the least, confusing, and traditional cues, like the party label, are of little use in interpreting the outcomes. Under these circumstances, media coverage of primaries has become an integral part of the Presidential nomination process. On the basis of rather nebulous standards, winners and losers are defined (sometimes in contradiction to the election results), front-runner status is conferred or withdrawn, and candidates are declared by media analysts to be "finished" or "still alive." Media expectations about candidates' primary performances are apparently based on a combination of historical experience, pre-primary polls, geographic proximity, and seat-of-the-pants judgments.[39]

The whimsical nature of media interpretations of primary elections can be significant because of the potential of news media for generating self-fulfilling prophecies. Multi-candidate contests, with no clearly established standards of victory, permit substantial leeway in media interpretation and emphasis, which can thrust one candidate into prominence while disrupting the momentum of another.[40] In Orwellian fashion, victory can become defeat, losing can become winning, and winning can come to mean 28% of the vote.

The contest between Senators George McGovern and Edmund Muskie for the Democratic nomination in 1972, and Jimmy Carter's success in 1976, are likely to become classic illustrations of the impact of media on the fortunes of candidates vying for the Presidential

39. Donald R. Matthews, "'Winnowing': The News Media and the 1976 Presidential Nominations," in Lengle and Shafer (eds.), *Presidential Politics*, pp. 279–281.

40. Herbert Asher, *Presidential Elections and American Politics* (revised ed.). Homewood, Ill.: Dorsey, 1980, pp. 250–251.

nomination.   Prior to the pivotal Wisconsin primary in April, 1972, Edmund Muskie had beaten George McGovern 5 out of 5 times— in the Iowa caucuses, in Arizona, New Hampshire, and Florida (where both lost badly to George Wallace), and, more importantly, head-to-head in Illinois.   In the early going, Muskie had scored 4 victories out of 5 overall, and was the only Democratic candidate to run ahead of President Nixon in the polls.[41]   Ironically, however, Muskie's candidacy was crippled and losing momentum while McGovern's was preparing to take off.   The reasons are complex.   In addition to McGovern's organizational superiority, Muskie was partly the victim of front-runner status conferred upon him by the media. It hardly seems reasonable that Muskie (or anyone else) could have won all 22 Democratic primaries, but this seems to be what the news media had come to expect of the man they had designated as the Democratic front-runner. McGovern, being an underdog, was not expected to do well, thus assuring that even modest successes would receive favorable media coverage.

This resulted in an unusual series of events in which Muskie's primary and caucus victories were discounted by the media (because he was, after all, the front-runner), and, in the case of the New Hampshire primary, a triumph by Muskie at the polls was converted into a media defeat. This happened because media analysts judged Muskie's victory margin to be insufficiently large when measured against expectations established by the media.   As front-runner, Muskie had been expected to get at least 50% of the vote in the New Hampshire primary, so his victory over McGovern by a margin of 47% to 37% was interpreted as a setback rather than a victory.   In combination with Muskie's penchant for emotional outbursts and his organizational weaknesses at the grass-roots level, this media defeat in the New Hampshire primary began to unravel his campaign for the Democratic nomination.   Newspapers began reporting that Muskie "had stumbled on his own turf," that he was "slipping," and that his campaign was "deteriorating."   An exasperated Muskie campaign official summed it up: "Once the press gets negative, the people you canvass get negative, then the staff gets negative, then you feel it sagging all around you, and you begin to feel utterly help- less to do anything about it."[42]   Then came the Florida primary,

41. Lanny J. Davis, "The Primaries: Which Winners Lost and Which Losers Won?" in Lengle and Shafer (eds.), *Presidential Politics*, pp. 283–292.

42. *Ibid*, p. 290. The staffer quoted by Davis is Keith Haller.

dominated by George Wallace and the school-busing issue. Muskie's poor fourth-place finish received considerably more media attention than McGovern's sixth-place showing. In the subsequent Illinois primary, Muskie's impressive win received scant media attention, making it, in the words of Muskie-staffer Lanny Davis, "the great non-event of the 1972 campaign."[43] In any event, it was too little, too late. A negative bandwagon was already rolling, and McGovern's extensive organization of loyalists was waiting to bury Muskie in Wisconsin. With the vote divided among 6 candidates, McGovern was the winner (with 30%), while Muskie finished fourth again and was effectively out of it.

The significance of McGovern's nomination under the new party rules was immediately apparent to Jimmy Carter and his campaign organizer, Hamilton Jordan, as they devised a strategy in 1974. Being nominated for President in 1976 was, in large part, a matter of organizing and planning for the primaries. Low name recognition and the lack of a national following were not necessarily an insurmountable obstacle. The primaries, and the media coverage that accompanies them, could be used to create popular support. Relying on a tight-knit personal organization, the Carter forces hoped to do well enough in the crowded early primaries to generate good press and establish their candidate's credibility. By defeating George Wallace in Florida, Carter would emerge as the moderate alternative, generating more good publicity, campaign contributions, and public acceptance.[44]

This strategy worked even better than expected, and the politically unemployed former Governor of Georgia was off and running. Carter's candidacy received a boost from the news media when he unexpectedly finished ahead of the other candidates in the New Hampshire primary. In contrast with 1972, when Senator Muskie's 47% of the vote was deemed a setback, the media awarded victory to Jimmy Carter after he received 28% of the 82,381 votes cast in the New Hampshire Democratic primary. Donald Matthews has de-

43. *Ibid*, p. 296. For an extensive discussion of the impact of media on Presidential politics, see James David Barber, *The Pulse of Politics*: *Electing Presidents in the Media Age*. New York: W.W. Norton & Co., 1980.

44. The complete text of Hamilton Jordan's 1974 memo to Jimmy Carter on campaign strategy is available in Wayne, *The Road to the White House*, pp. 104–105. See, also, Jules Witcover, *Marathon: The Pursuit of the Presidency 1972-1976*. New York: Viking Press, 1977, pp. 135–136.

scribed the "Great New Hampshire Overkill" as the surge of media attention focused on one of the nation's smallest and least typical states.[45] This phenomenon, in combination with Carter's dark-horse status, produced a media bonanza for the Carter campaign, including cover stories in both *Time* and *Newsweek*. Media coverage of second-place finisher Morris Udall, who received only 5% fewer votes than Carter, was infinitesimal by comparison.[46] With these initial successes in Iowa and New Hampshire, Carter was able to win 8 of the first 9 primaries and establish himself as a front runner. For the remainder of the campaign, the other Democratic candidates were chasing him.

In summary, whereas primary elections were formerly used selectively by Presidential aspirants to demonstrate voter appeal, they now provide a basis for little known candidates to build support through organization and to win delegates in the process. Selection of convention delegates by primary elections, and the media coverage and interpretation accompanying this process, has opened up Presidential nominations to lesser known regional candidates and Washington outsiders who might formerly have been excluded.

FINANCING PRESIDENTIAL NOMINATIONS

The progression of patterns of financing for Presidential campaigns has moved from dependence primarily on large contributors to greater involvement of small contributors and public funds. This has been accompanied by greater expenditures in the pre-convention phase of the campaign. In 1968 and 1976, when there were nomination contests in both parties, pre-nomination spending exceeded expenditures for the general election. Prenomination expenditures totaled $45 million in 1968 and nearly $67 million (about 60% of the total) in 1976.[47] Campaigns for Presidential nomination now cost as much as, or more than Presidential elections. While partly due to inflation, equally important is the increasing number of primaries and the growing costs of the media and public-relations-oriented services purchased by the candidates.

45. Matthews, " 'Winnowing': The News Media and the 1976 Presidential Nominations," p. 280.

46. Wayne, *The Road to the White House*, p. 101.

47. *Ibid*, p. 28.

A distinctive feature of modern political campaigns is the independence of candidates from the party. Campaigns are now candidate-oriented, directed and run by the candidates' personal organizations rather than by party professionals. Consequently, candidates must raise money to pay for services formerly provided by the party. The decreasing effectiveness of party organizations, and advances in communications technology, have caused party professionals to be supplanted by professional management specialists, whose services are expensive. Candidates now contract with private firms for campaign and information services, including public relations and media consultants, fund solicitation, and public-opinion polling. These services require professional management personnel, computerized mailing lists and data analysis, telephone banks, and television air-time. Candidates must also employ accountants and lawyers to keep track of campaign contributions and expenditures in order to comply with Federal campaign regulations.

Prior to 1964, both major parties relied primarily on large contributors to finance Presidential campaigns. Approximately three-fourths of all contributions to Presidential campaigns were in amounts of $500 or more, and contributions of $10,000 or more were not unusual. A handful of individuals made huge contributions. In 1968, Nelson Rockefeller received nearly $1.5 million from his stepmother, Mrs. John D. Rockefeller. The Nixon campaign in 1972 received at least two contributions in excess of $1 million (from insurance millionaire W. Clement Stone and oil and banking heir Richard Mellon Scaife), while McGovern got $400,000 from General Motors heir Stewart Mott and nearly as much from Xerox stockholder Max Palevsky.[48]

Beginning in 1964, Presidential candidates rediscovered the small contributor. Barry Goldwater's television and direct-mail appeals produced nearly $6 million in small contributions. Prior to that time it was assumed that appeals for small contributions would not produce enough money to cover the cost of the mail-out or television time. Subsequently, George Wallace in 1968, George McGovern and Richard Nixon in 1972, and Ronald Reagan in 1976 mounted successful campaigns to tap the small contributor.[49]

48. The figures are from Herbert E. Alexander, *Financing Politics: Money, Elections and Political Reform.* Washington, D.C.: Congressional Quarterly Press, 1976, pp. 69–75.

49. Huckshorn, *Political Parties in America,* pp. 192–195.

Federal Matching Funds

A significant development in the Presidential nominating process is the availability of public funds in the pre-nomination phase. The Federal Election Campaign Act of 1971, as amended in 1974 and 1976, makes public tax money, in the form of matching funds, available to Presidential candidates in the primaries. The goal is to make candidates less dependent upon large contributors by providing public funds to match private contributions of $250 dollars or less. To qualify for Federal matching funds, candidates must raise at least $5000 (in small contributions) in 20 different states. Contributions from committees and organizations are not eligible to be matched, and only the first $250 of individual contributions are matched. Public matching funds are financed from money collected from the $1 check-off on the Federal income tax form. At present, about one-fourth of American taxpayers are contributing to this fund, which finances much of the cost of Presidential primaries and nominating conventions and provides nearly all the money candidates can legally spend in Presidential elections.

In 1976, the Federal Election Commission disbursed in excess of $24 million in matching funds to 15 Presidential candidates in the primaries, and $4 million to the national parties for nominating conventions. The Presidential nominees of each major party received roughly equal shares of nearly $44 million in the general election campaign. In 1980, each candidate was eligible to receive up to $7.36 million of public money during the pre-convention phase. This constituted a national spending ceiling of $14.7 million each (plus 20% for fund-raising costs and an unlimited amount for legal and accounting costs).[50]

The matching-funds provisions, plus limits on campaign contributions, assure that candidates must raise money in small amounts. A Presidential candidate cannot legally receive individual contributions greater than $1000, and direct contributions from Political Action Committees cannot exceed $5000. This contrasts dramatically with days past when candidates could quickly gather hundreds of thousands of dollars from a few wealthy contributors.

50. *Congressional Quarterly Weekly Report,* February 23, 1980, p. 569.

Financing Jimmy Carter's Nomination

The rise of Jimmy Carter from a one-term governor of Georgia to President illustrates the potential of Federal matching funds for boosting the prospects of a well organized, but relatively unknown, candidate. Since Carter's first unsuccessful campaign for governor in 1966, a small group of influential Georgia lawyers (some with banking connections) has formed the core of his financial support. These individuals contributed personally to his campaigns, solicited contributions from friends and associates, and borrowed money from banks on their signatures to finance Carter's gubernatorial bids. These loans were later repaid from campaign funds. Several of these individuals, or members of their families, were subsequently appointed to state government positions by Governor Carter.[51] While still governor, Carter and his aides raised $47,000 in late 1974 as seed money for a small staff to get his Presidential bid off the ground. During 1975, Carter's supporters raised more than $700,000 to pay for nationwide campaigning by the former governor. This money was raised by a combination of personal solicitation, telethons aimed at small contributors, and rock concert benefits by the Allman Brothers Band. (Governor Carter had personally cultivated a relationship with Phil Walden, owner of Capricorn Records in Macon, Georgia.) Revenue from the rock concerts and Federal matching funds totaled about $800,000.[52] This money kept the Carter campaign going through the Iowa and Maine caucuses and the New Hampshire primary. After his early successes, Carter inherited the media benefits of front-runner status, and the pace of campaign contributions quickened as the smart money began to shift his way.

Independent Spending

Under the Federal Election Campaign Act (FECA) the need for candidates to do well early involves more than favorable media

51. Nicholas M. Horrock, "Carter Campaign Funds Raised by a Group of Georgia Lawyers," in Lengle and Shafer (eds.), *Presidential Politics,* pp. 166–168.

52. Robert Sam Anson, "Will Phil Walden Rise Again?" *Esquire,* June, 1980, p. 44.

coverage and momentum.   A candidate drawing less than 10%
of the vote in two consecutive primaries becomes ineligible to
receive public funds 30 days later.   Although this law has probably
increased the number of candidates in Presidential primaries by
encouraging more people to run, it has also assured that those unable to attract a following will be eliminated quickly, or forced to
rely entirely on private funds to finance their campaigns, as John
Connally did in 1980.

The limits on campaign contributions in this law have altered
patterns of campaign spending.   While individuals are permitted
to contribute a maximum of $1000 to each candidate in a single
election, political committees may contribute up to $5000 to a
candidate in each election.   This provision has led to the proliferation
of more than 2000 Political Action Committees (PACs).   Under a
1976 Supreme Court decision, spending by individuals and groups in
support of a candidate is considered a form of political expression
and is protected by the First Amendment.[53]   A candidate's supporters can legally spend an unlimited amount to help elect the candidate, provided that the spending is done *independently* (i.e.,
without any contact with the candidate or coordination by the candidate's campaign committee).   By maintaining the fiction of independent spending, individuals and groups can spend as much as they
want to help elect a candidate, and their expenditures are not legally
considered to be campaign contributions.

Independent spending in 1976 totaled slightly more than $750,000,
but the pace quickened in 1980.   A survey of Federal Election Commission records showed that more than $2 million was spent inde-
pendently in the first 3 months of 1980 alone.   The leaders in independent expenditures are ideologically oriented committees with
conservative political sympathies, such as the National Conservative
Political Action Committee and the Fund for a Conservative
Majority.[54]   Other PACs function specifically to support the candidacy of a single individual, such as Ronald Reagan's Citizens for the
Republic.   Independent PACs spent more than $11 million helping
elect Reagan in 1980.

While most of the party reforms of the 1970's are widely regarded

53. *Buckley* vs. *Valeo* (424 U.S.1, 1976).

54. *Congressional Quarterly Weekly Report,* June 14, 1980, p. 1635.   The
    $11 million in expenditures for Reagan was cited by ABC News, Tuesday
    evening, February 24, 1981.

(Photo by S. M. Wakefield)

as being damaging to the parties as institutions,[55] the FECA does have one feature designed to encourage candidacies within the two major parties by limiting funds for third-party candidacies. A minor party is required to obtain at least 5% of the vote in the last Presidential election to be eligible for public funding in the next election. However, in the case of John Anderson's Independent candidacy in 1980, the Federal Election Commission ruled that if Anderson won at least 5% of the popular vote in the 1980 Presidential election, he would be eligible for reimbursement of campaign expenses after the election. On this basis, Anderson was able to borrow money to keep his campaign alive.

In summary, reforms in financing Presidential nominations have had a number of effects. In assessing the impact of the FECA, polit-

55. See, among others: Huckshorn, *Political Parties in America*, pp. 140–142; Wayne, *The Road to the White House*, pp. 45–46; Kirkpatrick, "Dismantling the Parties . . .," pp. 18–28; "Is There a Better Method of Picking Presidential Nominees," in *The New York Times*, December 2, 1979, p. E5.

ical scientist Stephen J. Wayne concluded that the law had reduced secret contributions, encouraged lesser-known candidates to run, and increased the probability that an incumbent President would be challenged for renomination.[56]

NATIONAL NOMINATING CONVENTIONS

Delegates from the various state parties convene every four years for a traditional American political spectacle, the national nominating convention. At the convention they approve the party's platform, adopt party rules, nominate candidates for President and Vice President, and attempt to generate party support for those candidates. Of these functions, nomination of the candidates is presumably the most important but is the least likely to be affected by convention deliberations. The system of primaries and open caucuses results in most delegates being committed in advance to one candidate or another. The importance of pre-convention activity is shown by the decline of the multiballot convention. From 1832 until 1952, 32 Democratic conventions took an average of 12 ballots to nominate Presidential candidates. This average is inflated by the 103 ballots the Democrats took to nominate John W. Davis in 1924. The nomination of Adlai E. Stevenson on the third ballot in 1952 was the last time either party took more than one ballot to nominate a Presidential candidate. From 1856 until 1952, 24 Republican conventions averaged 4 ballots per nominee. The nomination of Thomas E. Dewey on the third ballot in 1948 was the last multiballot Republican convention. The nomination of Wendell L. Willkie by the Republicans in 1940 on the sixth ballot is generally regarded as the last dark-horse convention at which an unexpected candidate emerged as the nominee.

Nominating conventions of the post World War II era have, with only these two exceptions, chosen their candidates on the first ballot. Modern conventions have been characterized either by ratification of candidates whose nomination on the first ballot was assured by overwhelming delegate support, or by nomination of a front-runner who was heavily favored, but faced substantial opposition on the first ballot.

56. Wayne, *The Road to the White House,* pp. 43–45.

Convention Committees

Much of the work of conventions is done by committees, and frequently before the opening of the convention. The most prominent of these committees are Credentials, Rules, and Platform (Resolutions). In the case of competing delegations from the same state, the Credentials Committee recommends which delegates will be seated and permitted to vote. Credentials fights are not uncommon, but the recent pattern has been for the faction in control of the convention to overrule the Credentials Committee by a floor vote if the committee renders an unfavorable decision. This occurred in 1952 when the Republican Credentials Committee supported a delegation from Texas sympathetic to Senator Robert Taft, but this decision was overturned by a floor vote and a pro-Eisenhower delegation was seated. Likewise, the McGovern forces at the 1972 Democratic convention were able to reverse, by floor vote, an unfavorable credentials ruling on the California delegation.

The Rules Committee drafts the procedures of the convention, which are subject to approval by the convention. Consequently, the dominant faction can usually control the rules. A rules change of some significance occurred at the 1936 Democratic convention when the two-thirds rule was repealed, permitting nomination of Presidential candidates by simple majority. The effect of this change was to reduce the threat that a candidate could be vetoed by the Southern bloc.[57] Another notable change occurred in 1980 when the Democratic convention adopted the Rules Committee's recommendation that delegates be bound by the results of primaries in their states.

The Platform Committees of both parties meet prior to the start of the conventions to draft statements of principles for the parties. Since the platforms are drafted by party activists, they frequently take stands on important and controversial issues because the elite of the two parties differ substantially from one another on matters of policy. Party principles and promises written into the platform are not binding on the candidates running under the party label. The people running the government are, by and large, different from the people running the convention, and writing a plank into the party's platform is a far cry from enacting a policy into public law.

57. Huckshorn, *Political Parties in America,* p. 145.

Party Unity

Platforms are not always reliable guides to policies the party's candidate will eventually support, but they are instructive because they indicate: (1) which factions of the party are in control of the convention; (2) to which interest groups they plan to appeal; and (3) what the prospects are for party unity. The contents of platforms, especially the acceptance by the majority faction of minority planks on some issues, indicates the willingness of those in control to compromise with the losers to promote unity. Since there can be only one Presidential nominee, dissident party factions and supporters of losing candidates need to be granted some concessions if the party is to unify behind its nominee. The Vice-Presidential nomination may be one such concession, and balancing the ticket is a long-standing tradition in American party politics. Compromises on the contents of the party platform is another approach to party unity which was used successfully by the Carter forces at the 1980 Democratic convention to placate Senator Edward Kennedy and his supporters. Within a few days after the convention, the Senator was campaigning for the President. After personally greeting Carter at Boston's Logan International Airport, Kennedy addressed members of the American

(Photo by S. M. Wakefield)

Federation of Teachers, urging them to work for the reelection of President Carter and other Democratic candidates. The President won the endorsement of the 550,000-member union the same day.[58] Surveys taken shortly after the convention showed that the President had come from behind and pulled nearly even with challenger Ronald Reagan in the polls. This provided a stark contrast with both 1968 and 1972 when the Democratic candidate left a badly divided convention to begin campaigning far behind in the polls.

CONCLUSION

The disappearance of multiballot conventions reflects the displacement of brokered conventions by a new Presidential nominating process in which pre-convention activity is crucial to success. This, in turn, indicates the extent to which control of party institutions has passed from party leaders and government officials to political activists and candidates who have reshaped party nominating processes to their benefit. Brokered conventions, smoke-filled rooms and all, permitted party leaders to scrutinize prospective Presidential candidates before turning over party machinery to them. Convention bargaining, encouraged by large blocs of uncommitted delegates, provided a final test of a candidate's negotiating and persuasive skills in a setting which required intimate contact with powerful politicians and government officials. The politics involved in vying for support of influential political leaders required skills that are not as rigorously tested by the primary system.

Prior to 1972, primaries were a limited device which permitted candidates to demonstrate their voter appeal to party leaders. Popular support among party voters was only one factor in gaining the nomination. Since then, primaries have become the whole ball game so that the *overriding* criterion for nominating Presidents is their ability to win multicandidate elections. This wide-open system of Presidential nomination emphasizes primarily campaign skills which test the effectiveness of a candidate's electoral organization and media image.

The result of this process is, in the words of commentator David Broder, perpetual candidacy, with Presidential aspirants

---

58. "Carter Receives Backing of Teachers' Group," in *Dayton Daily News*, August 22, 1980, p. 4.

announcing their candidacies up to two years before the election. Thirty-five primary elections undoubtedly test an individual's campaign skills and physical endurance.   It is difficult to argue that such a system adequately tests a candidate's potential for Presidential leadership, or prepares the nominee for the rigors of the Presidency. This system does not require Presidential nominees to persuade party leaders and elected officials, nor to build alliances with other influential politicians. The victorious candidate may enter the Presidency without the allies who may help him succeed in the job.[59]

Policy analysis and campaign strategy are different and distinctive sets of skills. Once the victorious candidate assumes the Presidency, the finely tuned campaign organization may begin to sputter in dealing with the complexities of policy decisions and budgetary priorities. The candidate's personal organization will prove, in all likelihood, better suited to attaining Presidential power than to utilizing it successfully.

59. David S. Broder, "Primaries Add Up to Perpetual Candidacy," in *Dayton Journal Herald*, June 13, 1980, p. 20.

Chapter 3

Presidential Elections: An Uncertain Mandate

THE ELECTORAL COLLEGE

Given the considerable attention paid by the media and the public to Presidential elections, it is possible to lose sight of the fact that the President is not directly elected by the voters. The Electoral College, consisting of Presidential electors from each state, meets on the first Monday after the second Wednesday in December to choose the President. The College has, on occasion, chosen as President individuals who received fewer popular votes than their opponents in Presidential elections. Deadlocks in the Electoral College have permitted the House of Representatives to choose the President on two occasions. In numerous elections, the shift of a few thousand votes in key states would have produced either victory for the loser, or a deadlock in the College, requiring the House of Representatives to select the President.

This curious institutional arrangement, like much else in the Constitution, is a product of compromises made at the Constitutional Convention in 1787. To promote independence of the executive, selection of the President by the Congress was rejected. Even more unsatisfactory was the then-radical option of direct election by the voters. After considerable debate, the convention approved the principle of selecting the President by a body created especially for that purpose.[1]   It matters little that the Electoral College has seldom functioned as envisioned by the framers of the Constitution. The system of indirect election they created is a crucial consideration in any close Presidential election.

The system of Presidential electors was created to permit popular preferences to be expressed without determining the selection of the President.   As originally conceived, Presidential electors were to exercise independent judgment to assure that the most qualified individual was selected President.   The subsequent development of political parties undermined the independence of the College by ensuring election of Presidential electors pledged to support candidates of a particular party.   Electors were chosen by the states according to a variety of methods approved by the state legislatures. For example, in 1796 Presidential electors were chosen by the voters in 6 states and by the legislatures in 10 others, but in each case they were pledged to one candidate or another.[2]

Compromises at the Constitutional Convention created two features of the Electoral College that work to the advantage of small states. The number of electors is equal to the representation of each state in Congress; there is one elector for each Representative and Senator.   Since each state has two Senators, this feature over-represents small states.   The greatest political advantage for the smaller states is found in the contingency provision permitting the House of Representatives to choose the President if no candidate wins a majority of electoral votes.   The House is then free to choose from among any of the three Presidential candidates receiving the most electoral votes, with each state's Congressional delegation casting a single vote. Regardless of the size of a state's population, each Congressional delegation has an equal voice in selecting the next President. Congressional delegations evenly divided and unable to choose forfeit their votes.   The votes of an absolute majority of state delegations (26) are required to select a President.   The Twelfth Amendment to the Constitution stipulates that if the House of Representatives is unable to choose a President by March 4, then the Vice President shall act as President.   If no Vice Presidential candidate has received a majority of electoral votes, the Senate is authorized to select a Vice President by majority vote.   The Senate must choose between the

1. Roger Lea MacBride, *The American Electoral College.*   Caldwell, Idaho: Claxton Printers, 1963, pp. 13–23.

2. *Ibid.,* p. 28

two Vice-Presidential candidates with the most electoral votes. (The Senate has selected the Vice President only once—in 1837.)

The advantages afforded small states by the Electoral College system are balanced by the winner-take-all feature which works to the benefit of the larger states. There are a number of conceivable methods by which a state's Presidential electors may be allocated, including proportional representation, districts, or the general ticket. Under a system of proportional representation, the Presidential candidates share each state's electoral votes in proportion to their share of the popular vote. The district method awards electoral votes to whichever Presidential candidate carries each Congressional district, with the likely result that candidates would share the electoral vote of some states. In modern practice, no states use either of these systems, although the district method was used by some states prior to the Civil War.[3] States have abandoned both the practice of permitting the legislature to select Presidential electors and the allocation of electors by district. Every state now uses the general-ticket system, which permits voters of the state to cast their ballots for slates of electors pledged to various Presidential candidates. The slate receiving the most votes is elected, and it is these electors who convene in the state capital in December to cast the state's electoral votes for President and Vice President.

The general-ticket system permits all of a state's electoral votes to be cast for the same Presidential candidate by electors pledged to that candidate. This system is literally winner-take-all, and in a three-way race, a Presidential candidate can capture all of a state's electoral votes with as little as 34% of the popular vote. This is not a hypothetical situation. In the 1968 Presidential election, involving a three-way race between Richard Nixon, Hubert Humphrey, and George Wallace, slates of electors pledged to Nixon carried Tennessee and North and South Carolina with popular pluralities of less than 40%. George Wallace won all of Arkansas' electoral votes with 38% of the popular vote.[4] Richard Nixon was elected President in 1968 with a majority of 56% in the Electoral College while receiving a popular plurality of slightly more than 43%.

3. *Ibid.*, pp. 60–61.

4. Lawrence D. Longley and Alan G. Braun, *The Politics of Electoral College Reform* (2nd ed.). New Haven: Yale University Press, 1975, p. 8. Nixon's percentages in Tennessee and North and South Carolina were 37.8%, 39.5%, and 38.1%, respectively.

On occasion, the electoral vote of a state may be split between two or more Presidential candidates, most often because of a faithless elector not voting as pledged. In most Presidential elections since 1948 (excepting 1952 and 1964), there have been instances of Presidential electors, mostly from the South, not honoring their pledges. In 1976, an elector from Washington, pledged to President Ford, voted for Ronald Reagan.[5]   In addition, Alabama's electoral votes were split in 1960 when the slate elected consisted of five Democratic electors pledged to John Kennedy and six unpledged Democratic electors, who eventually voted for Independent Democrat Senator Harry Flood Byrd of Virginia.[6]

The Electoral College and Election Outcomes

There have been 15 Presidential elections in which no candidate received a majority of the popular vote.[7] Most often, the distortions produced by the Electoral College system have functioned to inflate the victory margin of the winner, producing electoral College majorities for the candidate with the largest popular plurality. This is not inevitable, however, and in three of these elections the Electoral

5. *Presidential Elections Since 1789* (2nd ed.).   Washington, D.C.: Congressional Quarterly, Inc., 1979, p. 7.

6. Longley and Braun, *Politics of Electoral College Reform*, pp. 4–5.

7.   These elections were:

Date	Winning Candidate	Percentage of Popular Vote
1824	John Quincy Adams	31.9
1844	James Knox Polk	49.6
1848	Zachary Taylor	47.3
1856	James Buchanan	45.6
1860	Abraham Lincoln	39.8
1876	Rutherford Hayes	47.9
1880	James Garfield	48.3
1884	Grover Cleveland	48.5
1888	Benjamin Harrison	47.8
1892	Grover Cleveland	46.0
1912	Woodrow Wilson	41.9
1916	Woodrow Wilson	49.3
1948	Harry Truman	49.6
1960	John Kennedy	49.5
1968	Richard Nixon	43.4

Source: Neal R. Peirce, *The People's President: The Electoral College in American History and the Direct-Vote Alternative.* New York: Simon and Schuster, 1968, pp. 302–307. Used with permission of the publisher. The figures for 1968 are from the Statistical Abstract of the United States, (100th ed.), 1979, p. 496.

College system has led directly (in 1876 and 1888), or indirectly (in 1824), to selection as President of a candidate not receiving the most popular votes. On one other occasion (1800), a deadlock in the College forced the House of Representatives to choose between two candidates of the same party who received the same number of electoral votes. In 1960, it is not completely certain which Presidential candidate received the most popular votes.[8] Moreover, there have been 22 Presidential elections in which shifts in a relatively small number of popular votes could have produced a different outcome, resulting in either a deadlock in the Electoral College, or the election of a different President. (Popular and Electoral College vote totals for Presidential elections since World War II are contained in the Appendix.)

Reversal of Election Results As shown in Table 3.1 there have been two instances when the Electoral College chose as President a candidate who did not receive a plurality of popular votes. In both cases, the College selected a Republican over a Democrat who had more popular votes. The election of 1876 was further complicated

Table 3.1   Popular and Electoral College Results in 1876 and 1888

Election	Candidates	Popular Vote	Percent	Electoral Vote
1876	Hayes (R)	4,035,924	47.9	185
	Tilden (D)	4,287,670	50.9	184
	Others	94,935	1.1	
1888	Harrison (R)	5,445,269	47.8	233
	Cleveland (D)	5,540,365	48.6	168
	Fisk (P)	299,813	2.2	
	Others	155,121	1.4	

Source: Extracted from data in *Presidential Elections Since 1789* (2nd ed.). Washington, D.C.: Congressional Quarterly, Inc. 1979, pp. 77, 80. Used with permission of the publisher.

8. Aside from questions of fraudulent votes in Illinois and Texas, the popular vote totals in 1960 differ, depending on how one chooses to count the election returns from Alabama. Voters in Alabama elected six unpledged Democratic electors and five pledged to Kennedy. If all the votes for unpledged Democratic electors are given to Kennedy, then he received more popular votes than Nixon. If votes for unpledged Democratic electors are not included in Kennedy's popular vote totals, then Nixon received the most popular votes. See Longley and Braun, *The Politics of Electoral College Reform*, pp. 2–6.

when the Congress intervened to settle the issue of disputed electoral votes. After the election, most newspapers announced that Samuel Tilden of New York had secured popular and Electoral College majorities, but Republican headquarters insisted that Rutherford B. Hayes of Ohio was elected by one electoral vote. The controversy centered around disputed election returns from three Southern states, still occupied by the Union Army, and one electoral vote from Oregon. Twenty electoral votes were contested, two sets of election returns being received from Florida, South Carolina, and Louisiana. The Republicans had to control all 20 of the disputed electoral votes in order for Hayes to be elected President by one electoral vote.

An electoral commission was created by the Congress to decide which sets of electoral votes were valid. The rules under which the commission operated provided that its decision was final unless both houses of Congress voted to override it. This proved to be critical, because the Republicans controlled the Senate and the Democrats controlled the House of Representatives. The commission was composed of 15 members (10 Congressmen and 5 Supreme Court Justices) of whom 8 were Republicans and 7 were Democrats. By straight party vote the commission upheld every Republican claim. The Democratic House rejected, but the Republican Senate upheld, the commission's decisions. All 20 electoral votes were awarded to Hayes, who was selected President by a majority of one electoral vote.[9]

The election of 1888 did not involve as much political intrigue. Rather, it seems to have been a straightforward case in which distortions inherent in the Electoral College caused the winner in popular votes to lose the Presidency. President Grover Cleveland, the popular vote winner, carried a number of states by large margins. Benjamin Harrison, the challenger, won in the Electoral College by carrying a number of larger states, including New York, Ohio, and Pennsylvania by small margins, producing large blocs of electoral votes.[10] Cleveland attained a measure of revenge when he defeated President Harrison in the election of 1892.

Deadlock The Electoral College has, on two occasions, been unable to produce majorities for any Presidential candidate, the result

9. MacBride, *American Electoral College*, pp. 35–36.

10. Longley and Braun, *Politics of Electoral College Reform*, p. 35.

being that the House of Representatives selected the President. This first occurred in 1800 under rules that were subsequently changed by constitutional amendment. As the Electoral College was originally conceived, each elector cast two votes, one for President and one for Vice President. The candidate receiving the most electoral votes was elected President and the second-place finisher became Vice President. In 1800, the newly formed Republican party was supporting Thomas Jefferson and Aaron Burr as its candidates for President and Vice President, respectively. The Republican electors loyally voted for the party's chosen men with the unexpected result that Jefferson and Burr received the same number of electoral votes. Consequently, the President was chosen by the House of Representatives, which was under the control of the Federalist party. House deliberations took a week, the issue not being decided until the 36th ballot after Alexander Hamilton threw his support to Jefferson.[11] Vice President Burr later repaid Hamilton by shooting him in a duel.

After Jefferson's party gained control of the Congress, they passed the Twelfth Amendment to the Constitution, which was quickly approved by the states. It provides that electors will cast separate ballots for the offices of President and Vice President, making it unlikely that a Vice-Presidential candidate will erroneously be elected President.

The four man Presidential race in 1824 produced another deadlock with no candidate having a majority in the Electoral College. Andrew Jackson won the most popular votes (41%) and the most electoral votes (99), but was 32 votes short of a majority in the Electoral College. The House of Representatives selected as President second-place finisher John Quincy Adams, who had received 31% of the popular vote and 84 electoral votes. Speaker of the House Henry Clay, who finished fourth in the Electoral College balloting, supported Adams and was subsequently appointed Secretary of State by the President amidst charges of a shady deal.[12]

Close Calls   There have been 22 Presidential elections since 1828 in which shifts of 75,000 or fewer voters could have altered the outcome. The closest of these was in 1876, when a shift of 116 votes

11. MacBride, *American Electoral College,* p. 31.

12. The election returns for 1824 are from *Presidential Elections Since 1789,* p. 25. On Clay's role in support of Adams, see Longley and Braun, *Politics of Electoral College Reform,* p. 36.

in South Carolina would have elected Tilden instead of Hayes.[13] Five of these close Presidential elections have occurred since 1916, and are listed in Table 3.2. In 1916, less than 2000 additional Republican votes in California would have cost President Woodrow Wilson reelection by denying him California's electoral votes. The outcomes of the Presidential races in 1948, 1960, and 1976 might have been altered by shifts of less than 13,000 votes in key electoral states.

Results of a computer analysis of the relationship between popular votes and electoral votes indicate that in an election as close as 1960, there is only a fifty-fifty chance that the popular vote winner will also obtain a majority in the Electoral College. When the victor's winning margin is 500,000 votes, there is still a one-in-three chance of losing in the Electoral College, and a Presidential candidate with a victory margin as great as 1.5 million votes still stands a one-in-four chance of losing in the Electoral College.[14]

Third Parties In close Presidential elections, it is the electoral vote of the states and not the popular vote that is decisive. This fact is fundamental to the strategy of Presidential candidates of both major parties, but it severely limits the prospects of third parties and independent candidates for electoral success. The relationship between electoral and popular votes in four Presidential elections is displayed in Figs. 3.1—3.4. These are relatively recent elections in which third-party candidates drained away significant numbers of popular votes and electoral votes from the major-party candidates. As these elections illustrate, the necessity of winning pluralities within states in order to gain electoral votes can reduce the candidate of a third party to an also-ran, unless that candidate has a large national following, or strong regional support. In every Presidential election there are a handful of minor parties able to pull votes. The Socialists, for example, won as much as 6% of the popular vote in 1912. With the possible exception of the Progressive Party in 1924, the most successful third parties in the twentieth century have been splinter parties, based on personalities and factions which split off from either the Republican or the Democratic party.

13. Results of these elections are available in Peirce, *The People's President*, pp. 317–321, and in Longley and Braun, p. 40.

14. Longley and Braun, *Politics of Electoral College Reform*, p. 3.

Table 3.2   Close Calls: Recent Presidential Elections in Which a Small Shift
             in Popular Votes Would Have Changed the Electoral College
             ·Outcome

Election	Shift	Where	Result
1916	1983	California	Hughes elected instead of Wilson
1948	12,487	California Ohio	Electoral College deadlock
	29,294	California Ohio Illinois	Dewey elected instead of Truman
1960	8971	Illinois Missouri	Electoral College deadlock
	11,424	Illinois Missouri New Mexico Hawaii Nevada	Nixon elected instead of Kennedy
1968	53,034	New Jersey Missouri New Hampshire	Electoral College deadlock
1976	9246	Ohio Hawaii	Ford elected instead of Carter

Source: The figures for the 1916, 1948, 1960 Presidential elections are extracted from
          Neal R. Peirce, *The People's President: The Electoral College in American His-*
          tory and the Direct-Vote Alternative. New York: Simon and Schuster Inc.,
          1968, pp. 317–321. They are used with the permission of the publisher. The
          figures for 1968 are cited by Longley and Braun, p. 11. The figures for 1976 are
          cited in Stephen J. Wayne, *The Road to the White House: The Politics of Presi-*
          dential Elections. New York: St. Martin's Press, 1980, p. 11.

The only third-party candidate to win more votes than one of
the major-party Presidential candidates was former President Theodore Roosevelt in 1912 (see Fig. 3.1). As outgoing President in
1908, Roosevelt used his influence to help William Howard Taft win
the Republican nomination. Four years later, Roosevelt, disgruntled
with Taft's Presidency, returned to challenge him. Roosevelt sound-
ly defeated both President Taft and Progressive Republican Senator
Robert La Follette in primaries in Illinois, Pennsylvania, Nebraska,
Oregon, Maryland, California, New Jersey, South Dakota, and Ohio
(Taft's home state). However, most of the delegates to the Republi-

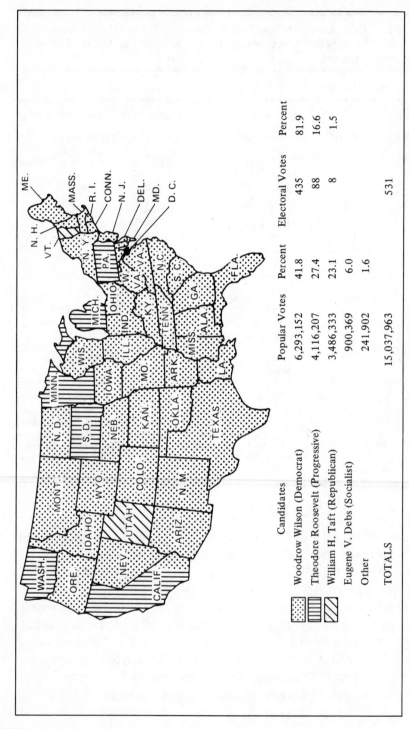

Figure 3.1 Results of the 1912 Presidential election: Electoral and popular votes. Source: *Presidential Elections Since 1789* (2nd ed.) Washington, D.C.: Congressional Quarterly, 1979, pp. 45 and 86. Reproduced by permission of the publisher.

Candidates	Popular Votes	Percent	Electoral Votes	Percent
Woodrow Wilson (Democrat)	6,293,152	41.8	435	81.9
Theodore Roosevelt (Progressive)	4,116,207	27.4	88	16.6
William H. Taft (Republican)	3,486,333	23.1	8	1.5
Eugene V. Debs (Socialist)	900,369	6.0		
Other	241,902	1.6		
TOTALS	15,037,963		531	

can convention were chosen by state party organizations, which supported President Taft.[15]

A few hours after the Republican convention renominated President Taft, a horde of Roosevelt's followers packed themselves into Chicago's Orchestra Hall to nominate Teddy by acclamation as an independent candidate for President. Determined to destroy Taft politically, the popular former President joined with dissident liberal Republicans in the Progressive Republican League to mount the 20th century's most impressive third-party Presidential bid.[16] Feeling "fit as a bull moose," Roosevelt ran as the nominee of the Progressive Party, fighting vigorously to defeat Taft's old guard. By and large he succeeded, as President Taft finished last in the three-way race, losing even his native Ohio and receiving only 8 electoral votes. Roosevelt won 27% of the popular vote and 88 electoral votes, but the prime beneficiary of Roosevelt's candidacy was Democrat Woodrow Wilson. With a shade under 42% of the popular vote, Wilson carried all but 8 states, winning 435 electoral votes.

Senator Robert La Follette's third-party candidacy in 1924 had its roots in progressive Republicanism, but it is regarded by some historians as a true third-party candidacy rather than as a splinter movement.[17] The Conference for Progressive Political Action launched the new Progressive Party in 1924, offering as its Presidential nominee "Fighting Bob" La Follette. The American Federation of Labor endorsed his candidacy and the Socialist party supported him. The results of this election (Fig. 3.2) are a classic illustration of the impact of the Electoral-College system on third-party Presidential candidacies. The senator, 69 and in failing health, could not command the same broad popular appeal as the dynamic and popular Theodore Roosevelt did in 1912. Despite winning nearly 17% of the vote nationwide, the senator was able to garner only the 13 electoral votes of his home state of Wisconsin. The remainder of his popular vote was not sufficiently geographically concentrated to control the electoral votes of any other states.

Except for Theodore Roosevelt, who was able to run strong nationally by virtue of being a popular former President, third-party

15. Howard P. Nash, Jr., *Third Parties in American Politics.* Washington, D.C.: Public Affairs Press, 1959, p. 249.

16. *Ibid.*, pp. 255–256.

17. William Best Hesseltine, *The Rise and Fall of Third Parties: From Anti-Masonry to Wallace.* Gloucester, Ma.: Peter Smith, 1957, pp. 28–33.

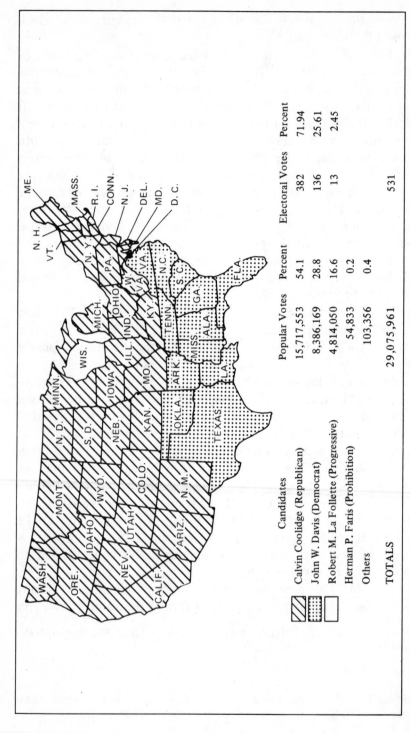

Figure 3.2 Results of the 1924 Presidential election: Electoral and popular votes. Source: *Presidential Elections Since 1789* (2nd ed.). Washington, D.C.: Congressional Quarterly, 1979, pp. 48 and 89. Reproduced by permission of the publisher.

Presidential candidates have needed a strong regional base in order to command significant numbers of electoral votes. The 1948 Presidential election (Fig. 3.3), in which two dissident Democrats challenged President Truman, is an almost ideal illustration of the advantages of a regional candidacy. Former Vice President Henry A. Wallace, running as a Progressive, attracted more than 2% of the popular vote, but won no electoral votes because his support was scattered throughout the country.

Unhappy over a liberal civil-rights plank in the Democratic platform, the Southern wing of the party also challenged the President. After walking out of the Democratic convention, the Dixiecrats nominated Governor J. Strom Thurmond of South Carolina as their candidate for President, intending to prove that the Democratic party could not win without the solid South. Running as a States' Rights Democrat, Thurmond got only 12,000 more votes than Henry Wallace, but won 39 electoral votes—7% of the total—because he carried four Southern states. Although the Electoral College system generally makes life difficult for third parties, those with a strong regional base are likely to fare better than a nationally oriented minor party with similar voter strength. The results of the 1980 Presidential election re-emphasized this fact. Independent candidate John Anderson won 7% of the popular vote nationwide but did not control any electoral votes because he was unable to carry any states.

The most impressive showing by a modern regionally based third party occurred in the 1968 Presidential election, again involving a dissident Southern Democrat. Alabama Governor George C. Wallace, running as the candidate of the American Independent Party, attracted nearly 14% of the popular vote, carried 5 Southern states, and won 46 electoral votes (Fig. 3.4). As close as this election was, it is conceivable that Wallace's electoral votes could have been crucial in the Electoral College. If neither Richard Nixon nor Hubert Humphrey won a majority of electoral votes, then Wallace would have controlled the balance of power, perhaps forcing the other candidates to deal with him before the Electoral College met in December to choose the President.[18] It did not work out that way, and Wallace's electors proved to be irrelevant. Even though Nixon led Humphrey by less than 1% of the popular vote, the Electoral College provided the Republican candidate with a comfortable majority, denying Wallace any leverage.

18. Longley and Braun, *Politics of Electoral College Reform*, pp. 17–18.

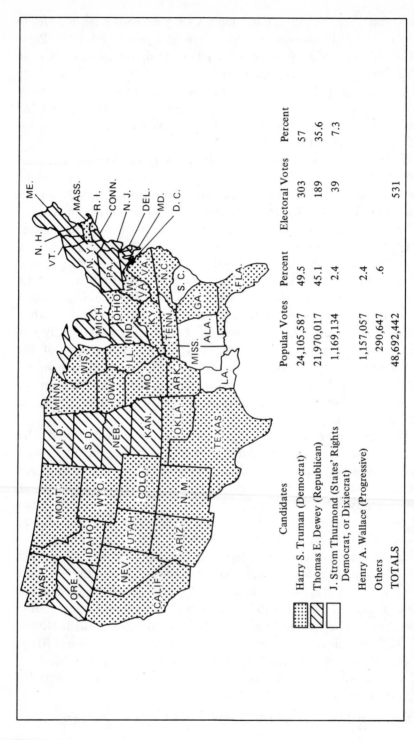

Candidates	Popular Votes	Percent	Electoral Votes	Percent
Harry S. Truman (Democrat)	24,105,587	49.5	303	57
Thomas E. Dewey (Republican)	21,970,017	45.1	189	35.6
J. Strom Thurmond (States' Rights Democrat, or Dixiecrat)	1,169,134	2.4	39	7.3
Henry A. Wallace (Progressive)	1,157,057	2.4		
Others	290,647	.6		
TOTALS	48,692,442		531	

Figure 3.3 Results of the 1948 Presidential election: Electoral and popular votes. Source: *Presidential Elections Since 1789* (2nd ed.). Washington, D.C.: Congressional Quarterly, 1979, pp. 54 and 95. Reproduced by permission of the publisher.

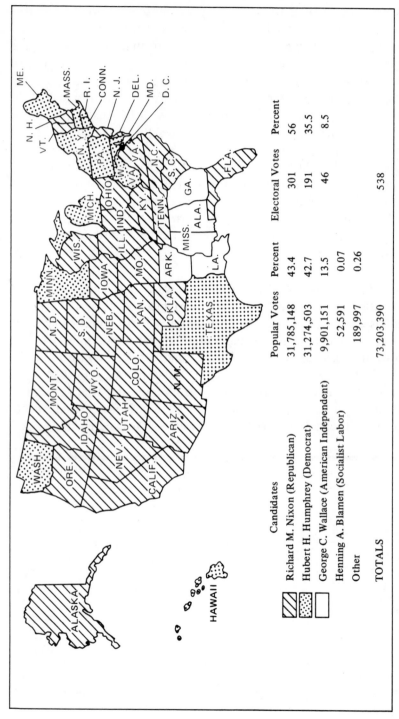

Candidates	Popular Votes	Percent	Electoral Votes	Percent
Richard M. Nixon (Republican)	31,785,148	43.4	301	56
Hubert H. Humphrey (Democrat)	31,274,503	42.7	191	35.5
George C. Wallace (American Independent)	9,901,151	13.5	46	8.5
Henning A. Blamen (Socialist Labor)	52,591	0.07		
Other	189,997	0.26		
TOTALS	73,203,390		538	

Figure 3.4 Results of the 1968 Presidential election: Electoral and popular votes. Source: *Presidential Elections Since 1789* (2nd ed.). Washington, D.C.: Congressional Quarterly, 1979, pp. 59 and 100. Reproduced by permission of the publisher.

Given the realities of the Electoral College system, third parties would seem to be faced with three alternatives: (1) nominate a nationally known candidate with a large personal following who can perhaps win enough electoral votes to force the Democratic, or Republican, candidates to make a deal before the Electoral College meets; (2) nominate a strong regional candidate, control most of the electoral votes of that region and bargain with the major parties; or (3) failing either of these, drain off votes from one of the major parties, causing them to lose the Presidency, perhaps with the aim of restructuring that party's goals and principles in the future. There is a fourth logical possibility, however, remote, that a popular third party candidate could actually win the Presidency for forging a new Presidential coalition, perhaps by capturing most of the Independent vote. This would seem to be a realistic strategy only during a time of partisan realignment.

The Importance of Large States The development and institutionalization of the practice of slates of pledged electors voting as blocs has great significance for Presidential electoral politics. Except for unusual instances involving election of faithless, or unpledged, electors, it means that a Presidential candidate can control all of a state's electoral votes by winning a popular plurality in that state. This makes it virtually impossible for serious Presidential candidates to ignore the large states and have any hope of being elected. Table 3.3 displays the ranking of the "Big Seven" states and their electoral

Table 3.3   The Large States and Their Electoral Votes

State	Electoral Votes	State's Percentage of Total Electoral Votes	State's Percentage of Electoral College Majority
California	45	8.4	16.6
New York	41	7.6	15.2
Pennsylvania	27	5.0	10.0
Texas	26	4.8	9.6
Illinois	26	4.8	9.6
Ohio	25	4.6	9.3
Michigan	21	3.9	7.8
TOTALS	211	39.1	78.1

Source: Computed from figures in the *Statistical Abstract of the United States* (100th ed.), 1979, p. 497.

Table 3.4   Victorious Party in Large States in Presidential Elections
from 1948 to 1976

State	Victorious Party in Presidential Election									Percentage of Republican Victories
	1948	1952	1956	1960	1964	1968	1972	1976	1980	
California	D	R	R	R	D	R	R	R	R	78
New York	R	R	R	D	D	D	R	D	R	56
Pennsylvania	R	R	R	D	D	D	R	D	R	56
Texas	D	R	R	D	D	D	R	D	R	44
Illinois	D	R	R	D	D	R	R	R	R	67
Ohio	D	R	R	R	D	R	R	D	R	67
Michigan	R	R	R	D	D	D	R	R	R	67

Source: Extracted from the *Statistical Abstract of the United States* (100th ed.), 1979,
p. 497. Updated by the author.

votes. The total of 211 electoral votes controlled by these seven
states constitutes more than three-fourths of the 270 needed for a
majority in the Electoral College. The rankings of these states will
change somewhat after the results of the 1980 census are implemented and the size of each state's Congressional delegation is adjusted in response to population shifts. Texas' and California's share
of electors will increase at the expense of the others, and Florida
(which presently has 17 electoral votes) may gain enough to join the
elite as a member of the "Big Eight."

The impact of large states on electoral strategy is considerable because a Presidential candidate is far better off to win large states by
small margins than small states by large margins. This reality forces
any serious Presidential candidate to contest the large states since it
is difficult to put an Electoral College majority together without
winning at least two, or three, of these pivotal states. A strategy of
ignoring the large states (Goldwater style) results in almost certain
defeat in the Electoral College, no matter how many popular votes it
generates. Such a strategy is not very prudent in any event, since the
large states have reasonably competitive party systems, and mainstream Presidential candidates of either party have a chance to win
some of the pivotal states. Table 3.4 shows which party carried each
of the large states in Presidential elections since World War II. All of
the large states have been reasonably competitive except for California, which has gone Republican 78% of the time.

The Presidential race within these states is usually closely contested, the margin between victory and defeat often being only a few thousand votes. For example, John Kennedy carried Illinois in 1960 with a plurality of less than 9,000 votes; in 1976, Jimmy Carter won Ohio by 11,000; and in 1948, President Truman carried California by less than 18,000 votes. In close Presidential elections, most of the large states are literally up for grabs by either party. This has resulted in Presidential candidates of both parties spending disproportionately large shares of campaign time and resources in these states.

Which states are targeted by each party depends partly on the specifics of the election—the issues and, especially, the candidates. In nine Presidential elections from 1948 to 1980, the Republicans have nominated candidates from Big-Seven states a total of eight times, the Democrats only three times.[19] This has worked to the Republicans' advantage, giving their candidates an electoral base within a pivotal state.

A candidate with a solid base of regional support (Kennedy in the East in 1960, Carter in the South in 1976, Reagan in the West in 1980) can adopt a strategy of holding onto this base and selectively targeting large states. In 20 Presidential elections since 1900, the winning candidates have carried, on the average, 5 of the 7 largest states, and no President has been elected without winning at least 3 of them. Conversely, a strategy focusing only on large states is not likely to succeed because it requires the candidate to carry all of them. This is very difficult for anyone other than a popular incumbent President to do. Only Herbert Hoover (1928), Dwight Eisen-

19. The states of residence of the Presidential nominees were:

	Presidential Nominee	
Date	Democrats	Republicans
1948	Harry Truman, Missouri	Thomas Dewey, New York
1952	Adlai Stevenson, Illinois	Dwight Eisenhower, New York, Pennsylvania
1956	Same as 1952	Same as 1952
1960	John Kennedy, Massachusetts	Richard Nixon, California, New York
1964	Lyndon Johnson, Texas	Barry Goldwater, Arizona
1968	Hubert Humphrey, Minnesota	Richard Nixon, California, New York
1972	George McGovern, South Dakota	Richard Nixon, California, New York
1976	Jimmy Carter, Georgia	Gerald Ford, Michigan
1980	Same as 1976	Ronald Reagan, California

(Photo by Michael Evans, The White House)

hower (1952), and Ronald Reagan (1980) have been able to do it without the advantages of Presidential incumbency. Presidents Franklin Roosevelt (1936), Dwight Eisenhower (1956), Lyndon Johnson (1964), and Richard Nixon (1972) carried all 7 of these states in their reelection bids.

Although these large states are diverse socially and economically, they share some similarities which affect Presidential elections. In addition to being politically competitive and available to candidates of either party, they have diversified urban economies characterized by industrial development, large financial centers, and, except for Texas, heavily unionized labor. Each is populated by significant numbers of ethnic and racial minorities.

To carry the large states, candidates attempt to piece together a coalition by appealing to social, economic, and racial groupings for support. Cohesive groups, particularly those with high rates of voter turnout, are of special concern to Presidential candidates because of the necessity of winning closely contested pivotal states. The Presidential constituency has, of necessity, a somewhat more urban, industrialized, and ethnic flavor than the nation as a whole. Consequently, various groups, rather than the individual voter, frequently become the focus of Presidential campaigns.

In summary, a unique feature of American Presidential elections is the indirect system of election whereby the President is chosen not by the voters, but by an institution especially created for that purpose. In practice, the Electoral College frequently awards exaggerated majorities to the Presidential candidate with the largest popular plurality, although, on occasion, the College has selected Presidents who did not win popular pluralities. On other occasions, the College has been unable to select a President, leaving the choice to the House of Representatives. In a majority of Presidential elections since 1828, shifts of a relatively small number of votes in key states might have changed the outcome. The winner-take-all feature of the Electoral College results from election of slates of electors pledged to Presidential candidates. This magnifies the importance of a handful of states which control large blocs of electoral votes. The social, economic, and ethnic diversity of these pivotal states encourages Presidential candidates to assemble and activate voter coalitions composed of social and economic groupings.

THE PRESIDENTIAL ELECTORATE

Since only one candidate can win a Presidential election, campaign politics involves coalitions of groups of voters. There is little incentive for each group, or faction, to nominate its own candidate because a broad base of electoral support is necessary to produce the pluralities within states required by the Electoral College. For social, economic, and historical reasons, most voter groups are, to a certain extent, predisposed to support one, or the other, of the major parties. The parties come to rely upon this voter support and conduct their Presidential campaigns in a manner compatible with their traditional group basis of support. Generally, neither party commands total loyalty from any group, and both parties attempt to appeal to nearly all groups for votes, although the conservative wing of the Republican party seems to have written off the black vote. The configuration of group support that defines modern Presidential coalitions first began to take shape during the early 1930's and continues to influence Presidential election outcomes.

Alignment and Realignment

Presidential electoral coalitions are the product of historical circumstances and events, changing in response to social and economic development.   Voter alignments may change as gradually, or as suddenly, as the partisan preferences of the groups and individuals composing them.   Historical development and major events periodically converge to produce significant alterations in the voter alignments defining the party system and Presidential coalitions.   Changes in partisan alignments are occasionally so dramatic and significant in their long-run implications that Presidential elections associated with these extensive partisan shifts have become known as critical elections.

Critical Elections   Characterized by intensive disruption of traditional patterns of voting as large blocs of voters shift their partisan allegiances, critical elections are associated with abnormal social and economic stress.   Involving a high level of political intensity, critical elections are preceded, or accompanied, by major third-party movements indicating the inability of politics as usual to aggregate political demands.   Ideological polarizations occur within, and between, parties, and various segments of the electorate are mobilized, or activated, to higher levels of participation.   Most fundamentally, however, critical elections are associated with significant alterations in the party balance.   As voters realign themselves in response to historical developments, the party balance is altered, the minority party may gain strength, perhaps even becoming the majority party.   New parties may emerge as old ones disintegrate, and new voter coalitions form which prove to be relatively durable.   Such changes are likely to be associated with new directions in government policies.[20]

Historically, five major realignment eras are associated with the Presidential elections of 1800, 1828, 1860, 1896, and 1932.   Periods between critical elections are characterized by relatively stable partisan alignments.   During this stable phase in the electoral cycle, one party has generally predominated, being preferred by a large portion of voters.   The other party may find itself consigned to the status of minority party, heavily outnumbered by voters of the other party, or the party balance may be reasonably competitive, as in the period prior to the critical election of 1896.   This election, which Republican William McKinley won by a landslide, is regarded as an affirmation of the control of national political institutions by Eastern commercial and industrial interests.   Democrat William Jennings Bryan

20. Walter Dean Burnham, *Critical Elections and the Mainsprings of American Politics.* New York: W. W. Norton & Co., 1970, pp. 6–10.

attempted to forge a winning Presidential coalition of debt-ridden small farmers in the West and South and urban industrial workers in the Northeast. Bryan's attempt to merge rural populism and urban proletarian discontent wilted in the face of the financial and organizational resources of the urban Republican machines. Republicans carried working-class, as well as middle- and upper-class neighborhoods in the urban industrial states.[21]

The loss of the industrial states to the Republicans was a defeat from which the Democrats did not fully recover until 1932. In the interim, the Democrats were a minority party, almost perpetually out of power. They were able to control the Congress, or the Presidency only occasionally, having consistent support only in the South, Texas, and some border states. Democrat Woodrow Wilson was able to win the Presidency only because Theodore Roosevelt split the dominant Republican party in 1912. Wilson and the Democrats were barely able to hold on to the White House in a close election in 1916. By 1928, Democratic support had shrunk to encompass only the solid South, with Republican Herbert Hoover winning even Texas, Florida, Tennessee, and North Carolina.

Then it happened. In October, 1929, the stock market crashed, resulting in bankruptcy for investors and businesses. Next, the banks failed, and many of those not already wiped out by the crash lost their savings. More businesses closed, and within a short time one-fourth of the work force was unemployed. There were no jobs, no money, no credit, and no place to get any. America was caught in a worldwide depression, and the Republican party had the misfortune to be in power when it happened. The Republican public philosophy of unregulated industrial expansion was suddenly discredited. Herbert Hoover's inactivity and ineffectiveness in alleviating the economic misery wrought by the Great Depression would earn the Republicans a reputation as the party of big business with no concern for the common people.

The New Deal Alignment The New Deal voter alignment was the product of a single event (the economic catastrophe) and a single personality—Franklin Delano Roosevelt. After his landslide victory over President Hoover in 1932, Roosevelt and the Democratic-controlled Congress produced a series of innovative and pragmatic social

21. V. O. Key, Jr., *Politics, Parties and Pressure Groups.* New York: Thomas Y. Crowell, 1942, pp. 185–191.

programs aimed at alleviating the economic chaos by stabilizing the banking system, regulating the stock market, making credit available to farmers and businesses, and putting people back to work. To cope with the crisis, the President and the Congress produced an out-pouring of legislation during the first 100 days of Roosevelt's administration that was unparalleled in the nation's history.

This series of legislative enactments and Presidential actions collectively came to be known as the New Deal. Even a partial listing of New Deal legislation is impressive. Within a few days after his inauguration Roosevelt declared a banking holiday and called the Congress into special session to enact an emergency banking measure which extended government assistance to private bankers to reopen their banks. Within four days, citizens were depositing more money in banks than they were withdrawing. "Capitalism," observed Raymond Moley, "was saved in eight days."[22] The next day, fulfilling a pledge dear to the hearts of Democratic voters, Roosevelt asked Congress to end prohibition of alcoholic beverages, which it did as impatient Congressmen chanted, "Vote! Vote! We want beer!"[23]

This was followed shortly by farm bills subsidizing farm staples and making credit available to farmers to avoid foreclosures. Help for the unemployed came in the form of public-works projects and a half billion dollars in direct Federal grants to states for relief. Within two months, the Congress passed the Home Owners' Loan Act, which prevented massive foreclosures by eventually refinancing one of every five mortgaged private dwellings in America's cities. Rural electrification was begun by creation of the Tennessee Valley Authority, and industrial mobilization was initiated through the National Industrial Recovery Act, an unprecedented program of governmental—industrial cooperation which contained extensions of collective bargaining rights for labor.

Few of these experimental programs worked exactly as had been anticipated, but they were indicative of Roosevelt's ability to galvanize the political system into action during a crisis. In addition to his great skill as a politician, Roosevelt possessed another rare attribute—the capacity for inspiring his fellow countrymen through eloquent rhetoric. Audiences in excess of 60 million Americans sat around radio sets to hear the President's fireside chats as he called for

22. William E. Leuchtenburg, *Franklin D. Roosevelt and the New Deal: 1932-1940.* New York: Harper and Row, 1963, p. 45.

23. *Ibid*, p. 46.

sacrifice, discipline, and action. It may well be that the President's ability to inspire public confidence and instill hope was his greatest contribution to American politics. He had created the impression of a man who knew how to lead and had faith in the future.[24]

Voters flocked to the Democratic party, and by 1936 the electoral transformation was complete. Roosevelt's personal popularity, his ability to reestablish public confidence, and the popularity of New Deal programs converged in 1936 to produce one of the most one-sided Presidential elections in history. Roosevelt was victorious in every corner of the country, winning 61% of the vote. The Republican opponent, Alfred M. Landon, was unable to carry even his native Kansas and received only 37% of the popular vote and 8 electoral votes. Democrats controlled both houses of Congress by large majorities.

Seeking unprecedented third and fourth terms as President, Roosevelt easily disposed of Republican dark horse Wendell Willkie (1940) and New York's Governor Thomas Dewey (1944) by comfortable popular majorities and huge margins in the Electoral College. The Democrats, who had languished as a minority party for 80 years, were now the new majority. By forging a coalition between Southern whites (who had been Democrats since enduring reconstruction under the Republicans after the Civil War) and Northern urban working-class ethnics and minorities, the Democrats dominated Presidential politics uninterruptedly, until 1952.

The New Deal Coalition Since World War II The theory of critical elections postulates that voter realignments are followed by periods of relative partisan stability. Periods between major partisan realignments are not static, however, and voters within regions or discrete social groups may move from one party to another. These trends are known as secular realignments.[25] The New Deal coalition was composed partly of incompatible elements (Southern whites, Northern blacks, and liberals), and over the course of time, the internal contradictions have necessitated some adjustments within this voter alignment. Not surprisingly, there has been movement of groups both into and away from the Democratic coalition. Secular realignments along regional and racial lines have occurred, modifying the New Deal coalition. These trends are shown in Table 3.5, which

24. *Ibid.*, pp. 45–61.

25. Burnham, *Critical Elections*, p. 5.

Table 3.5   Presidential Votes by Groups, 1952–1980

Group	1952 Stevenson (Percent)	1952 Eisenhower (Percent)	1956 Stevenson (Percent)	1956 Eisenhower (Percent)	1960 Kennedy (Percent)	1960 Nixon (Percent)
National	44.6	55.4	42.2	57.8	50.1	49.9
Sex						
Male	47	53	45	55	52	48
Female	42	58	39	61	49	51
Race						
White	43	57	41	59	49	51
Nonwhite	79	21	61	39	68	32
Education						
College	34	66	31	69	39	61
High school	45	55	42	58	52	48
Grade school	52	48	50	50	55	45
Occupation						
Professional and business	36	64	32	68	42	58
White-collar	40	60	37	63	48	52
Manual	55	45	50	50	60	40
Age						
Under 30	51	49	43	57	54	46
30–49	47	53	45	55	54	46
50 and older	39	61	39	61	46	54
Religion						
Protestant	37	63	37	63	38	62
Catholic	56	44	51	49	78	22
Politics						
Republican	8	92	4	96	5	95
Democrat	77	23	85	15	84	16
Independent	35	65	30	70	43	57
Region						
East	45	55	40	60	53	47
Midwest	42	58	41	59	48	52
South	51	49	49	51	51	49
West	42	58	43	57	49	51
Members of labor union families	61	39	57	43	65	35

Table 3.5 *Continued*

Group	1964 Johnson (Percent)	1964 Goldwater (Percent)	1968 Humphrey (Percent)	1968 Nixon (Percent)	1968 Wallace
National	61.3	38.7	43.0	43.4	13.6
Sex					
Male	60	40	41	43	16
Female	62	38	45	43	12
Race					
White	59	41	38	47	15
Nonwhite	94	6	85	12	3

Table 3.5 *Continued*

	1964		1968		
Group	Johnson	Goldwater	Humphrey	Nixon	Wallace
	(Percent)			(Percent)	
Education					
College	52	48	37	54	9
High school	62	38	42	43	15
Grade school	66	34	52	33	15
Occupation					
Professional and business	54	46	34	56	10
White-collar	57	43	41	47	12
Manual	71	29	50	35	15
Age					
Under 30	64	36	47	38	15
30–49	63	37	44	41	15
50 and older	59	41	41	47	12
Religion					
Protestant	55	45	35	49	16
Catholic	76	24	59	33	8
Politics					
Republican	20	80	9	86	5
Democrat	87	13	74	12	14
Independent	56	44	31	44	25
Region					
East	68	32	50	43	7
Midwest	61	39	44	47	9
South	52	48	31	36	33
West	60	40	44	49	7
Members of labor					
union families	73	27	56	29	15

Table 3.5 *Continued*

	1972		1976		
Group	McGovern	Nixon	Carter	Ford	McCarthy
	(Percent)			(Percent)	
National	38	62	50	48	1
Sex					
Male	37	63	53	45	1
Female	38	62	48	51	a
Race					
White	32	68	46	52	1
Nonwhite	87	13	85	15	a
Education					
College	37	63	42	55	2
High school	34	66	54	46	a
Grade school	49	51	58	41	1
Occupation					
Professional and business	31	69	42	56	1
White-collar	36	64	50	48	2
Manual	43	57	58	41	1

Table 3.5 *Continued*

	1972		1976			
Group	McGovern	Nixon	Carter	Ford	McCarthy	
	(Percent)			(Percent)		
Age						
Under 30	48	52	53	45	1	100%
30–49	33	67	48	49	2	100%
50 and older	36	64	52	48	a	100%
Religion						
Protestant	30	70	46	53	a	100%
Catholic	48	52	57	42	1	
Politics						
Republican	5	95	9	91	a	100%
Democrat	67	33	82	18	a	
Independent	31	69	38	57	4	100%
Region						
East	42	58	51	47	1	
Midwest	40	60	48	50	1	
South	29	71	54	45	a	100%
West	41	59	46	51	1	
Members of labor union families	46	54	63	36	1	

Table 3.5 *Continued*

	1980		
Group	Reagan	Carter	Anderson
		(Percent)	
National	51	42	7
Sex			
Male	54	37	7
Female	46	45	7
Race			
White	55	36	8
Nonwhite	14	82	3
Education			
College	53	35	10
High school	48	46	4
Grade school	N.A.	N.A.	N.A.
Occupation			
Professional and business	56	33	9
White-collar	48	42	8
Manual	47	46	5
Age			
Under 30	43	43	11
30–49	54	37	7
50 and older	54	40	5
Religion			
Protestant	56	37	6
Catholic	51	40	7

Table 3.5 *Continued*

	1980		
Group	*Reagan*	*Carter* *(Percent)*	*Anderson*
Politics			
Republican	84	11	4
Democrat	26	66	6
Independent	54	30	12
Region			
East	47	43	8
Midwest	51	41	6
South	51	44	3
West	52	35	10
Members of labor union families	44	47	7

[a] Less than 1%   N.A., not available.

Source: "Presidential Votes by Groups, 1952–1976." *Gallup Opinion Index*, December, 1976, pp. 116–117. Reprinted by permission. Figures for 1980 are from *The New York Times/CBS News Poll*, reported in *The New York Times*, November 9, 1980, p. 18.

shows the votes of various regional and social groupings in the United States from 1952 to 1980.

Region

One of the most readily apparent trends is the desertion of the Democrats at the Presidential level by the formerly solid South. Once heavily Democratic in Presidential voting, that area of the country is now up for grabs. Within the South there are at least two separate trends relevant to Presidential politics. First, among white voters, large numbers of former Democrats have become Independents who switch parties in Presidential elections, depending on the candidates. In 1968, a third of white Southern votes went to George Wallace, accounting for more than half his votes. Democratic identifiers have declined from 80% of Southern whites in 1952 to 47% in 1976.[26]   Black Southerners are very loyal Democrats and are participating in greater numbers. Jimmy Carter's victory in the South in 1976 rested on the support of a large majority of black voters and a substantial minority of white support.[27]

26. Herbert B. Asher, *Presidential Elections and American Politics* (revised ed.). Homewood, Ill.: Dorsey, 1980, p. 85.

27. *Ibid.*, pp. 209–210.

Although Republicanism has gained strength in the South (due largely to migration of Northerners to the region), the Democrats remain the majority party in terms of voter preferences, as well as Congressional voting. In recent Presidential elections, however, the Democrats have been able to carry the region only by nominating a Southerner for President or Vice President. Lyndon Johnson's presence on the Democratic ticket in 1960 contributed to John Kennedy's electoral success in parts of the South, especially Texas. President Johnson won the majority of Southern votes in 1964, but lost five states to Goldwater. Although Jimmy Carter won the region in 1976, the South abandoned him in 1980 and gave a majority of its votes to Ronald Reagan.

The urban Northeast and industrial Midwestern cities continue to constitute the core of the Democratic Presidential constituency. Republican support is especially strong in the West, rural areas in the Midwest and East, and the suburbs. In Presidential elections since 1952, excluding only the Johnson landslide of 1964, the Republicans have repeatedly carried most of the states west of the Missouri River, except Texas.

Race

From the Civil War until the Great Depression, black votes supported the party of Lincoln. Even in 1932, a majority of black votes supported Herbert Hoover.[28] After moving tentatively into the Roosevelt coalition in 1936, their support of Democratic Presidential candidates has steadily increased. Republican candidate Eisenhower was able to attract the support of a substantial minority of black votes (39%) in 1956, as was Richard Nixon (32%) in 1960. Black voter support for Democratic candidates has increased dramatically since the 1964 Presidential election. In that election, the Republican nominee was Senator Barry Goldwater, whose vote in the Senate against the 1964 Civil Rights Act put him on record as opposed to Federal enforcement of civil rights. President Johnson sponsored this legislation and fought for its passage, subsequently receiving 94% of the black votes in the 1964 election. After his reelection, the President and the Democratic controlled Congress followed up with the 1965 Voting-Rights Act, leading to rapid increases in registra-

28. Mark R. Levy and Michael S. Kramer, *The Ethnic Factor: How America's Minorities Decide Elections.* New York: Simon and Schuster, 1972, p. 40.

tion and participation of Southern black voters. These events seem to have cemented the relationship between black voters and the Democratic party.

As a result of these developments, the parties are nearly polarized by race at the Presidential level. Black voters constitute about one-fifth of the Democratic Presidential constituency, and only once since 1952 has a Democratic Presidential candidate (President Johnson in 1964) won majority support from white voters. Conversely, nearly all votes (97%) for Republican Presidential candidates come from white voters.[29] The Democrats now lead Republicans in party identification among black voters by a margin of 75% to 5%. Blacks were the only social group to give President Carter a substantial majority of votes (88%) in his reelection bid in 1980.

Social Class

About one-third of Americans say that they never think of themselves as members of a social class. Even at the height of New Deal politics, American parties were not class-polarized. The Democrats drew greater support from the working class, poor, and union households, but these groups were not unanimous in supporting the Roosevelt coalition. The Republicans were able to enlist the support of a minority of voters in these categories, just as Democrats were able to attract votes from a minority of white-collar and upper middle-class voters. There has been a lessening of class differences in party voting for President since 1948, although the political significance of social class fluctuates from one election to another. A majority of manual workers supported Republican candidates in 1956 and 1972, both landslide reelections of incumbent Presidents, and a majority of white-collar workers and professionals supported Democrat Lyndon Johnson for reelection in 1964. Class differences in Presidential voting followed the more traditional pattern in 1952, 1960, and 1976. Manual workers were evenly divided between Reagan and Carter in 1980.

Within working-class occupations, members of union households have been the most dependable supporters of Democratic Presidential candidates, based primarily on the party's defense of

29. Robert Axelrod, "Where the Votes Come From: An Analysis of Electoral Coalitions, 1952–1968," in James I. Lengle, and Byron E. Shafer (eds.), *Presidential Politics: Readings on Nominations and Elections.* New York: St. Martin's, 1980, p. 421.

union rights to strike and bargain collectively. Even so, union members' support for Hubert Humphrey in 1968 and Jimmy Carter in 1980 was not as great as in the past, and in 1972 a majority of union households supported President Nixon for reelection. Organized labor remains an important component of a winning Democratic Presidential coalition, and its return to the Democratic camp in 1976 was crucial to Jimmy Carter's narrow victory. In the closely contested states of Ohio, New York, and Pennsylvania, union-voter-registration drives contributed to Democratic majorities.[30]

Religion

Only twice (1972 and 1980) during the postwar era have a majority of Catholic voters not supported the Democratic Presidential candidate. Their consistent support is attributable partly to social class and partly to the fact that most of the immigrant Catholics from Ireland, Poland, and Italy settled in urban population centers at a time when these cities were controlled by old-style Democratic political machines. Unlike many other voting groups, Catholics retain their Democratic preferences even after moving to the suburbs.[31]

Except for blacks, Jewish voters are the most pro-Democratic of any group, having been attracted into the Democratic coalition by the party's opposition to Hitler and the Nazis, and remaining there on the basis of the Democrats' general liberalism and support of the state of Israel. Jewish voters, nearly one-fourth (23%) of the New York electorate, constitute a key component of the Democratic Presidential coalition because of the importance of New York's electoral votes.

In summary, the Democratic coalition that dominated Presidential politics through the 1960's consisted of diverse, overlapping minorities: the poor, the working class, union members, blacks, Catholics, Jews, city dwellers, and Southerners. The Republican Presidential coalition depends primarily on the support of whites, Protestants, Westerners and Midwesterners, and middle- and upper

30. Gerald M. Pomper, "The Presidential Election," in Gerald M. Pomper et al., *The Election of 1976: Reports and Interpretations.* New York: David McKay Co., Inc., 1977, p. 62.

31. Robert J. Huckshorn, *Political Parties in America.* North Scituate, Ma.: Duxbury, 1980, p. 241.

middle-class voters outside the central cities.[32]   The Democratic coalition is fragile and has proven increasingly unstable. Southern whites have become more independent in Presidential voting, and working-class white voters are not as staunchly Democratic as in the past.   The internal contradictions within the Democratic coalition have been heightened by struggles over government policies regarding racial integration and equality, which alienated many Southern whites, as well as by tension between liberal and conservative Democrats over matters of life style and morality. Only once since 1964 has a Democratic Presidential candidate been able to win majorities among all the groups that comprised the New Deal coalition. In 1976, Jimmy Carter carried the South as well as the other components of the New Deal alignment, but he was not completely successful in reassembling the coalition. Despite being a native son of the region, Carter was not able to command the support of a majority of Southern whites. Instead, he relied on heavy support by newly enfranchised Southern black voters. Jimmy Carter's resurrection of the New Deal coalition proved only temporary. Among traditionally Democratic groups, President Carter received majority support only from liberals and blacks in 1980.[33]

Dealignment   The era since the last major voter realignment has been one of Democratic dominance, modified by secular trends, including the departure at the Presidential level of many Southern whites from the Democratic party and nearly all black voters from the Republican party. Equally important is the trend, affecting both parties, of growing voter independence. As discussed in the previous chapter (see Table 2.3), this has been manifested by decreases in both the number of voters expressing a partisan preference and the intensity, or strength, of voters' party identifications.

A major reason for this dealignment, or weakening of partisan ties, is simply the passage of time. For reasons already discussed, the perception of political parties and Presidential candidates by citizens of voting age was profoundly affected by the Great Depression, resulting in a voter alignment favorable to the Democrats. The De-

32. Axelrod, *Where Votes Come From*, pp. 415–416.

33. According to *The New York Times/CBS News Survey*, 57% of self-described liberals voted for President Carter, 27% for Ronald Reagan, and 11% for John Anderson.   Reported in *The New York Times*, November 9, 1980, p. 18.

pression generation was, by and large, fairly successful in transmitting its partisan preferences to its children, who did not experience the economic catastrophe directly, but were socialized by their parents into the partisan alignment it produced. The New Deal-voter alignment began to break down as increasing numbers of younger voters two generations removed from the Great Depression came of age politically and began behaving in a more independent and less partisan fashion.[34]   Research on the relationship between age and party identification shows that, in 1952 about one-fourth of those under 30 were Independents. Twenty years later, about half of the citizens under 30 were Independents.[35]

This is a development of some significance for Presidential electoral politics since, throughout much of the postwar era, party identification was the single most important variable influencing the voting choices of the Presidential electorate. As the influence of partisanship has declined, voters' perceptions of issues and candidates have become more influential, and voting behavior has become more volatile and unpredictable.

PRESIDENTIAL ELECTIONS

In theory, Presidential elections might be regarded as a means by which voters can express their preferences about parties, issues, and candidates, and thereby direct the future course of public policy. If parties and candidates consistently took unequivocal positions on issues, and if most voters were aware of issue alternatives and voted for President on that basis, then it might be feasible to contend that Presidential elections provide the public with a means for shaping public policy. This conception of elections (associated with the responsible party advocates) is better regarded as an ideal situation, which may occasionally be approximated, than as a realistic description of the functioning of Presidential elections. The lack of cohesive and responsible political parties has become a trademark of the American political system, and the public's lack of awareness

34. On the causes of dealignment, see Paul W. Beck, "Partisan Dealignment in the Postwar South," *American Political Science Review,* 71. June, 1977, pp. 477–496.

35. Louis M. Seagull, *Youth and Change in American Politics.* New York: New Viewpoints, 1977, p. 96.

about national policy questions is exceeded only by the ability of Presidential candidates to obfuscate their issue positions. The platforms of the national party conventions frequently offer competing alternatives to the public, but the inability of the parties to make their platforms binding on candidates, and the willingness of candidates to promise everything to everybody on some issues, makes it difficult to attribute clear policy significance to Presidential voting. Moreover, the fragmented governmental structure confronting victorious Presidential candidates creates a public–policy process which assures a major role for numerous other politicians and institutions.

While there are instances of parties enacting campaign pledges into law, it is equally likely that campaign goals will be modified by the policy process and by the necessity of responding to changing circumstances. The final outcome of the public-policy process may, or may not, resemble promises made by Presidential candidates. It was difficult to foresee, for example, that, as President, Richard Nixon would move to establish detente with the Soviet Union, open relationships with China, and impose peacetime wage and price controls. Likewise, it must have been unexpected by a large portion of the public that Lyndon Johnson, after being reelected as a peace candidate, would escalate America's Vietnam commitment into a major war.[36]

The diverse nature of Presidential electoral coalitions and the large number of issues in an election permit winning candidates a great deal of discretion in interpreting the outcome to suit their predispositions. An election victory becomes a mandate for change, or an endorsement of the *status quo* (keep up the good work) largely on the basis of how the President chooses to interpret it. For these reasons, a number of political scientists have concluded that Presidential elections should be interpreted not as referenda on policy questions, but more generally as mechanisms whereby citizens choose their leaders and express approval or dissatisfaction with the past performance of incumbents.[37]

In the most general terms, elections are decisions about who should rule. Presidential elections specifically decide which individuals will control the Presidential apparatus, Cabinet posts, and top-level executive positions within the national government for the

36. As Professor Herbert Asher has pointed out, President Johnson's escalation of the Vietnam War was not totally inconsistent with his electoral support since, in the 1964 election, the President received majority support from Hawks as well as Doves. See Asher, *Presidential Elections and American Politics*, p. 29.

next four years. This has indirect, but real, implications for public policy because politicians and activists in the two parties represent different constituent groups favoring competing policy alternatives.

Presidential elections are more than decisions about government personnel. In addition, they permit voters to express approval or disapproval of incumbents by retaining them or voting them out of office. Admittedly, this is retrospective judgment, permitting voters to remove incumbents only after the damage has been done. Nonetheless, the right of citizens to reject their rulers is fundamental to the concept of representative democracy. Finally, elections provide a system for the orderly transfer of power from one administration to another. Actions taken by the President become legitimate partly because of the procedures followed to gain the mantle of power.

Voter Participation in Presidential Elections

Figure 3.5 charts participation rates of American citizens in national elections since 1932 and reflects two distinct patterns. Overall voter turnout in national elections, while fluctuating considerably, has gradually declined despite recent efforts to make voter registration and participation easier. The pool of eligible voters has expanded steadily as women, blacks, and youth have been enfranchised. However, the percentage of eligible voters who participate has shrunk to little more than half.

The downward trend in turnout overlays a regular pattern of fluctuations between Congressional and Presidential elections. Participation in Congressional mid-term elections is consistently about 15% less than turnout during Presidential election years. This pattern of voter behavior, known as "surge and decline," reflects the surge of voter and media interest accompanying Presidential elections, which produces higher rates of participation. This voter surge is regularly followed by a decline in interest and turnout in Congressional mid-term elections two years later. Both of these factors—declining voter involvement and surge and decline in turnout—have consequences for Presidential elections.

37. Of the many political scientists adopting this position, among the most prominent are: Herbert Asher, *Presidential Elections and American Politics,* pp. 27–31, and Thomas R. Dye and Harmon L. Zeigler, *The Irony of Democracy* (4th ed.). North Scituate, Ma.: Duxbury, 1980, pp. 159–187. See, also, Gerald M. Pomper, *Elections in America.* New York: Dodd, Mead and Co., 1968.

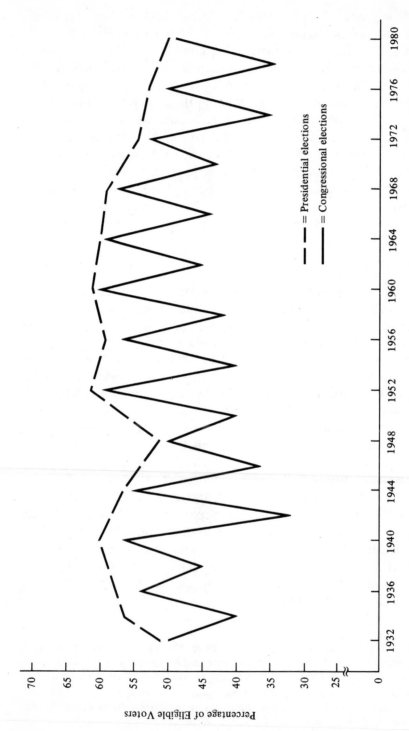

Figure 3.5 Participation in national elections from 1932 to 1980. Source: *Statistical Abstract of the United States* (100th ed.), 1979, p. 513, Table No. 835. Updated for 1980 by the author.

Turnout   Low voter participation in American elections results from a combination of factors, including difficult registration procedures, voter apathy and alienation, and the feeling on the part of an increasing number of citizens that it makes no difference whether they participate or not.   Since most people who are registered also vote, considerable attention has been devoted to facilitating voter registration.   Numerous barriers to registration have been eliminated or lessened, including residency requirements, literacy tests, and poll taxes.   A 1978 study concluded that voter registration procedures have the greatest effect on the least educated, and that if all states adopted procedures similar to the most permissive states, turnout might be as much as 9% higher in Presidential elections.[38]

Since voter turnout peaked in the 1960 election, there has been a gradual decline, despite increasingly permissive registration laws. This is partly attributable to the tendency of newly enfranchised groups to participate less than those who have been socialized into voting regularly.   In 1920, the Nineteenth Amendment was added to the Constitution, permitting women to vote.   Until recently, their participation rates were lower than men's and still are among lesser-educated and older women.   Prior to the passage of the 1965 Voting Rights Act, black citizens were systematically excluded from registering and voting in many Southern states.   Although their participation has increased significantly, it is still lower than average.   The most recent expansion of the pool of eligible voters occurred in 1971, when the Congress passed, and the states approved, the Twenty-sixth Amendment, lowering the voting age to 18.   The newly enfranchised young voters stayed away from the polls in droves, less than half of those under 25 voting in the 1972 and 1976 Presidential elections.   The United States Census Bureau estimated that about one-third of the decline in voter turnout since 1964 is due to the changing age distribution of the population.[39]

There is evidence that increasing cynicism and futility among voters have taken their toll.   A survey conducted in 1976 estimated that 10 million eligible Americans, many of them young people, had dropped out of the electorate. Feelings of cynicism and futility were especially pronounced in this group, over half of whom agreed that "it doesn't make any difference who is elected."[40]

38. Huckshorn, *Political Parties in America*, p. 223.

39. Asher, *Presidential Elections and American Politics*, p. 53

40. Huckshorn, *Political Parties in America,* pp. 230–231.

Many attitudes affecting political participation are related to voters' sociological characteristics. Political interest, information, ideology, sense of civic duty, party identification, and feelings of cynicism, or efficacy, are all linked to social class, age, race, education, religion, and ethnic-group membership. Consequently, the Presidential electorate is disproportionately white, middle-aged, and of higher education and social status than the public at large. Individuals predisposed to be Republicans are more likely to vote than those having the social attributes of Democrats, somewhat offsetting the numerical advantage enjoyed by the Democrats.

Surge and Decline The cyclical pattern of surge and decline is a distinctive feature of American elections. Within the electorate there is a core of voters (about 40%–45%) who vote in most national elections, Congressional as well as Presidential. The political makeup of this group reflects the distribution of party identification among the electorate, these voters being both more partisan and more interested in politics than those voting only during Presidential years.[41] This core of partisan voters is predominantly Democratic simply because there are so many more Democrats than Republicans, even taking into account higher turnout rates of Republican voters. This is the primary reason that, except for two brief interludes (1947-1949 and 1953-1955), the Democrats controlled the Congress from 1933 until 1981.

Differences between the Presidential and Congressional electorates have prevented similar Democratic dominance of the Presidency. Presidential elections, being more visible and better publicized, create a surge of interest within the electorate that attracts additional voters to the polls, many of whom are less partisan and more likely to vote on the basis of candidate and issue orientations.[42] Although strong partisans participate at a greater rate, their declining numbers mean that Independents and weak partisans constitute an increasing share of the Presidential electorate. Independents swing from one party to the other, depending on the candidates and issues of the election. As Table 3.6 shows, Independents have given greater support to Republican than Democratic Presidential candidates since 1952—

---

41. Angus Campbell, "Surge and Decline: A Study of Electoral Change," in Angus Campbell *et al., Elections and the Political Order.* New York: John Wiley & Sons, 1966, pp. 40–62.

42. *Ibid.,* pp. 42–43.

Table 3.6   Support for Presidential Candidates by Independent Voters, 1948-1980.

	1948	1952	1956	1960	1964	1968	1972	1976	1980
				Percent					
Democratic	57	33	27	46	66	32	33	45	30
Republican	43	67	73	54	34	47	65	55	54
Wallace (1968)						21			
Anderson (1980)									12

Source: William H. Flanigan and Nancy H. Zingale, *Political Behavior of the American Electorate* (4th ed.). Boston: Allyn and Bacon, 1979, p. 62. Used with permission of the publisher. Figures for the 1980 election are from *The New York Times/CBS News Poll* reported in *The New York Times,* November 9, 1980, p. 18.

four times overwhelmingly so. In 1960 and 1976, Democrats won despite majority support by Independents for the Republican candidate. This regular surge of participation by less-partisan voters, along with the increase in split-ticket voting in Presidential elections, enhances Republican prospects for winning the Presidency. By nominating attractive candidates and seizing the initiative on issues, the Republicans can overcome the Democrats' numerical advantage.

In summary, weakening of partisan ties and increasing numbers of Independent voters mean a greater role for candidate and issue orientations as determinants of the Presidential vote. Presidential election outcomes are heavily influenced by the behavior of swing voters consisting mostly of Independents and weak partisans. Voting behavior of swing voters fluctuates from one election to another, depending on their reactions to Presidential candidates and issues. As the minority party, the Republicans must be particularly concerned with nominating strong candidates able to appeal to Independents and weak Democrats. A configuration of candidates and issues which divides the electorate along traditional party lines works to the Democrats' advantage because of their numerical superiority.

The Vote Choice

A number of environmental and sociological factors influence the likelihood that individuals will vote and predispose them to cast ballots for one party or the other. Actual voting behavior fluctuates more than partisan attachment, and citizens' vote choices in any particular Presidential election are influenced by immediate psychological factors, including their perceptions of parties, candidates, and issues.

Candidate Image Presidential elections, involving choices between politicians as well as parties and ideologies, are heavily influenced by voters' perceptions of the candidates. Although voters' partisan preferences color their reactions to candidates, there are in any Presidential election a number of dissatisfied partisans who defect in response to their evaluations of the candidates. It is difficult to sort out the effects of voters' candidate orientations independently from the impact of issues and incumbency. Candidate orientation refers to voters' opinions about the candidates' personal qualities, considered apart from party affiliation and issue positions. The most popular candidates have tended to be incumbent Presidents, and, on occasion, a controversial candidate has become the major issue in the election.

The University of Michigan election surveys have attempted to systematically assess voters' reactions to Democratic and Republican Presidential candidates since 1952. Three generalizations are supported by this research:[43]

Republican Presidential candidates were more positively evaluated than Democratic candidates in every election except 1964 and 1976. President Lyndon Johnson enjoyed a huge advantage in 1964 over Senator Barry Goldwater, the least popular Republican nominee during the survey period. Jimmy Carter was slightly more positively evaluated than President Ford in 1976, although both candidates were perceived positively by the electorate. Preliminary analysis of 1980 election surveys indicates that Ronald Reagan was evaluated more positively by the voters than was President Carter. A post-election survey of 12,782 voters by *The New York Times* and CBS News found that 38% of those who voted for Ronald Reagan were motivated primarily by dissatisfaction with President Carter.[44]

43. For an extensive discussion of the impact of voters' candidate orientations and election outcomes, see Asher, *Presidential Elections and American Politics*, Chapters 5, 6, and 7.

44. Adam Clymer, "Displeasure with Carter Turned Many to Reagan." *The New York Times*, November 9, 1980, p. 18.

The greatest differences in candidate appeal occurred in 1956,
1964, and 1972. In each case a popular incumbent President
was reelected by a landslide. In 1956, President Eisenhower
recorded the highest level of popular appeal of any candidate.
Presidents Johnson (1964) and Nixon (1972) overwhelmingly
defeated unpopular opponents who were not positively evaluated by a majority of their own party's rank and file.

The candidate having the more positive evaluation by voters
won 7 of the 8 Presidential elections from 1952 to 1980. The
only exception was in 1960, when Democrat John F. Kennedy
narrowly defeated Republican Richard Nixon despite Nixon's
more positive voter evaluations.

Issues and Ideology   Major election analyses conducted during
the 1950's and early 1960's portrayed the American electorate as
generally being little interested in, or aware of, political issues and
ideology.[45]   Voters were most likely to define their self-interest in
terms of group affiliations and voted for the President primarily on
the basis of traditional party ties or candidate orientation.   This
image of the American voter began to change after the 1964 Presidential election.   Surveys since that time have shown greater voter
interest and awareness of issues and an increase in the potential for
issue voting.   Civil rights was a major issue in the 1964 campaign, and
Vietnam, law and order, and other social issues were important to
increasing numbers of voters in 1968 and 1972.

During that period, more voters began to think about political
issues within an ideological framework, adopting issue positions more
likely to be consistent with one another.   Research indicates that
the number of ideologues in the electorate more than doubled between 1964 and 1972, a development not confined to the well-
educated stratum of voters.[46]   This development is probably attributable, also, to the unequivocal ideological and issue positions es-
poused by Presidential candidates Goldwater, Wallace, and McGovern
during this period.

45. See Angus Campbell et al., *The American Voter.* New York: John Wiley
& Sons, 1964, as well as *Elections and the Political Order.*

46. Norman H. Nie, Sidney Verba, and John R. Petrocik, *The Changing Ameri-*
can Voter (enlarged ed.).   Cambridge, Ma.:   Harvard University Press,
1979, Chapter 7.

Each party has enjoyed political advantages from its association with certain broad issue areas, a traditional configuration that has remained relatively stable. Voter perceptions of the parties' competence in the areas of domestic and foreign policy, and the parties as managers of government, have been repeatedly surveyed since 1952. Republican Presidential candidates have consistently been perceived more favorably by the public as managers of government and foreign policy, except in 1964, when the Republicans surrendered this advantage by nominating Goldwater.[47]   Democratic Presidents have assisted the Republicans in maintaining their advantage in foreign policy by involving the nation in large-scale and unpopular Presidential wars in Korea and Vietnam.

Democrats have enjoyed long-standing advantages in domestic politics, being perceived by the electorate as the party that better represents the ordinary person. Until recently, this image was reinforced by the association of Democratic administrations with prosperity and Republican Presidents with recession and hard times. The nation's economic difficulties during the Carter administration eroded this partisan advantage.

In a Gallup survey in March, 1980, three-quarters of the sample mentioned inflation as the number-one problem facing the United States. By a margin of 32% to 28%, those interviewed preferred the Democrats to the Republicans as the party best able to handle this problem. Twenty-eight percent perceived no difference between the parties on this issue. However, by September, 1980, 35% of those interviewed chose the Republicans as the party best able to deal with inflation, 32% chose the Democrats, and 22% saw no differences between the parties.[48]   Results of a *New York Times/CBS News* survey indicate that 34% of the voters in the 1980 election considered themselves to be worse off economically than in the previous year. Of this group, only 25% voted for President Carter.[49]

In summary, party identification appears to have been the most important factor explaining the behavior of the Presidential electorate during the postwar era. Party identification is linked to group membership and structures Presidential elections by providing a

47. Asher, *Presidential Elections and American Politics*, pp. 132–142.

48. See *The Gallup Opinion Index*, March, 1980, pp. 25–26; and September, 1980, p. 9.

49. *The New York Times,* November 9, 1980, p. 18.

foundation of relative stability amidst short-term fluctuations related to voters' perceptions of candidates and issues. Voters are more likely to depart from their party in Presidential elections whenever their evaluations of candidates or issues are in conflict with their party identification, or when they are cross-pressured by conflicting group affiliations. Presidential candidates are frequently evaluated by voters in terms of personality, image, character, and traditional values (such as religion and family life), and only secondarily on the basis of their politics and issue positions. The issue dimension of Presidential politics has assumed greater importance since 1964. Voters have become better educated and more issue oriented, and Presidential candidates have more often taken ideological positions on controversial issues.

Presidential Campaigning

Active personal campaigning by Presidential candidates is a 20th century phenomenon, becoming a regular feature of American politics since the turn of the century. Changes in American society and politics have affected the conduct, financing, and impact of Presidential campaigns.

Conduct of Campaigns Presidential campaigning has evolved through three relatively distinct phases:

> *Front-Porch Campaigning* In the days of William McKinley, Presidential candidates were not expected to campaign for their party's nomination, but to remain quietly at home until officially notified by the convention. The Presidential campaign began in earnest after Labor Day and lasted only 2 months.[50] Not wanting to degrade the office to which they aspired, most Presidential candidates adopted a low-key style of front-porch campaigning. The dominant mode of campaigning from the time of McKinley (1896) until Franklin Roosevelt (1932) consisted of addresses by the Presidential candidate to groups of visitors and newspaper reporters who came to the candidate's home.
>
> *Whistle-Stop Campaigning* The party realignment that put the

---

50. James David Barber, *The Pulse of Politics: Electing Presidents in the Media Age.* New York: W. W. Norton & Co., 1980, p. 10.

Democrats in power was accompanied by a change in Presidential campaign style.   In addition to an increasing use of radio as a campaign tool, Presidential candidates personally became more active in whistle-stop campaigning. Candidates, crisscrossing the nation by rail, addressed crowds of voters at stops along the way, frequently giving the same speech half a dozen or more times a day. Franklin Roosevelt began extensive whistle-stop campaigning in 1932. President Harry Truman conducted the last great whistle-stop tour in the 1948 campaign, traveling 32,000 miles in 8 weeks.[51]

Media Campaigning As discussed in the previous chapter, political campaigns have increasingly become candidate oriented and media based. Television began to be a factor in Presidential electoral politics during the 1952 campaign, and by 1960, television sets had proliferated to the point where television advertising was the most cost-efficient method for reaching large masses of the public.

Typically, both major party Presidential candidates spend at least half of their total campaign budgets on television production and advertising costs, concluding with an intensive media blitz during the last 2 weeks of the campaign.

If the old politics consisted of meeting the voters, the new politics is directed at reaching the voters.[52] Modern Presidential campaigns involve elements of both. Contact with the voters has not been outmoded, but it has taken a back seat to media campaigning. Old-style campaigning involves reaching the voters by means of door-to-door canvassing.   The objectives are to identify potential supporters and activate them by supportive personal contacts, mobilizing as many as possible for voter registration and election-day participation.   Party unity is important in this aspect of a Presidential campaign because the regular party organization can help in providing this service.   The candidate usually attempts to supplement the party's precinct organization with newly recruited volunteers. Active support by interest groups is welcomed at this stage as a source of free labor for the campaign. Personal campaigning by the candidates (working the crowds, addressing campaign rallies and friendly

51. Wayne, *Road to the White House*, p. 157.

52. Huckshorn, *Political Parties in America*, p. 151.

audiences) has long been important for activating supporters, and·it has assumed new importance because of the media exposure it generates.

Campaign Finance Table 3.7 displays the amounts spent by national-level committees for Presidential candidates in general elections since 1936. Costs of Presidential elections began escalating rapidly during the postwar era, out-racing the rate of inflation. The decrease in campaign costs since the peak in 1972 has resulted directly from public financing of Presidential elections and spending limits imposed by the Federal Election Campaign Act. Secret campaign spending, illegal and unreported contributions, laundered money, and other violations have occurred frequently enough in the past to warrant caution in taking these figures too literally, but authorities regard them as reasonable estimates. The figures reported for 1976 and 1980 are approximations, including only the amount of public funds Presidential candidates were entitled to spend under the provisions of the FECA. Independent spending by Political Action Committees on behalf of the candidates is not included.

Impact of Presidential Campaigns The campaign is important during any close election, the growing independence of the electorate having increased the pool of potential swing voters. Most voters make up their minds before the Presidential campaign begins, but an increasing number are deciding how to vote during the later stages of the campaign. Surveys indicate that the number of voters making

Table 3.7   Presidential General Election Spending at the National Level, 1948–1980

Year	Republican		Democratic	
1948	Dewey	$ 2,127,296	Truman	$ 2,736,334
1952	Eisenhower	6,608,623	Stevenson	5,032,926
1956	Eisenhower	7,778,702	Stevenson	5,106,651
1960	Nixon	10,128,000	Kennedy	9,797,000
1964	Goldwater	16,026,000	Johnson	8,757,000
1968	Nixon	25,402,000	Humphrey	11,594,000
1972	Nixon	61,400,000	McGovern	30,000,000
1976	Ford	21,800,000	Carter	21,800,000
1980	Reagan	29,400,000	Carter	29,400,000

Source: 1948–1972 figures are from Herbert E. Alexander, *Financing Politics: Money, Elections, and Political Reform.* Washington, D.C., Congressional Quarterly, Inc., 1976, p. 20. Used with permission of the publisher.

up their minds during the Presidential campaign increased from 25% in 1948 to 45% in 1976. A significant portion (24%) decided during the last 2 weeks of the 1976 campaign and 23% decided in the final week of the 1980 campaign.[53]

There were significant shifts in the candidate preferences of voters during the last weeks of the campaign in the Presidential elections of 1948, 1968, 1976, and 1980, and smaller shifts in 1960. In 1968 and 1976, Nixon and Carter began their campaigns with huge leads, only to see them slip away. In 1948 and 1960. Truman and Kennedy, the eventual winners, trailed early, with President Truman not overtaking Thomas Dewey until the last week of the campaign. The 1980 Presidential election was considered by pollsters to be too close to call until the final week of the campaign. After the televised debate between President Carter and Ronald Reagan, voter opinion began to crystallize in favor of Reagan. Other elections have been so one-sided that it is difficult to see how any amount of campaigning could have reversed the outcome. The elections of 1936, 1964, and 1972 are examples, all involving reelection of incumbents. Landslide reelection victories for incumbent Presidents were facilitated in 1964 and 1972 when the opposition party nominated candidates not acceptable to their own rank and file.

The changing nature of Presidential campaigns has consequences for the candidates and the government, as well as for the voters. The extensive system of primary elections forces candidates, even incumbent Presidents, into lengthy campaigns for their party's nomination. In combination with the general election campaign, this creates a situation of perpetual candidacy, transforming "a quadrennial event into a saga lasting two or three years."[54] Aside from consuming too much of the President's time, this has the undesirable side effect of disconnecting campaign politics from the context of forces in Washington. The lengthy campaign, and the manner in which the media choose to cover it, distracts both the public and the press from the Presidential implications of what the candidates are saying. Campaign maneuver itself becomes the featured story as the media focus on the horse-race aspects of the campaign, devoting little attention to the implications that candidate and issue

53. *Ibid.*, CPS surveys cited p. 175. 1980 figures cited in *The New York Times,* November 9, 1980, p. 18.

54. Barber, *Pulse of Politics*: *Electing Presidents in the Media Age*, p. 10.

alternatives have for governing the country. The battle story has drifted away from Washington and "lost its connection with the reality the victor would encounter there."[55]

Incumbency

The advantages of campaigning as an incumbent President are so great as to constitute one of the most important factors in a Presidential campaign. Advantages of incumbency can be grouped into three categories.

Status When incumbency is a factor, the candidates are not on an equal footing, one being "Mr. President," the other simply "the challenger." Although the Presidency no longer commands unquestioning respect, the incumbent derives an air of legitimacy as the chief of state and head of government. The incumbent is free to run as President, statesman, and partisan at the same time, while attempting to portray the challenger as poorly informed, inexperienced, unrealistic, and without grasp of the intricacies of national government and foreign relations.

Pork The President, as executive head of the United States governmental departments, can influence a portion of the Federal pork barrel. The timely announcements of new Federal public works projects, grants to cities, low-interest loans to farmers, and increases in pay or benefits for government employees are part and parcel of being chief executive. These kinds of incentives, and the implicit threat to slow the flow of Federal dollars, can produce endorsements by prominent government officials as well as voter support. For example, in his battle with Ronald Reagan for the 1976 Republican nomination, President Ford awarded Federal patronage and pork to generate support among Republican leaders and voters. Shortly before the New Hampshire primary, the President announced his intention to retain the Portsmouth Naval Shipyard, which the Department of Defense had intended to close. Ford also appointed New Hampshire's Attorney General, Warren Rudman, as Chairman of the Interstate Commerce Commission, and pledged to New England fishermen to fight for extension of the territorial limit from 12 miles to 200 miles. On the stump in Florida, the President promised that

55. *Ibid.*, p. 313.

Brevard County would receive serious consideration as a site for a solar-research facility. Shortly before the Florida primary, the Air Force awarded $33.6 million in contracts to Florida companies, and the Department of Transportation granted $15 million for a rapid transit system for the Miami area. To the voters of Illinois the President promised more Federal spending for agriculture animal research.[56]

Media   Extensive free media coverage is afforded the incumbent simply because the President is news. The President can focus media coverage in a manner that permits an incumbent to co-opt a challenger's ideas and programs. Should an issue prove popular, it can quickly be embraced by submitting a Presidential proposal to Congress. In the area of foreign relations, the President can generate media coverage that no challenger can match. The coverage afforded Presidential trips abroad to mingle with other heads of state is not available to the challenger at any price.

As the 1980 campaign heated up, President Carter drew on all these resources in an attempt to save his Presidency. Within a two-week time span the President took the following actions:

> With an eye on the ethnic vote, the President approved $670 million worth of new credit guarantees for the purchase of grain by Poland. In a televised announcement (which also received front-page coverage by the *New York Times*), the President declared his action to be "proof of the solidarity between the American people and the Polish people."[57]
>
> Two weeks later, in an attempt to bolster his campaign in the pivotal industrial states, the President approved a comprehensive aid package for the steel industry.
>
> This was followed in two days by a campaign visit to Flint, Michigan, where the President urged the public to buy new fuel-efficient cars made in America. Network coverage concluded with footage of members of the United Auto Workers serenading Carter on his 56th birthday to the strains of "Happy Birthday, Mr. President."

56. Reported in *Time*, March 22, 1976, p. 8.

57. *The New York Times,* September 13, 1980, p. 1.

Perhaps the greatest testament to the power of incumbency as a campaign tool is the track record of Presidents who have sought reelection. As shown by Table 3.8, incumbents have been victorious in 11 of 15 Presidential elections since 1900, a success rate of 73%. The majority–minority party affiliation of Presidents has made little difference in their success, minority-party incumbents winning 75% of the time compared with 73% success for majority-party Presidents.[58] Minority-party incumbents have had greater electoral success than majority-party non-incumbents, who have won 50% of the time. Minority non-incumbents naturally have the lowest victory rate, winning only 29% of the time. Of the three Republican Presidents losing reelection contests, Taft had to contend with a badly divided party, Hoover was caught in an economic catastrophe, and Ford was an appointed President, never having been elected to the Presidency or the Vice Presidency. Only the second Democratic President since Franklin Roosevelt to win a majority of the popular vote, Jimmy Carter subsequently became the only Democratic incumbent to be defeated in this century.

Table 3.8 Electoral Success of Incumbent and Non-Incumbent Presidential Candidates, 1900–1980

| | Incumbents | | Non-Incumbents | |
	Majority Party	Minority Party	Majority Party	Minority Party
Wins	1900 (R) 1940 (D) 1904 (R) 1944 (D) 1924 (R) 1948 (D) 1936 (D) 1964 (D)	1916 (D) 1956 (R) 1972 (R)	1908 (R) 1920 (R) 1928 (R) 1960 (D) 1976 (D)	1912 (D) 1932 (D) 1952 (R) 1968 (R) 1980 (R)
Losses	1912 (R) 1932 (R) 1980 (D)	1976 (R)	1916 (R) 1952 (D) 1956 (D) 1968 (D) 1972 (D)	1900 (D) 1936 (R) 1904 (D) 1940 (R) 1908 (D) 1944 (R) 1920 (D) 1948 (R) 1924 (D) 1960 (R) 1928 (D) 1964 (R)
Winning Percentage	0.73	0.75	0.50	0.29

58. The 1932 election presents some difficulties since the nation was in the midst of a partisan realignment, and it is difficult to know with certainty which party was the majority party. Treating the Democrats rather than the Republicans as the majority party in 1932 will slightly alter the percentages in Table 3.8, but not the general conclusion that incumbency is of greater significance than the majority–minority party status of the Presidential candidates.

Not since the elections of 1888 and 1892, had two successive incumbent Presidents been defeated for reelection. The consecutive defeats of President Ford in 1976, and President Carter in 1980, reflected the extent of popular dissatisfaction with Presidential leadership, and emphasized the limits to the effectiveness of incumbency as a campaign tool. The primary liability of incumbency is the necessity for the administration to defend its record. President Ford's association with the Nixon administration and his controversial pardon of the former President contributed to his defeat in 1976. The association with some of the worst economic conditions since the Great Depression and President Carter's inability to effectively deal with this problem were crucial to his defeat. Interviews of voters in the 1980 election indicate that only about 11% supported Ronald Reagan primarily for ideological reasons (responding, for example, "He's a real conservative."). A much larger group of Reagan voters (38%) said that one of their main reasons for supporting him was simply that "It's time for a change."[59]

The willingness of incumbent Presidents to confront their challengers in televised debates may serve to diminish some of the advantages of incumbency. Presidents Ford and Carter, as well as incumbent Vice President Richard Nixon in 1960, debated their challengers and lived to regret it. Even should the debate result in a draw, this works to the challenger's advantage by placing both candidates on a relatively equal plane. Even though the greatest impact of televised Presidential debates has been to reinforce partisan predispositions of voters, this tends to reassure the challenger's supporters that their candidate is an even match for the President. By debating their challengers face to face, Presidents risk surrendering some of the advantages of incumbency, including the superior status and experience attributed to the Presidency, as well as the benefits of unequal media exposure.[60]

CONCLUSION

American Presidential elections are a unique institution, requiring the participation of an increasingly disinterested electorate whose

59. Clymer, *Displeasure with Carter*, p. 18.

60. The literature researching Presidential debates is voluminous. For an authoritative assessment, see Asher, *Presidential Elections and American Politics*, pp. 164–168 and pp. 205–207.

preferences are filtered through an Electoral College which may, or may not, honor them. Reforms in the nominating process have created an ironic situation in which voters may have more influence over who is nominated for President than who is elected. Scholars and commentators are not in agreement about the significance and meaning of Presidential elections. In addition to permitting voters to express disapproval of incumbents, Presidential elections provide for the orderly transfer of power by deciding who will control the national executive apparatus. Because of the diverse nature of Presidential electoral coalitions, the multitude of issues, and a lengthy campaign process that disconnects electoral politics from the context of forces in Washington, it is difficult to assess the policy implications of Presidential elections. Armed with this uncertain mandate, the President confronts a fragmented governmental structure and a multifaceted policy process where the only certainty is the inevitability of compromise.

Chapter 4

Presidential Popularity and Political Influence

Citizens' political beliefs and values define the political culture of a nation. The political culture includes attitudes and orientations of citizens toward their country, its political institutions, and leaders. As part of the political environment in which leaders must function, popular beliefs provide support, as well as some constraint, for the choices of action available to the President. While many of the values and beliefs defining American political culture are relatively stable, significant features, including popular images of the Presidency, are in transition.

POST-WORLD WAR II AMERICAN POLITICAL CULTURE

In the two decades between the end of World War II and the Vietnam conflict, American political culture was generally characterized by:

> High levels of public trust in government and political institutions generally, and high levels of public confidence in the Presidency
> Substantial public approval of Presidential performance
> Widespread acceptance of the two-party system, and a stable partisan alignment

Moderately high levels of public participation in Presidential elections and low public acceptance of unconventional means of political participation.

POST-VIETNAM AMERICAN POLITICAL CULTURE

The impact of historical events and social forces has significantly transformed aspects of American political culture, particularly citizen beliefs and perceptions relating to the Presidency. Distinguishing features of post-Vietnam American political culture include:

Substantially lower levels of trust in government, increasing political cynicism in general, and diminished public confidence in the Presidency

Low levels of public approval of Presidential performance

Decreasing acceptance of the two-party system and increasing preference for political independence, especially among younger citizens, resulting in a more volatile partisan alignment

Declining levels of public participation in Presidential elections and increasing public acceptance of unconventional means of political participation

Explanations for these developments are necessarily complex, but some of the political and social forces contributing to these modifications in the public's attitudes and political orientations include:

The emergence in the 1970's of a younger generation of citizens considerably less partisan and more independent politically

The increasing impact of television and peer groups as agents of political socialization

Public reactions to government policies dealing with Vietnam, urban unrest, and racial integration

The impact of the Watergate revelations on public confidence in government

The discussion in this chapter focuses on public confidence and approval of the Presidency and the utility of public opinion as a political resource for the President.

PUBLIC CONFIDENCE IN GOVERNMENT

That public trust and confidence in political leaders and institutions, including the Presidency, have significantly decreased since the mid-1960's hardly seems subject to dispute. This has been a consistent finding in survey after survey. The impact of the Watergate scandal should be viewed as one contributing factor accelerating this trend rather than as the primary cause. The decreasing confidence of the public in the national government is depicted in Fig. 4.1. Clearly the trend of declining public trust in government predates the Watergate affair by several years. The data in Fig. 4.1 include six surveys at different points in time. In each survey a representative national sample was asked to respond to this question: "How much of the time do you think you can trust the government in Washington to

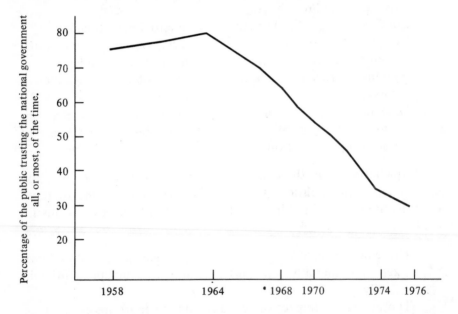

Figure 4.1 Public trust in government, 1958–1976. Source: The data in this figure consist of responses of samples of the public to the question: "How much of the time do you think you can trust the government in Washington to do what is right?" The graph plots the percentage of the public responding "always," or "most of the time." The data were extracted from SRC/CPS election surveys in 1958, 1964, 1968, 1970, 1974, and 1976; reported in Herbert Asher, *Presidential Elections and American Politics: Voters, Candidates, and Campaigns Since 1952* (revised ed.). Homewood, Ill.: Dorsey, 1980, p. 9. Used with permission of the University of Michigan.

do what is right?" Fig. 4.1 displays the percentage of citizens answering "always" or "most of the time."

Similar patterns of declining public confidence in governmental institutions, including Congress and the Presidency, as well as increasing feelings of futility and political ineffectiveness, have been documented by extensive research.[1] There is no single explanation for these trends, but research suggests there are at least three contributing factors:

Public dissatisfaction with the performance of government and political leaders in specific policy areas

Public sense of disillusionment and betrayal resulting from revelations of misconduct by government officials, especially the President

Social processes of modern society associated with increasing detachment from institutions

Policy Dissatisfaction

A number of commentators have contended that distrust of government arises out of dissatisfaction with the nature of decisions made by political leaders.[2] Research on public perceptions of, and response to, Presidential leadership on controversial national issues suggests that this is true. On the basis of public response to government policies dealing with Vietnam, urban unrest, racial integration, and individual and minority rights, a substantial minority of the public was found to be not only distrustful, but polarized into two groups preferring opposing policy alternatives. Disillusioned with the failure of the government's policies promoting social equality, and opposed to the escalation in Vietnam, cynics of the left favored fundamental

---

1. See, for example, Arthur H. Miller, "Public Policy and Political Cynicism: 1964–1970," in Norman R. Luttbeg (ed.), *Public Opinion and Public Policy* (revised ed.). Homewood, Ill.: Dorsey Press, 1974, pp. 453–477; Phillip E. Converse, "Change in the American Electorate," in Angus Campbell and Phillip Converse (eds.), *The Human Meaning of Social Change*. New York: Russell Sage Foundation, 1972; Ada W. Finter, "Dimensions of Political Alienation," *American Political Science Review*, XLIV, 2. June, 1970, pp. 389–410.

2. In addition to Arthur H. Miller, "Public Policy and Political Cynicism," see William A. Gamson, *Power and Discontent*. Homewood, Ill.: Dorsey Press, 1968, pp. 42–48, 178 ff.

social changes.   Fearful of social changes, supportive of political authority, but dissatisfied by the inability of the government to maintain order and control dissenters, cynics of the right constituted a much larger group of alienated individuals.   Political cynicism and mistrust characterized both disillusioned liberals and fearful conservatives, frustrated Hawks and outraged Doves.[3]

This issue polarization overlaps social groupings and so reflects more than ideological and policy differences between individual citizens. Of the cynics of the left, one-third were under 30 years old, 38% were black, and 28% had some college education. Cynics of the right were almost all white and not as well educated. This is further compounded by the fact that those most desirous of social change perceived the legitimate means of influence as ineffective. Part of the sharp drop in trust among black citizens after 1966 is attributable to frustration arising out of the failure of government civil rights and economic policies to fulfill expectations.[4]

Under this interpretation, the widespread public cynicism and mistrust characteristic of American political culture during the 1970's is partly attributable to the actions of the Democratic administrations of the 1960's. Public expectations were raised to unrealistic levels by liberal policies and then dashed by the urban riots and destruction of the late 1960's and the protracted war in Vietnam, which drained away resources and commitment from the Great Society programs. That war, initiated by an American President recently reelected as a peace candidate, further fueled the development of public cynicism and mistrust. The failures of these policies not only disillusioned liberals, but also generated cynicism among those opposed to the social policies whose priorities were the maintenance of social order and victory in Vietnam.[5]

These developments should not be interpreted to mean that most citizens are dissatisfied with government policy most of the time. On the contrary, there is abundant evidence that a substantial

3. Miller, "Public Policy and Political Cynicism," pp. 459–474.

4. *Ibid.*, p. 461

5. For further development of this thesis, see Louis M. Seagull, *Youth and Change in American Politics.* New York: New Viewpoints, 1977, pp. 65–67, 85–95. For a more general historical discussion of the decline of liberalism during this era, see John Frederick Martin, *Civil Rights and the Crisis of Liberalism: The Democratic Party: 1945-1976.* Boulder, Col.: Westview Press, 1979, pp. 183–216.

number of citizens are largely indifferent to many issues of public policy, and that public attitudes may be described as "permissive," if not enthusiastic, about many government programs.[6] The existence of a substantial minority of individuals who are mistrustful, polarized, and opposed to middle-of-the-road policies does sugest that, in the future, policy alternatives acceptable to the public may be increasingly difficult to discover.

Government Misconduct

The Watergate scandal and the attempted coverup resulted in a wide assortment of governmental actions of questionable legality. Revelation of the scope and extent of such activities, many of them authorized by the President or his subordinates, has undoubtedly contributed to growing public cynicism and mistrust of government. The impact of the Watergate revelations on the public's political orientations has been extensively studied, and findings indicate that the widespread publicity about governmental misconduct was damaging not only to citizens' trust in government, but to public confidence in the Presidency and other political instituions as well. At the height of the Watergate scandal, more than one-third of those interviewed in a Harris survey expressed little, or no, confidence in the executive branch of the government.[7] In a survey in April, 1979, only 38% of the respondents agreed that "the office of the President has done some good," whereas nearly half (45%) thought the Presidency in need of reform.[8]

Declining public esteem for the Presidency may have long-run implications of some significance for the American political system because the President apparently plays a central role in linking citizens to political authority and institutions. The Presidency is the most visible and personalized political institution and, to a great extent, the President, as Chief of State, symbolizes the United States government. For some citizens, the President is the only cognitive

---

6. On the nature of permissive opinion, see William H. Flanigan and Nancy H. Zingale, *Political Behavior of the American Electorate* (4th ed.). Boston, Ma.: Allyn and Bacon, 1979, p. 98.

7. Cited in Robert E. DiClerico, *The American President*. Englewood Cliffs, N. J.: Prentice-Hall, 1979, p. 168.

8. Jack Dennis, "Who Supports the Presidency," *Society* 13. July, 1976, pp. 51–52.

link to the political system, and, for nearly all citizens, the President is the first link to the government.   Research on childhood political socialization has shown that early political learning is not very specific in content and is characterized by development of general values and beliefs about political authority and government.   Childhood is frequently described as a period when basic commitments occur which affect the legitimacy and stability of the political system.[9] The President is by far the most visible political authority figure as children develop their images of government.

Prior to the Watergate scandal, numerous surveys indicated that most American children tended to have positive, even benevolent, perceptions of the President and political authority.   The post-Watergate generation, now coming of age politically, has been socialized into a different set of assumptions.   Survey evidence indicates that the idealistic benevolent image of the Presidency formerly characteristic of many children has been shattered by the Watergate revelations.   The prevalence of widespread cynicism and negative evaluations of the President is a significant departure from most earlier socialization research.[10]

9. The political socialization literature is voluminous. The best-known surveys of children's political attitudes and orientations include: Fred Greenstein, *Children and Politics*.   New Haven, Conn.: Yale University Press, 1965; David Easton and Jack Dennis, *Children and the Political System: Origins of Political Legitimacy*.   New York: McGraw Hill, 1969; Robert D. Hess and Judith V. Torney, *The Development of Political Attitudes in Children*. Garden City, N.Y.: Doubleday and Co., Inc., 1968; M. Kent Jennings and Richard G. Niemi, "The Transmission of Political Values from Parent to Child," *American Political Science Review*, LXII. March, 1968, pp. 169–184. For research findings challenging the benevolent-image interpretation of political socialization, see: Dean Jaros et al., "The Malevolent Leader: Political Socialization in an American Subculture," *American Political Science Review*, LXII. June, 1968, pp. 564–575; and Schley R. Lyons, "The Political Socialization of Ghetto Children: Efficacy and Cynicism," *Journal of Politics*. May, 1970, pp. 288–304.

10. A survey of children ages seven to ten in an upper middle–class Boston suburb in December, 1973, explicitly documented the impact of Watergate on the benevolent image of political authority and the Presidency.   See F. Christopher Arterton, "The Impact of Watergate on Children's Attitudes Toward Political Authority," *Political Science Quarterly*, Vol. 89, No. 2 June, 1979, pp. 269–388.   Arterton reported that as early as December, 1973, over half of the fifth–grade children in his sample agreed that President Nixon should be impeached. See Table 9, p. 282.

It is not yet possible to assess accurately the long-range impact of these episodes of governmental misconduct. It is obvious that public mistrust was not confined to President Nixon, since his departure from the Presidency has not been followed by a significant increase in public confidence in government. A long-run question of significance for the American political system is whether public dissatisfaction with Presidential performance and misconduct goes beyond specific policy failures and scandals and has begun to deplete that reservoir of favorable public attitudes, or goodwill toward the political system that has so long been a characteristic of American political culture.[11]

Social Processes of Modern Society

Increasing public mistrust of government and political institutions may be viewed as resulting, in part, from the evolution of modern society, as well as a response to particular policies or events. Specifically, the rapid changes in behavior patterns characteristic of modern technological society, in juxtaposition to the conservatism of political institutions, results in discontinuities which contribute to detachment, or alienation, of individuals from social institutions.[12] According to this interpretation, decreasing public confidence in government is part of a larger pattern of growing alienation and detachment from institutions that is produced by social and economic dislocations associated with advanced technological society. Additional support for this view is found in evidence documenting declining public respect for nongovernmental institutions in the United States, as well as declining public trust in government and confidence in institutions in numerous other developed nations.[13]

POPULAR EVALUATIONS OF PRESIDENTS

Probably no aspect of the President's relationship with the public is better documented than "Presidential Popularity," or the Pres-

---

11. "Diffuse Support" in David Easton's sense of the term. See Easton's *A Systems Analysis of Political Life.* New York: John Wiley & Sons, 1965, p. 278.

12. Seagull, *Youth and Change in American Politics,* pp. 56–70.

13. Flanigan and Zingale, *Political Behavior of the American Electorate,* p. 189.

ident's standing in the polls. With great regularity since 1945, the Gallup organization has asked representative samples of Americans the same question: "Do you approve, or disapprove, of the way (the incumbent) is handling his job as President?" The responses to this question form an index (known as Presidential Popularity) consisting of the percentage of citizens approving the President's performance at any given point in time. Systematic data is available for all Presidents since Harry S Truman. The pattern of public responses is displayed in Figs. 4.2–4.9.   Several generalizations are supported by these data:

1. *On the average, public approval of Presidential performance has diminished considerably.* Assessments of the performance of incumbent Presidents fluctuate, but (as shown in Figs. 4.2–4.5) the public had generally favorable evaluations of American Presidents prior to the Vietnam War. The limited polling data available during Franklin Roosevelt's Presidency indicates that public assessment of him was quite positive. Not only was he elected President four times, his popularity never dropped below 50% approval.[14]   Likewise, Eisenhower and Kennedy were popular Presidents.   Eisenhower's public approval dipped as low as 49% only once during his second term, and during his first term, he accomplished the unprecedented feat of gaining popularity, finishing that term higher in the polls than he started. John Kennedy was the last President to maintain at least 50% approval for his entire term of office. Harry S Truman was the only President during this era to receive the low public evaluations that have recently become commonplace.   Not coincidentally, Truman also presided over a period of rampant inflation and an unpopular and indecisive Presidential war.

Just as formerly high levels of public confidence in government have been eroded, popularity ratings of Presidents have suffered for some of the same reasons. Figure 4.6 should not necessarily be interpreted to mean that Lyndon Johnson's popularity declined only because of opposition to American military involvement in Southeast Asia.   There is substantial evidence that President Johnson's war policies were unpopular with some segments of the public (the

14. Fred I. Greenstein, "Popular Images of the President," in Aaron Wildavsky (ed.), *The Presidency*. Boston, Ma.: Little, Brown and Company, 1969, p. 290.

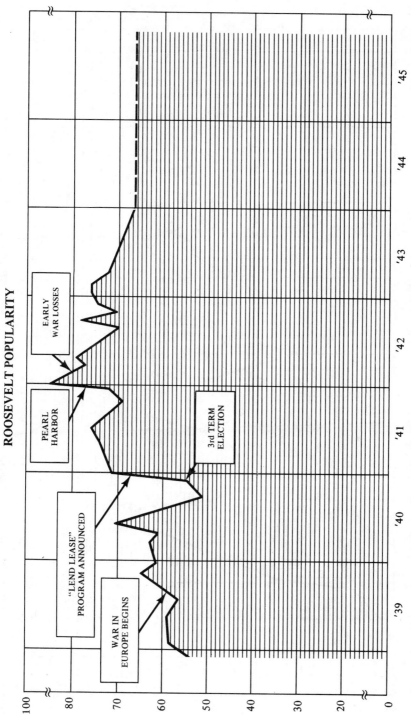

Figure 4.2 Public approval of President Roosevelt, 1939–1944. Source: *The Gallup Opinion Index*, October/November, 1980, p. 39.

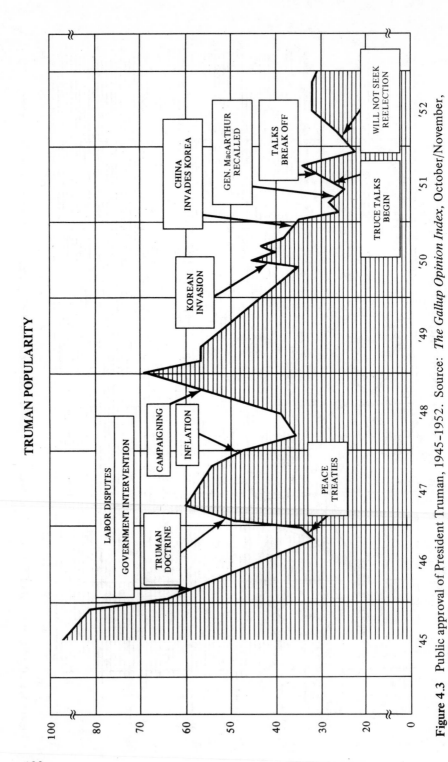

TRUMAN POPULARITY

LABOR DISPUTES

GOVERNMENT INTERVENTION

TRUMAN DOCTRINE

CAMPAIGNING

INFLATION

PEACE TREATIES

KOREAN INVASION

CHINA INVADES KOREA

GEN. MacARTHUR RECALLED

TALKS BREAK OFF

TRUCE TALKS BEGIN

WILL NOT SEEK REELECTION

Figure 4.3 Public approval of President Truman, 1945–1952. Source: *The Gallup Opinion Index*, October/November, 1980, p. 36.

EISENHOWER POPULARITY

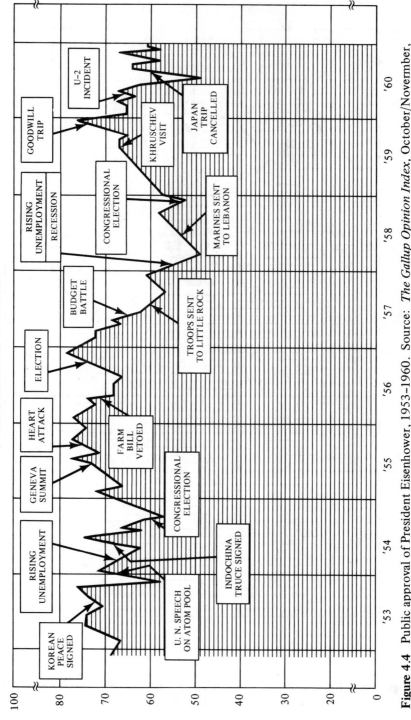

Figure 4.4 Public approval of President Eisenhower, 1953–1960. Source: *The Gallup Opinion Index*, October/November, 1980, p. 33.

KENNEDY POPULARITY

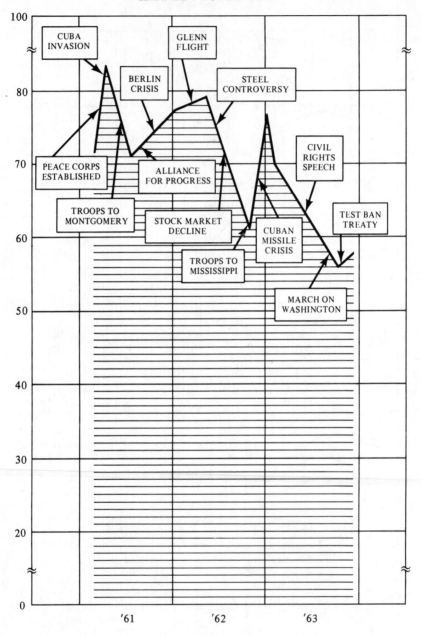

Figure 4.5 Public approval of President Kennedy, 1961–1963. Source: *The Gallup Opinion Index,* October/November, 1980, p. 28.

JOHNSON POPULARITY

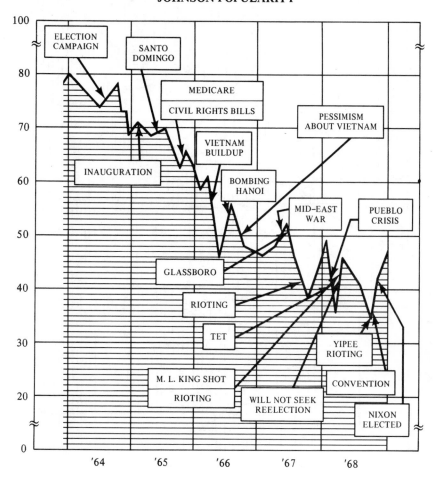

Figure 4.6 Public approval of President Johnson, 1964–1968. Source: *The Gallup Opinion Index,* October/November, 1980, p. 25.

Hawks) because they believed America should win at all costs. By pursuing a policy of gradual escalation, rather than total commitment to victory, Johnson lost support not only among those opposed to United States' military involvement, but also among those convinced that, once committed, America should do whatever was necessary to win.[15] Erosion of the President's support was inevitable, given the increasing polarization of the public on this issue.

15. Flannigan and Zingale, *Political Behavior of the American Electorate,* pp. 112–113.

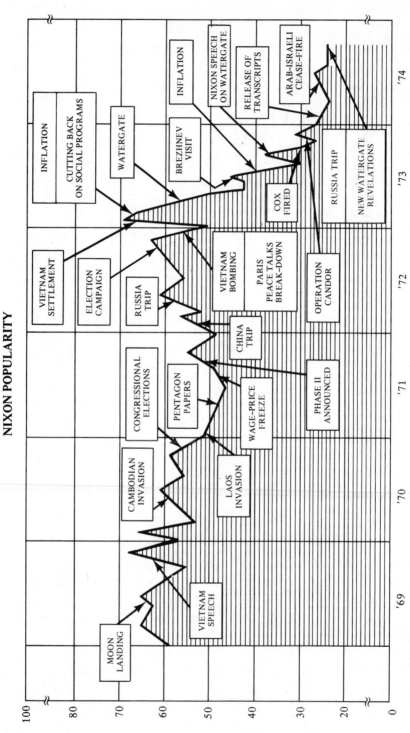

NIXON POPULARITY

100 — 80 — 70 — 60 — 50 — 40 — 30 — 20 — 0

'69   '70   '71   '72   '73   '74

MOON LANDING

VIETNAM SPEECH

CAMBODIAN INVASION

CONGRESSIONAL ELECTIONS

PENTAGON PAPERS

LAOS INVASION

WAGE-PRICE FREEZE

CHINA TRIP

PHASE II ANNOUNCED

RUSSIA TRIP

ELECTION CAMPAIGN

VIETNAM SETTLEMENT

INFLATION

CUTTING BACK ON SOCIAL PROGRAMS

WATERGATE

BREZHNEV VISIT

VIETNAM BOMBING

PARIS PEACE TALKS BREAK-DOWN

OPERATION CANDOR

COX FIRED

RUSSIA TRIP

NEW WATERGATE REVELATIONS

INFLATION

NIXON SPEECH ON WATERGATE

RELEASE OF TRANSCRIPTS

ARAB-ISRAELI CEASE-FIRE

Figure 4.7 Public approval of President Nixon, 1969–1974. Source: *The Gallup Opinion Index*, October/November, 1980, p. 21.

FORD POPULARITY

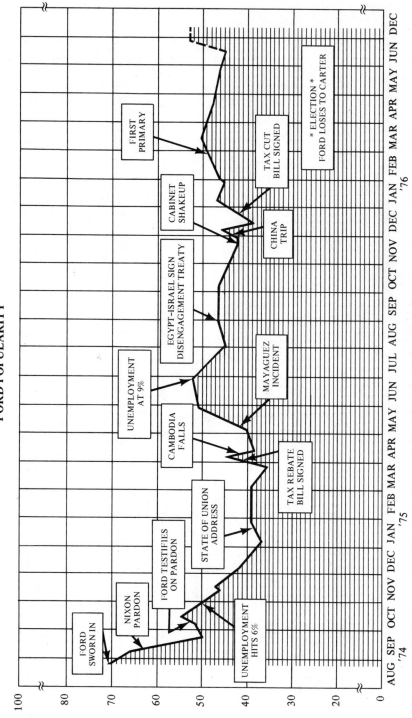

Figure 4.8 Public approval of President Ford, 1974–1976. Source: *The Gallup Opinion Index*, October/November, 1980, p. 16.

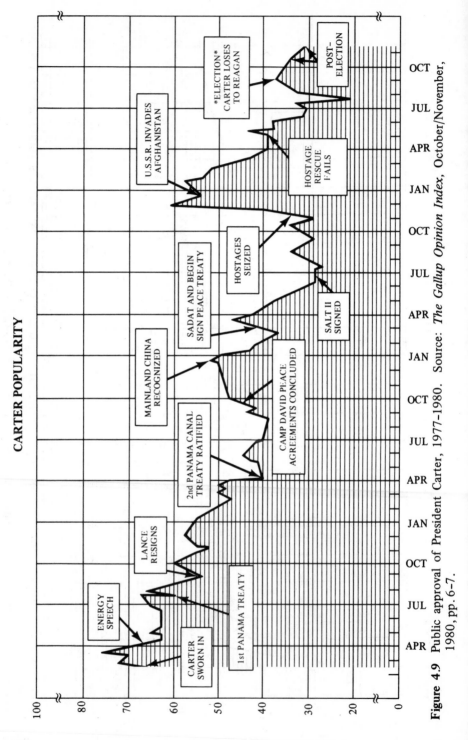

Figure 4.9 Public approval of President Carter, 1977–1980. Source: *The Gallup Opinion Index,* October/November, 1980, pp. 6–7.

Of recent Presidents, Richard Nixon had perhaps the best prospects for maintaining high levels of public approval (Fig. 4.7). Nixon remained reasonably popular during his first term, and his level of public approval approached 70% after his reelection and announcement of a Vietnam settlement. Unfortunately for the President this was followed shortly by the emergence of one of the major political scandals in American history, and Nixon's approval ratings plunged more than 40 percentage points during the first year of his second term. When he left office, his rating of 24% approval was one of the lowest ever recorded by the Gallup poll.

President Ford's public-approval ratings, like Nixon's, were heavily influenced by the impact of a single event. One month after assuming office, Gerald Ford pardoned Richard Nixon for any and all crimes related to the Watergate affair. While this pardon was a legal exercise of executive authority, it was politically costly. Figure 4.8 shows that President Ford's public approval declined 22 percentage points in the months after the controversial pardon.

Jimmy Carter's popularity peaked after two months in office and then began a steadily downward slide as the economy worsened and Carter was increasingly perceived by the public as inept (Fig. 4.9). This downward trend was briefly interrupted by a temporary gain of 11 points after the President's impressive success in engineering the Camp David accord between Egypt and Israel. A more significant upturn in President Carter's popularity occurred late in 1979. In November of that year, Iranian militants seized the United States Embassy in Teheran, taking the American Embassy personnel as hostages. This event, which rapidly escalated into an international confrontation, gave a considerable (if temporary) boost to President Carter's level of public approval. From a low of 29% before the Iranian crisis, the President's approval rating skyrocketed to 61% within a month after the embassy takeover and remained high for several months, working to Carter's advantage as he began his campaign for the Democratic nomination in the spring of 1980.

2. *There is a tendency for citizens to rally to the support of the President during an international crisis.* The impact of the Iranian crisis on President Carter's approval ratings is one instance of a more general phenomenon known in political science parlance as the rally-round-the-flag effect.[16] Dramatic international events involving the

16. John E. Mueller, *War, Presidents, and Public Opinion.* New York: John Wiley & Sons, 1973, p. 208. The following discussion is based on Mueller's analysis, pp. 205–220.

United States, and the President directly, usually result in a temporary boost in the public's approval of the President *regardless* of how they are handled. Examples abound. Public approval of President Truman rose 9 points after his decision to resist the Communist invasion of Korea. Eisenhower's ratings improved 8% during the Suez Canal crisis. Within a month after his successful resolution of the Cuban missile crisis, public approval of President Kennedy increased 14 percentage points. Even foreign-policy fiascoes are frequently good for a temporary boost in the polls. Kennedy's popularity *increased* after the bungled Bay of Pigs invasion of Cuba (10 points), as did Eisenhower's after the U–2 incident.

3. *The President's election, or reelection, produces substantial increases in public approval.* Immediately after his inauguration, the President's public support is considerably greater than the percentage of the electorate that voted for him. Successful candidates supported by barely a majority of the voters usually begin their Presidencies with approval of nearly three-quarters of the public. Similarly, non-elected Presidents, succeeding after death or resignation, begin their terms with considerable public approval. It appears that a portion of the public who did not support the candidate is willing to grant a measure of approval to him as President. As in the case of the rally-round-the-flag effect, this honeymoon effect tends to be rather short-lived—erosion of the President's public approval beginning almost immediately as subsequent decisions alienate various components of the public.

4. *The long-term trend in Presidential popularity is almost inevitably in the direction of a decrease in public approval.* Presidential popularity is almost invariably lower at the end of a Presidential term of office than at the beginning, the only exception being Eisenhower's first term. From the Truman through the Nixon Presidencies, the average decline in public approval of Presidential performance was 6% per year, although there was wide variation around this average.[17] The pervasiveness of this pattern suggests that the dynamics between the President and the public are such that the Chief Executive can expect to lose popularity simply by exercising the powers and duties of office.

17. *Ibid.*, p. 220.

John E. Mueller's detailed analysis of trends in Presidential popularity suggests several reasons for the phenomenon of consistent decline in public approval of Presidential performance. In addition to scandals affecting the President's personal integrity, there could be indecisive, unpopular wars, or the alienation of minorities which may result from some particular action of the President. Even if an administration always acts with majority support (a rather tenuous assumption), it will gradually alienate enough components of the public to lose popularity. Controversial decisions inevitably make enemies for the President and, over a period of time, this takes a toll on public approval, converting former supporters into opponents.

Moreover, if the public is sufficiently polarized on an issue, the President may alienate substantial numbers of citizens on both sides of the issue. Mueller suggests that administration enforcement of school desegregation is this type of issue,[18] as was President Johnson's Vietnam policy. Applying this concept to the Carter administration, Robert DiClerico concluded that within his first year in office the President managed to generate substantial opposition from farmers, the National Urban League, the AFL–CIO and the liberal wing of the Democratic party.[19]

The condition of the nation's economy is another key variable affecting Presidential popularity. Public approval of the President declines in proportion to the severity of an economic slump.[20] The precipitous decline in public approval of President Carter is partly attributable to the association between his administration and the worst economic conditions since the Truman era. President Ford's popularity bottomed out during the economic recession of 1974–75, and Eisenhower's lowest level of public approval came during the recession of 1958. Despite the successful conclusion of World War II, President Truman's public approval declined dramatically following the war as economic conditions deteriorated.

"Stagflation" is the term used to describe the simultaneous conditions of economic stagnation (little or no real growth) and high

18. *Ibid.*, p. 205.

19. DiClerico, *The American President*, p. 158.

20. Mueller, *War, Presidents, and Public Opinion*, pp. 213–215.

inflation that characterized the American economy during the Ford and Carter administrations. This is a difficult economic condition for government to deal with, especially since prevailing economic orthodoxy suggests that an economic slump may be useful in combating inflation. For a President to choose, as Carter did in 1980, to encourage an economic slowdown in order to restrain rampant inflation, the net result may well be further erosion of public approval as unemployment increases and interest rates rise.[21]

PUBLIC SUPPORT AND POLITICAL INFLUENCE

After analyzing the dynamics of Presidential popularity, Mueller concluded that if the President wishes to leave office a popular man, he should either (1) resign the day after inauguration, or (2) be Dwight David Eisenhower.[22]   In addition, the President's relationship with the public will likely benefit from efforts to maintain a stable economy and to avoid scandal and even the appearance of impropriety, and to use the powers of Commander in Chief with restraint. Beyond this, the President is in a position to use his influence with the public to shape the agenda of politics and to mobilize the support of specific-issue publics on matters of public policy.

Television: Setting the Agenda of Politics

Television has become the dominant source of the public's information about Presidential politics. Nearly every American home has at least one television set, and events connected with Presidential politics are given network coverage several times a day. When asked in repeated surveys since the Eisenhower era to indicate their most important source of information about Presidential campaigns, about one-fourth of the public has consistently named newspapers. The

21. On President Carter's economic policies and recession, see Steven Rattner, "The Risky Politics of Recession," *The New York Times Magazine,* May 11, 1980, pp. 21 ff. The complexity of the "stagflation" problem, as well as the state of disarray of current economic theories for dealing with it, can be seen in a symposium of the views of twenty leading economists. See David Mermelstein, "The Threatening Economy," *The New York Times Magazine,* December 30, 1979, pp. 12 ff.

22. Mueller, *War, Presidents, and Public Opinion,* p. 233.

percentage choosing television, however, has more than doubled since 1952 to over two-thirds of the public. The percentage choosing radio as the most important source has decreased from one-third to less than 5%. Moreover, television is now the public's most trusted source of information about Presidential politics.[23]

Political commentators are not in agreement about the impact and importance of this development. Looking only at the impact of television on the level of public interest, involvement, and information about politics, it is feasible to conclude that television has not transformed American politics. Turnout in national elections has not increased appreciably during the era of widespread reliance on television (indeed, the opposite seems to be happening), nor does television seem to have activated political interest among its viewers. Rather, television seems to have supplanted radio as the dominant electronic advertising and entertainment medium.[24]

The impact of television on Presidential politics would seem to lie elsewhere than activation of the public to greater levels of political involvement. Professor Herbert Asher's penetrating analysis suggests that the importance of the relation between television and Presidential politics is to be found in the nature of the medium. The two primary characteristics of political presentations on network television are immediacy and oversimplification.[25] The organization of network television provides instant coverage and analysis of political events. This has advantages and disadvantages for the President's attempts to influence the public. For a substantial majority of the public, network television defines what is news. This can assist the President in one primary function—setting public and governmental priorities. Network television is a useful tool in the President's attempts to define the political and social issues society should confront. There is some evidence that issues emphasized by network news correspond with issues citizens come to consider important.[26]

23. These figures are extracted from a series of SRC/CPS surveys cited in Herbert Asher, *Presidential Elections and American Politics* (revised ed.). Homewood, Ill.: Dorsey Press, 1980, p. 229.

24. Angus Campbell, "Has Television Reshaped Politics?" *Columbia Journalism Review.* Fall, 1962, pp. 10–13.

25. Asher, *Presidential Elections and American Politics,* pp. 229–243.

26. *Ibid.*

The immediacy of television coverage, in combination with the President's practically unlimited access to network airwaves, provides instant direct communication with the public, permitting the President to convey his ideas in a manner he prefers. Television permits the White House to maximize the President's visibility by creating media events, including the staging of dramatic announcements, extensive coverage of ceremonial occasions, diplomatic and legislative triumphs, as well as press conferences and public addresses.

High visibility and extensive television coverage do not assure support for the President's policies among the public or the relevant political elite. The ability of the President to place some issues on the national agenda in no way assures that other pertinent political actors will be motivated to support the President's policies, or to take any action at all, for that matter. Even when the political elite are in agreement about goals, there is likely to be a wide range of competing policies acceptable to various segments of the public. Presidential attempts to use television to influence the public inevitably come up against the reality of widespread lack of public awareness and concern about many political issues. Presidential addresses on matters of military and foreign policy frequently have a measurable impact on public approval of the President's policies, but educating the public on the specifics of domestic policy issues has proven a difficult task for Presidents.[27]

Low public concern and awareness of policy issues is reinforced by the content of network television's presentations of political material which tends to oversimplify complex political issues, frequently not providing the in-depth analysis common in magazines and newspapers. The average network news story lasts for about a minute and a half. Citizens now rely most heavily on the medium with a format least able to present detailed information and analysis of political issues. One aspect of the incomplete, or oversimplified, nature of television news coverage of politics is that it tends to be negative, focusing on problems, controversies, and conflicts within government, and on the shortcomings of political leaders. In addition to possibly increasing public cynicism (or realism) about government and politicians, this means that the immediacy of television coverage does not always work to the President's advantage. Presidential mis-

27. For example, Gallup polls before and after President Carter's televised address on the energy crisis showed only a slight (11%) increase in public concern about the energy crisis. Cited in DiClerico, *The American President*, p. 169.

judgments, deceptions, and fiascoes, as well as staged media events and political triumphs, are now piped into the nation's living rooms to be contemplated with the evening meal.[28]

Mobilizing the Politically Relevant Public

Surveys of public opinion are naturally of interest to political scientists, commentators, and politicians. A note of caution is in order, however. Even though sampling error is slight (about 3%), public opinion polls can create misleading impressions about the structure of public opinion, especially in regard to issues of public policy. This is true for two reasons: polls *create opinions* while attempting to measure them, and polls do not adequately assess the *intensity* with which opinions are held. The survey approach to the analysis of citizens' opinions creates the likelihood that the pollster is, in part, measuring attitudes that do not exist, or, at least, did not exist before the survey. This is especially true regarding issue preferences because polling citizens about issues requires them to respond by indicating a preference among issue alternatives. This technique probably underestimates the number of people having no opinion, while inflating the number of citizens willing to offer an opinion in the absence of any real preference, or even awareness, among the alternatives presented. Consequently, on many issues there is little stability in individual responses, suggesting that considerable numbers of people respond essentially at random to surveys about issue preferences.[29]   Evidence also suggests that on many policy issues a substantial minority of the public either has no opinion, does not know what the government is doing in that policy area, or is simply volunteering opinions in response to questions asked by pollsters.[30]

The problem of individuals' differing levels of intensity of opinion cannot be remedied simply by asking respondents in a poll how strongly they feel about an issue. The intensity with which opinions are held is sufficiently important that it necessitates a different analytical conception of public opinion. Rather than

28. For an extensive discussion of television and Presidential politics, see Asher, *Presidential Elections and American Politics*, pp. 233–243.

29. Phillip E. Converse, "Attitudes and Non-Attitudes: Continuation of a Dialogue," in Edward R. Tufte (ed.), *The Quantitative Analysis of Social Problems.* Reading, Ma.: Addison-Wesley, 1970, pp. 168–189.

30. Flanigan and Zingale, *Political Behavior of the American Electorate,* p. 99.

grapple with the amorphous nature of public opinion, an alternative is to focus on the structure of opinions around particular issues. This conception assumes not only that opinions are specific to issues, but also that the intensity of issue preferences is reinforced by group affiliations. Consequently, the *politically relevant public* for many issues is composed primarily of activists and organized interests most immediately affected by those policies. The public that exists around tariff policy is substantially different from the publics concerned about farm-price supports, workmen's compensation, civil rights, or energy policies.[31]

For reasons of organization, finance, activism, and intensity, the publics specific to an issue are likely to have greater political impact than public opinion in general. Political influence flows disproportionately to those with the awareness, skills, organization, motivation, and finances sufficient to have an impact on decision makers. This is not to say that public opinion is irrelevant, but rather that it is frequently *permissive,* meaning that, on many issues, there is low public awareness and little widespread intensity of feeling. Consequently, on many policy issues, government decision makers may choose from a wide range of policy options acceptable to the largely indifferent public.

There are, of course, a minority of political issues on which public opinion is *directive* in the sense that a large portion of the citizenry has intense opinions and preferences about the various policy alternatives.[32] For this minority of policy issues elected officials need to be attentive to constituency preferences. Legalized abortions and the busing of school children for racial integration are examples of two such salient and controversial issues.

For issues falling within the permissive range of public indifference, the appropriate strategy for the President may be to attempt to influence the publics specific to those issues. Efforts directed at gaining support, or muting opposition, of influential organized interests will likely have a greater impact on the political decision-making process than will Presidential attempts to influence the perceptions of the disinterested public. Presidential attempts to raise the consciousness of the mass public frequently have limited impact, not only because of widespread indifference about many issues, but

31. This is the conception of public opinion developed by David B. Truman in *The Governmental Process: Political Interests and Public Opinion.* New York: Knopf, 1957, pp. 218–223.

32. Permissive and directive opinions are discussed in Flanigan and Zingale, *Political Behavior of the American Electorate,* pp. 98–99.

also because it is difficult to translate public sentiment into political action and influence. Interest group membership is much easier to activate politically, having been organized partly for that purpose.

Dealing with specific-issue publics has the added advantage of immersing the President into the substantive realities of policy issues, emphasizing political persuasion and bargaining required by the public-policy process. Because of the heavy emphasis on imagery and style, reliance primarily on public relations techniques to influence the general public may actually distract the President and his staff from the more profitable use of limited Presidential resources, as well as create the possibility of overexposure.

Issue publics may be energized through use of executive department liaison peronnel to mobilize clientele groups, or the President's persuasive efforts can be coordinated from the White House. Both the Kennedy and Johnson administrations actively employed these techniques to generate support for their legislative programs. President Kennedy met personally with 1,700 opinion leaders in seeking support for civil-rights bills, and both administrations worked closely with lobbyists from the AFL–CIO and civil-rights groups on mass transit, tax cuts, war on poverty, and civil-rights legislation. These groups organized local support, publicized issues in the media, stimulated constituency mail and pressured influential members of Congress.[33] Preliminary reports suggest that the ground swell of response to President Reagan's televised appeal for public support for his tax cut proposal was, in part, an organized telephone campaign orchestrated by local business leaders.[34] The successful mobilization of an issue public contributed to the impression of more general popular support.

Activation of interest groups is influential because it generates communication with political decision makers from the most politically relevant, activist, and organized components of their political constituencies. Political decision makers are, in general, likely to be more responsive to this type of influence than to more diffuse public opinion. Recent research has shown that the relationship between the President's public popularity and his success in Congress is indirect at best. Members of Congress respond less to the President's level of public approval and more to his popularity among their supporters, again emphasizing the importance of activating partisans,

33. George C. Edwards III, *Presidential Influence in Congress.* San Francisco, Ca.: Freeman, 1980, pp. 169–171.
34. See Cheryl Arvidson, "Reagan's Efforts Ring Tax-cut Bell," *Dayton Daily News,* July 30, 1981, pp. 1, 6.

opinion leaders and organized interests for generating support on issues.[35]   These techniques are useful in wooing members of the opposition party who may be less accessible to the administration. President Carter, for example, successfully activated outside interest groups in winning Republican Congressional support to sustain his veto of the 1978 public works bill.[36]

CONCLUSION

Presidents appeal to the public on many occasions to seek support on policy issues. In addition to generating support on specific issues, Presidential appeals to the public are effective in placing issues on the national agenda, dramatizing events, projecting an image or style, and maintaining public confidence. This latter task has become increasingly difficult in the face of growing public cynicism and mistrust of government and politicians.

Activation and mobilization of various issue publics, opinion leaders, and organized interests have proved to be effective ways for the President to translate influence with the public into power that will shape the direction of public policy. Electronic mass media, particularly television, provide the President with a leadership tool of considerable potential. The impact of the President's nearly unlimited access to the public through television has been diminished by the independent and frequently critical emphasis of network news coverage, growing public mistrust of government, and the generally mediocre and uninspiring quality of much recent Presidential rhetoric.

35. See two research reports by George C. Edwards III. "Presidential Influence in the House: Presidential Prestige as a Source of Presidential Power," *American Political Science Review,* LXX, pp. 101–113, and "Presidential Influence in the Senate: Presidential Prestige as a Source of Presidential Power," *American Politics Quarterly,* IV. October, 1977, pp. 481–500.

36. Edwards, *Presidential Influence in Congress,* p. 178.

FURTHER READING

PRESIDENTIAL POWER

Corwin, Edward S. *The President: Office and Powers 1787–1957* (4th rev. ed.). New York: New York University, 1957. A somewhat conservative historical and constitutional analysis of the office and its powers.

Cronin, Thomas E., and Tugwell, Rexford G. *The Presidency Reappraised* (2nd ed.). New York: Praeger Publishers, 1977. Seventeen prominent scholars discuss the powers, paradoxes, limitations, and responsibilities of the post-imperial Presidency.

Neustadt, Richard E. *Presidential Power: The Politics of Leadership.* New York: John Wiley and Sons, 1960. Illustrating his analysis with events from the Truman and Eisenhower Presidencies, Professor Neustadt concludes that Presidential power is essentially the power of persuasion.

Pious, Richard. *The American Presidency.* New York: Basic Books, 1979. A thorough consideration of the powers and responsibilities of the modern Presidency.

Reedy, George E. *The Twilight of the Presidency.* New York: New American Library, 1970. A former high-level Presidential advisor's thoughts on some of the difficulties inherent in the modern Presidency.

Schlesinger, Arthur M., Jr. *The Imperial Presidency.* Boston, Ma.: Houghton Mifflin, 1973. The eminent historian analyzes the events and personalities which transformed Presidential activism into imperialism.

OVERVIEWS OF THE PRESIDENTIAL SELECTION PROCESS

Barber, James David (ed.). *Choosing the President.* Englewood Cliffs, N. J.: Prentice-Hall, 1974. Seven distinguished scholars discuss the recruitment, nomination, and election of Presidents.

Barber, James David. *The Pulse of Politics: Electing Presidents in the Media Age.* New York: W. W. Norton & Co., 1980. A comprehensive analysis of Presidential nominations and elections by one of America's most respected Presidential scholars.

Ladd, Everett Carll, Jr., and Hadley, Charles D. *Transformation of the American Party System: Political Coalitions from the New Deal to the 1970's*

(2nd ed.). New York: W. W. Norton & Co., 1978. Changes in American political parties, Presidential coalitions, and voter alignments since the New Deal.

Polsby, Nelson W., and Wildavsky, Aaron. *Presidential Elections: Strategies of American Electoral Politics.* (5th ed.). New York: Charles Scribner's Sons, 1980. An analysis of the Presidential selection process emphasizing strategy, resources, and campaigning.

Watson, Richard A. *The Presidential Contest.* New York: John Wiley & Sons, 1980. A concise and current summary of the Presidential selection process.

Wayne, Stephen J. *The Road to the White House: The Politics of Presidential Elections.* New York: St. Martin's Press, 1980. A thorough and systematic analysis of Presidential nominations and elections, including an assessment of the impact of recent changes in rules for campaign finance and selection of convention delegates.

PRESIDENTIAL NOMINATIONS

Barber, James David (ed.). *Race for the Presidency.* Englewood Cliffs, N. J.: Prentice-Hall, 1978. Barber and three other scholars analyze the impact of news media on the Presidential-nominating process.

David, Paul T., and Ceaser, James W. *Proportional Representation in Presidential Nominating Politics.* Charlottesville, Va.: University of Virginia Press, 1980. A major study analyzing in detail the impact of delegate-selection processes on the Presidential nominating process in 1976.

David, Paul T., Goldman, Ralph M., and Bain, Richard C. *The Politics of National Party Conventions.* Washington, D.C.: The Brookings Institute, 1960. A valuable record of the history of Presidential nominating conventions.

Kirkpatrick, Jeane. *The New Presidential Elite.* New York: Russell Sage Foundation, 1976. Analysis of changes in Presidential nominating politics resulting from party reforms.

Lengle, James I., and Shofer, Byron E. (eds.). *Presidential Politics: Readings on Nominations and Elections.* New York: St. Martin's Press, 1980. A collection of research and writings by prominent scholars and journalists.

Sullivan, Denis G., et al. *The Politics of Representation: The Democratic Convention of 1972.* New York: St. Martin's Press, 1974. Survey of 1972 convention delegates.

CAMPAIGN FINANCE

Alexander, Herbert E. *Financing Politics: Money, Elections, and Political Reform.* Washington, D.C.: Congressional Quarterly, 1976. An overview of recent developments in Presidential campaign finance.

Alexander, Herbert E. *Financing the 1972 Elections.* Lexington, Ma.: D.C. Heath, 1976; *Financing the 1976 Election.* Washington, D.C.: Congressional Quarterly, 1979. These books are the authoritative source for data on finances of the 1972 and 1976 elections.

Heard, Alexander. *The Costs of Democracy.* Chapel Hill, N.C.: University of North Carolina Press, 1960. A source book on campaign finance prior to 1960.

ELECTORAL BEHAVIOR

Asher, Herbert. *Presidential Elections and American Politics: Voters, Candidates, and Campaigns Since 1952* (rev. ed.). Homewood, Ill.: Dorsey, 1980. Thorough survey of research on Presidential campaigns and elections since 1952.

Burnham, Walter Dean. *Critical Elections and the Mainsprings of American Politics.* New York: W. W. Norton & Co., 1970. A theory of critical elections and voter realignments.

Campbell, Angus, et al. *The American Voter.* New York: John Wiley & Sons, 1964. Detailed investigation into the psychology of Presidential voting using in-depth surveys of voters during the Eisenhower era.

Campbell, Angus, et al. *Elections and the Political Order.* New York: John Wiley & Sons, 1966. A collection of scholarly research which constitutes much of the basis of political scientists' understanding of electoral behavior.

Congressional Quarterly, *Presidential Elections Since 1789* (2nd ed.). Washington, D.C.: Congressional Quarterly, 1979. A source book with statistics on every Presidential election as well as information about the candidates.

DeVries, Walter, and Tarrance, Lance, Jr. *The Ticket-Splitter, A New Force in American Politics!* Grand Rapids, Mich.: Eerdmans, 1972. Research on a topic of increasing significance in American elections.

Flanigan, William H., and Zinglae, Nancy H. *Political Behavior of the American Electorate* (4th ed.). Boston, Ma.: Allyn and Bacon, 1979. Concise and current summary of research on American electoral behavior.

Key, V. O., Jr. *The Responsible Electorate: Rationality in Presidential Voting 1936–1960.* New York: Vintage Books, 1968. Contending that "voters are not fools," Key studied swing voters with special attention to why they switch parties in Presidential elections.

Nie, Norman H., Verba, Sidney, and Petrocik, John R. *The Changing American Voter* (enlarged ed.). Cambridge, Ma.: Harvard University Press, 1979. Updating the image of the American voter, the authors document both the increasing political independence of voters and the growing potential for issue-voting in Presidential elections.

Pomper, Gerald. *Voters' Choice: Varieties of American Electoral Behavior.*
New York: Dodd, Mead & Co., 1975. Systematic survey of American
electoral behavior.

THE ELECTORAL COLLEGE

Longley, Lawrence D., and Braun, Alan G. *The Politics of Electoral College
Reform* (2nd ed.). New Haven, Conn.: Yale University Press, 1975.
The impact of the Electoral College on Presidential politics, and considera-
tion of the possible impact of various reform proposals.
MacBride, Roger Lea. *The American Electoral College.* Caldwell, Idaho: Claxton,
1963. A concise historical treatment of the topic.

PRESIDENTIAL ELECTIONS

McGinniss, Joe. *The Selling of the President 1968.* New York: Trident, 1969.
Cynical account of Richard Nixon's 1968 media campaign.
Pomper, Gerald M., et al. *The Election of 1976: Reports and Interpretations.*
New York: David McKay Co., Inc., 1977. An assortment of assessments
and interpretations of the 1976 Presidential election.
Schram, Martin. *Running for President: A Journal of the Carter Campaign.*
New York: Pocket Books, 1977.
White, Theodore H. *The Making of the President 1960.* New York: Atheneum
Publishers, 1961; *The Making of the President 1964.* New York: Atheneum
Publishers, 1965; *The Making of the President 1968.* New York: Atheneum
Publishers, 1969; and *The Making of the President 1972.* New York:
Atheneum Publishers, 1973. White's series constitutes some of the best
reporting of American Presidential elections, particularly the 1960 book
which won a Pulitzer Prize.
Witcover, Jules. *Marathon: The Pursuit of the Presidency 1972-1976.* New
York: Viking, 1977. In the tradition of Theodore White's accounts, an
extensive report of the strategies and personalities contending for the
Presidency.

PUBLIC OPINION

Edwards, George C. *Presidential Influence in Congress.* San Francisco: Free-
man, 1980. An attempt to systematically investigate links between the
President's popularity and executive influence in Congress.
Mueller, John E. *War, Presidents, and Public Opinion.* New York: John Wiley
& Sons, 1973. An influential analysis of Presidential popularity from
Truman through Nixon's first term.

Seagull, Louis M. *Youth and Change in American Politics.* New York: New Viewpoints, 1979. Analysis of changing public perceptions of politicians and political institutions with special emphasis on the growing significance of generational differences.

The Gallup Opinion Index. A monthly chronicle of the state of public opinion on political, social, and economic matters. Presidential popularity is regularly assessed.

(National Archives 306–PS–49–8235)

Part Two

The Presidency

Chapter 5

Presidential Tenure and Succession

THE YEAR THERE WAS NO PRESIDENT

The year there was no President is the sum total of the periods—weeks and months—when the President was unable to exercise the powers and duties of the office.[1] Three Presidents have suffered lengthy periods of physical disability sufficient to disrupt the normal functioning of the government. After being shot, President James Garfield was bedridden for 80 days before he died. A period of 280 days elapsed from the time of Woodrow Wilson's stroke (September, 1919) until Cabinet meetings were resumed. The most recent period of physical disability was the 143 days between President Eisenhower's heart attack (in 1955) until his announced recovery.[2] Four other Presidents have suffered briefer periods of disability, ranging from several days to a week, before they died. In addition, Franklin Roosevelt's growing disability was clearly evident to his close associates even before his last election.[3] He served only three and a half months of his fourth term before he died.

1. Richard Hansen, *The Year We Had No President.* Lincoln, Neb.: University of Nebraska Press, 1972, p. 1.

2. *Ibid.*

3. Edward S. Corwin, *The President: Office and Powers*, 1787–1957 (4th ed.). New York: New York University Press, 1957, p. 54.

If "Presidential disability" is broadly interpreted to include not only incapacitating physical illness, but *any period of inability* which renders the President unable to exercise the powers and duties of office, then the final six weeks of President Nixon's tenure in office should be included. As the President battled for political survival during that period, he was in the White House for a total of only six days.[4] The responsibilities of running the government and managing the White House were assumed by Chief-of-Staff Alexander Haig, regarded by some commentators as a "surrogate President" during the final days of the Nixon administration.[5]

Several thorny questions arise during any lengthy period of Presidential disability, or inability. There are likely to be any number of matters in foreign and domestic policy requiring the President's attention. Some can be delegated to White House assistants and department heads, but others are likely to be more urgent, requiring the President's personal attention. This is especially true of foreign relations during the nuclear age. Deterrence, a key concept in America's defense strategy, depends upon the nation's capacity to retaliate immediately if attacked. During the period of President Eisenhower's convalescence, Vice President Nixon expressed concern about a possible nuclear confrontation with the Soviet Union: "Would the President be well enough to make a decision? If not, who had the authority to push the button?"[6]

An equally intriguing question during any future period of Presidential incapacity is whether the untested constitutional mechanism for dealing with this problem (the Twenty-Fifth Amendment) will be invoked, and, if invoked, how well will it work? This amendment permits a disabled President to voluntarily relinquish power to the Vice President, but also permits the Vice President to assume the powers of the Presidency if, in the collective judgment of the Cabinet, the President is no longer capable of exercising the powers and duties of office. This provision, enacted in 1967, has never been invoked.

Another dimension of the Presidential disability question was raised by Fletcher Knebel's novel *Night of Camp David*, in which

4. Theodore H. White, *Breach of Faith: The Fall of Richard Nixon*. New York: Dell Publishing Company, Inc., 1976, p. 389.

5. Bob Woodward and Carl Bernstein, *The Final Days*. New York: Avon Books, 1977, pp. 289, 355.

6. Richard M. Nixon, *Six Crises*. New York: Doubleday and Co., Inc., 1962, p. 139. Cited by Hansen, *The Year We Had No President*, p. 2.

President Mark Hollenback cracks under the strain of the job and loses his mind. A tense period ensues, during which the nation may be plunged into a nuclear holocaust. The crisis is finally resolved when the President, in one of his more lucid moments, decides to resign.[7] The possibility of serious mental illness in high office is not a totally farfetched scenario. At least one state governor developed a serious mental disorder while in office.[8] During President Nixon's final days in office there was considerable speculation about the condition of his mental health. Two things were clear: He was under a tremendous amount of pressure as he confronted the reality of a choice between resignation or impeachment, and there was considerable concern among White House assistants and the President's family that the pressure might become too much for him. A brief review of the circumstances and handling of Presidents Wilson's and Eisenhower's disabilities and the final days of the Nixon administration will illustrate the difficulties and ambiguities created by periods of Presidential incapacity.

Mrs. Wilson's Regency

In the fall of 1919, President Woodrow Wilson suffered a crippling stroke, leading to the nation's longest and most bizarre period of Presidential disability. For months the President lay stricken, his left side paralyzed. The executive branch entered a period of drift, functioning sporadically and uncertainly. After President Wilson fired Secretary of State Lansing for calling unauthorized Cabinet meetings, the Cabinet did not meet for eight months, numerous bills became law without the President's signature, and badly needed support for the Treaty of Versailles and the League of Nations was not forthcoming.[9] The situation was complicated by the lack of esteem the President felt for Vice President Marshall and Wilson's reluctance to delegate authority to the Cabinet during his disability.

7. Fletcher Knebel, *Night of Camp David.* New York: Bantam Books, Inc., 1966.

8. In 1959, after medical testimony that he was mentally ill, Louisiana Governor Earl K. Long was committed to Southeast Louisiana State Hospital on the basis of a court order signed by his wife. A week later, Long, acting under his authority as Governor, fired the superintendent of the hospital as well as the director of state hospitals. He then appointed two new officials who declared him sane and a free man. See Hansen, *Year We Had No President*, p. 101.

9. Hansen, *Year We Had No President*, pp. 29–41.

Out of this chaos the President's wife emerged as one of the more influential first ladies in history. Edith Bolling Wilson became chief-of-staff, if not acting President. On the advice of the President's physicians, to protect the President and permit him time to recuperate, Mrs. Wilson began to screen incoming communications and visitors to the White House, deciding the key question of which matters were important enough to warrant the President's attention. By her own testimony, she permitted only the most important matters to be brought to the President's attention.[10]   Eventually, the President recovered sufficiently to resume some of his duties during his last year in office.

Government by Committee

By the time of the next significant period of Presidential disability, the Presidency had evolved more elaborate institutional features which better enabled the administration to handle the crisis. The Eisenhower administration was hierarchically organized with considerable authority delegated through Chief-of-Staff Sherman Adams. President Eisenhower's first heart attack (September, 1955), coming as it did during the Cold War, had potentially world wide ramifications. Unlike the period of President Wilson's disability, there was considerable cooperation and teamwork during Eisenhower's illness. For two months, the administration was managed by a committee that included Adams, Vice President Nixon, three Cabinet secretaries (State, Treasury, and the Attorney General) and one general officer.

Most decisions that were pending could be handled either by this committee, or postponed. There was considerable concern, however, about whether this committee approach would be adequate to handle a major international crisis. This became a central concern again late in 1957 when the President suffered a stroke which temporarily affected his ability to speak. The President once again recovered completely.[11]

During the interval between his two illnesses, the President was unsuccessful in persuading the Congress to act on either a proposed constitutional amendment, or legislation to deal with the problem of Presidential disability. Unable to obtain the constitutional clarification he sought, Eisenhower developed a more personal solution

10. *Ibid*, p. 34.

11. *Ibid*, pp. 61–65.

in the form of a written agreement with Vice President Nixon on the terms and conditions under which the Vice President could assume the powers and duties of the Presidency in case of another serious Presidential disability. A similar agreement was signed by President Kennedy and Vice President Johnson.

The Final Days

Periods of Presidential disability caused by a heart attack or a stroke can be relatively clearly demarcated. President Nixon's final days in office were more ambiguous, being characterized by his gradual withdrawal from the powers and duties of office as the Watergate scandal slowly consumed his Presidency. Chief-of-Staff Alexander Haig assumed increasingly greater authority as the staff struggled to manage the White House and to keep the government running. Preoccupied with his own defense, the President began to seclude himself at San Clemente.

This creeping paralysis of the Presidency began with the release of the White House transcripts.[12] No other Presidential administration has had to withstand such intense scrutiny by the national media, the Washington community, and the public. The innermost thoughts of the President and his closest advisers were laid bare to the glaring light of publicity. A delight for Nixon haters and a shock to the President's supporters, the transcripts proved to be a chronicle of the administration's insecurities, prejudices, deceptions, and duplicity. Republican Congressional leader John Rhodes summed them up in one sentence: "I have never read such sleaziness in all my life."[13] The President was reduced to the status of an unindicted co-conspirator and stripped of the moral authority to govern. Although determined to "tough it out" and finish his second term, he was eventually overwhelmed by events—some of his own making.

As the impeachment inquiry in Congress picked up momentum, the President began to focus primarily on foreign relations to distract himself from "the Watergate problem." The Presidency continued to function, but not the President. By February, 1974, Chief-of-Staff Haig was described by Theodore White as "more than deputy Presi-

---

12. *Submission of Recorded Presidential Conversations to the Committee on the Judiciary of the House of Representatives by President Richard Nixon.* Washington, D.C.: U.S. Government Printing Office, April 30, 1974.

13. Woodward and Bernstein, *Final Days*, p. 161.

dent—from his desk, appointments, legislation, bills all moved to proper channels, sometimes with, and sometimes without, the consideration of the President."[14]

On July 24, 1974, the Supreme Court administered the coup de grace, ruling that the President must surrender additional tapes as evidence in the prosecution of those already indicted for Watergate offenses. Among these tapes were the conversations of June 23, 1972, which proved conclusively that the President had sanctioned the attempt to obstruct the Federal Bureau of Investigation's inquiry into the Watergate affair. In addition, this tape established that the President had lied repeatedly to the public about the extent of his involvement. When the contents were made public, the remnants of the President's political support disintegrated. The President, however, continued to insist privately, as well as publicly, that he had done nothing wrong. When his attorney, J. Fred Buzhardt, advised otherwise, Nixon became furious and would not talk to Buzhardt for a week.[15]

By the time the Judiciary Committee of the House of Representatives had voted three articles of impeachment against the President, it had become clear to Haig that he must go about relieving Richard Nixon of his Presidency. Consequently, on August 1, 1974, "Haig became acting President of the United States."[16] Haig's objectives were to keep the government running during the crisis and to give the President time to come to the only logical conclusion—resignation.

As the pressure continued to mount during the final two weeks of the Nixon Presidency there was increasing concern among the President's staff and family about the condition of his mental health, fears that the President might commit suicide, and reports of excessive drinking and bizarre behavior on the President's part.[17] As the President teetered on the brink of resignation, Haig continued to assume

---

14. White, *Breach of Faith*, p. 18.

15. *Ibid*, p. 20.

16. *Ibid*, p. 23.

17. For example: On August 6, 1974, the President's son-in-law, Edward Cox, reportedly said that the President had been drinking and acting irrationally. According to Cox, "The President was up walking the halls last night, talking to pictures of former Presidents—giving speeches and talking to the pictures on the wall." Source: Woodward and Bernstein, *Final Days*, pp. 437–438. See, also, pp. 100–102, 204, 230, 270.

increasing authority within the White House. As a precautionary measure Haig called the President's doctors and ordered all pills be denied the President.[18] Secretary of Defense Schlesinger elected to bypass the President on military matters by ordering all military commanders to accept no direct order from the White House unless countersigned by Schlesinger himself.[19]

Although President Nixon has been described during this period as an "unstable personality," not able to distinguish between real and fancied enemies, other well regarded commentators have contended that the President was mentally stable during the final days.[20] On balance, President Nixon seems to have weathered this difficult ordeal with considerable courage. On the evening of August 8, 1974, Richard Nixon addressed the nation for the last time as President. Acknowledging his inability to govern, he was resigning, he said, "because America needs a full-time President."

THE TWENTY-FIFTH AMENDMENT

The inevitable uncertainties associated with extended periods of Presidential disability and incapacity emphasize both the importance and imperfections of the constitutional procedures for handling succession. There are constitutional procedures permitting the President voluntarily to relinquish power, as well as mechanisms to force involuntary surrender of Presidential authority.

In instances when the President might choose voluntarily to relinquish authority, there is an option other than resignation. Section 3 of the Twenty-Fifth Amendment to the United States Constitution reads as follows:

> Whenever the President transmits to the President pro tempore of the Senate and the Speaker of the House of Repre-

---

18. Woodward and Bernstein, *Final Days*, p. 498.

19. White, *Breach of Faith*, p. 35.

20. Theodore White is probably the most respected commentator to describe the President as mentally unstable during this period. See *Breach of Faith*, pp. 50–51, and especially, pp. 422–423. Reportedly, Chief-of-Staff Haig indicated to Watergate prosecutor Leon Jaworski that the President was unstable. See Woodward and Bernstein, *Final Days*, pp. 270–271. In a radio interview broadcast on WAVI (Dayton, Ohio) in February, 1975, Dan Rather contended that the President was not mentally unbalanced during the final days.

sentatives his written declaration that he is unable to discharge the powers and duties of his office, and until he transmits to them a written declaration to the contrary, such powers and duties shall be discharged by the Vice President as Acting President.

This section of the amendment permits the President temporarily to relinquish the powers and duties of the Presidency while still retaining the office. This option provides the President with some middle ground between the alternatives of resigning, or clinging stubbornly to power. From the perspective of an ambitious politician who has devoted years to seeking the Presidency, this would likely be an attractive alternative that might encourage the President to acknowledge a serious disability.

It is easily conceivable that because of mistrust and contempt for the Vice President, the President might be reluctant to surrender authority. In addition, the voluntary yielding of power assumes a rational state of mind on the President's part. Certain severe physical and mental disorders make voluntary relinquishment of power less likely. Section 4 of the Twenty-Fifth Amendment outlines a set of (as yet untested) procedures for handling these contingencies:

Whenever the Vice President and a majority of either the principal officers of the executive departments or of such other body as Congress may by law provide, transmit to the President pro tempore of the Senate and the Speaker of the House of Representatives their written declaration that the President is unable to discharge the powers and duties of his office, the Vice President shall immediately assume the powers and duties of the office as Acting President.

Thereafter, when the President transmits to the President pro tempore of the Senate and the Speaker of the House of Representatives his written declaration that no inability exists, he shall resume the powers and duties of his office unless the Vice President and a majority of either the principal officers of the executive department or of such other body as Congress may by law provide, transmit within four days to the President pro tempore of the Senate and the Speaker of the House of Representatives their written declaration that the President is unable to discharge the powers and duties of his office. Thereupon Congress shall decide the issue, assembling within forty-eight hours for that purpose if not in session. If the Congress, within twenty-one days after receipt of the latter written declaration, or, if Congress is not in session, within twenty-one days after Congress is required to assemble, determines by two-thirds vote of both Houses that the President is unable to discharge the powers and duties of his office, the Vice President shall continue to discharge the same as Acting President; otherwise, the President shall resume the powers and duties of his office.

Difficulty of Execution

Under these unusual circumstances, the Vice President, with majority support in the Cabinet, can *assume* the powers and duties of the Presidency. In cases of open conflict between the President and the administration about the extent of a Presidential disability, the Congress must decide the issue. The difficulties inherent in these procedures are obvious at first glance. They require the determination of Presidential disability to be made by executive officials who are appointed by the President and accountable to him. Moreover, given the structure and organization of the modern Presidency, there is no assurance that either the Vice President or the Cabinet will have close enough access to the President to make a sound judgment of the extent of disability. The situation is likely to be especially touchy if the disability is mental rather than physical. During President Nixon's final days in office he was in close contact only with his family and a few White House assistants. Secretary of State Kissinger was the only Cabinet secretary with ready access to the President. Although the Twenty-Fifth Amendment attempts to provide for the orderly handling of Presidential disability or incapacity, the institutional nature of the modern Presidency makes it as likely as not that the President's personal White House assistants will also play a key role in managing any future disability crisis.

IMPEACHMENT

The constitutional provisions for impeachment permit the Congress to remove a President from office. A necessary last resort, this procedure is not without its drawbacks. The Constitution (Article II, Section 4) provides that Federal officials, including the President and Vice President, can be "removed from office on impeachment for, and conviction of, treason, bribery, or other high crimes and misdemeanors." Impeachment is the prerogative of the House of Representatives and requires only a majority vote. The question of guilt or innocence is then determined by a trial conducted in the Senate, with a two-thirds vote being required to convict and remove a Federal official from office.

Impeachment and removal of a President is so arduous a process that it is rarely used. Only President Andrew Johnson has been impeached. He narrowly escaped conviction by the Senate and remained in office to serve out his term. President Nixon, facing certain impeachment by the House and likely conviction by the Senate, resigned from office.

There are several difficulties inherent in the process, not the least of which is defining what constitutes an impeachable offense. Opinions of legal scholars and politicians run the gamut from Congressman Jerry Ford's assertion that "an impeachable offense is whatever the House of Representatives says it is"[21] to the more conservative view that impeachable offenses are limited to relatively serious criminal offenses. These difficulties arise partly because the Constitution is ambiguous and partly because the impeachment process is highly political. Partisan and political motives for supporting impeachment can never be completely separated from legal and constitutional issues. The impeachment of President Andrew Johnson supposedly revolved around his violation of the Tenure of Office Act by firing Secretary of War Stanton without the Senate's consent. This appears to have been as much an excuse as a reason for his impeachment. The real issue apparently was a political conflict between Johnson and the Radical Republicans in Congress over his post-Civil War reconstruction policy.[22] Likewise, the three articles of impeachment approved against President Nixon by the House Judiciary Committee cited both legal and political offenses.

Article I. Obstruction of Justice. In addition to making false and misleading statements and withholding evidence, the President was accused of misusing the Central Intelligence Agency and interfering with investigations by the Department of Justice and the Federal Bureau of Investigation.

---

21. As Vice President during Nixon's final months in office, Ford took a more conservative view of impeachment in defending the President.

22. See Michael Les Benedict, *The Impeachment and Trial of Andrew Johnson*. New York: W.W. Norton & Co., Inc., 1973, pp. 1–88.

Article II. Abuse of Executive Power. The President was accused of violating the constitutional rights of citizens, misusing Federal agencies for political purposes, and failure to take care that the laws were faithfully executed.

Article III. Defiance of Congressional Subpoenas. The President was charged with failing to produce papers subpoenaed by the House Judiciary Committee.[23]

Regardless of how an impeachable offense is defined, the process itself is a cumbersome one. The inquiry by the House Judiciary Committee into the charges against President Nixon took eight months. Had President Nixon chosen to face impeachment by the House and trial in the Senate rather than to resign, several more months would have passed before the issue was resolved. Even if the President had been acquitted by a Senate trial (an extremely unlikely outcome), he would have been so politically weakened as to be unable to govern. One of the results of the impeachment process was to contribute significantly to the state of paralysis characterizing the final months of the Nixon administration.

During such a period when the President is politically weakened and preoccupied, the administration is likely to drift aimlessly, unable to provide leadership, while being forced to respond to initiatives from external sources. Public trust and confidence in the President may be so low that support is not forthcoming if other nations seek to exploit the President's weakness. In addition, the President's motives for responding to a foreign policy crisis will likely be suspect, further aggravating an already dangerous situation.

Confronted with the difficulties inherent in the impeachment process, it is inevitably tempting to ponder simpler and more expeditious alternatives such as the vote of no confidence used to handle executive leadership transitions in parliamentary systems. Since the American system is not parliamentary but Presidential, it seems politically inadvisable to subject the chief executive to removal by a vote of no confidence without also assuring that the President's party will control the legislature, something our present system cannot do. However, there is an even more basic difficulty with the no-confidence vote. When a parliament ousts the Prime Minister or Chancellor by a vote of no confidence, it is merely removing the

23. The full text of the three Articles of Impeachment is available in White, *Breach of Faith*, pp. 437–441.

head of government, not the head of state. In the American system, the President serves both functions. Doubtless one of the factors making impeachment such a difficult process is that it involves removal of the American head of state, as well as the head of government. Barring major constitutional changes, the nature of the American Presidential system offers little possibility for a workable no-confidence mechanism. Given the difficulties and limitations inherent in the impeachment process, there is little wonder, and probably considerable virtue, in the fact that it is seldom used.

THE VICE PRESIDENCY

The Vice Presidency is a paradox. It is an office with virtually no power, whose incumbents have frequently languished in obscurity. The office has, on occasion, been a burial ground for troublesome reformers or party hacks. Modern Vice Presidents are frequently talented individuals who, despite Presidential assurances to the contrary, are under-utilized and assigned mostly ceremonial tasks. The office has been the object of considerable ridicule throughout American history. Daniel Webster, when offered the Vice Presidential nomination in 1848 replied, "I do not propose to be buried until I·am really dead."[24]

The frustrations of being second choice tell only part of the story. The Vice Presidency is also an office of considerable potential and has enjoyed something of a renaissance during the 20th century. Numerous influential politicians have actively sought the Vice Presidency, including John F. Kennedy, Hubert Humphrey, and Nelson Rockefeller. Others, including Lyndon Johnson, Harry Truman, and Franklin Roosevelt were willing to accept the nomination when their party offered it. Richard Nixon fought vigorously to keep his Vice Presidential nomination, defending his fitness for the job in the nationally televised "Checkers" speech, now widely regarded not only as a turning point in his career, but a classic video performance as well. Nixon also declined to accept a Cabinet position in Eisenhower's administration in exchange for relinquishing the Vice Presidency.

24. Michael V. DiSalle, *Second Choice*. New York: E.P. Dutton (Hawthorne Books), 1966, p. 14.

Route to the Presidency

Despite the ridicule and disclaimers, these men wanted the job because, in most instances, they wanted to be President. There are few more successful routes to the Presidency than the Vice Presidential nomination of one of the two major parties. Historically, nearly one Vice President out of three has become President—thirteen in all. Eight have succeeded to the Presidency upon the death of the President; one has succeeded when the President resigned, and four have subsequently been nominated and elected President. In this century, the odds have been even better. Presidents Theodore Roosevelt, Coolidge, Truman, Johnson, and Ford all succeeded from the Vice Presidency. Two former Vice Presidents were nominated by their parties to oppose one another in the 1968 Presidential election, with Richard Nixon prevailing over Hubert Humphrey.

A Vice Presidential nomination can prove useful in future electoral politics. In 12 of the 21 Presidential elections from 1900 to 1980, at least one of the Presidential candidates nominated by the major parties had either previously served as Vice President, or had been their party's candidate for that office.[25] This suggests that a Vice Presidential nomination has some value for those seeking the Presidency, because it provides an opportunity to build up party credit, visibility, and contacts for a future Presidential campaign. Franklin Roosevelt, the most successful Presidential candidate in history, first ran unsuccessfully as the Democratic Vice Presidential nominee in 1920.

Ideally, the Vice President should be the President's understudy, kept abreast of the administration's politics and decisions, prepared

---

25. Twentieth century Presidential candidates who were former Vice Presidents or Vice Presidential nominees include:
   1904 Theodore Roosevelt (Republican). Former Vice President
   1912 Theodore Roosevelt (Progressive). Former President and Vice President.
   1924 Calvin Coolidge (Republican). Former Vice President
   1932, 1936, 1940, 1944 Franklin D. Roosevelt (Democrat). Former Vice Presidential nominee.
   1948 Harry S. Truman (Democrat). Former Vice President
   1948 Henry A. Wallace (Progressive). Former Vice President
   1960 Richard M. Nixon (Republican). Former Vice President
   1964 Lyndon B. Johnson (Democrat). Former Vice President
   1968 Hubert H. Humphrey (Democrat). Former Vice President
   1968, 1972 Richard M. Nixon (Republican). Former Vice President
   1976 Gerald R. Ford (Republican). Former Vice President

to assume the duties and responsibilities of the Presidency, if necessary. Except for presiding over the Senate, this is the Vice President's only constitutional responsibility. Unfortunately, the ideal of the apprentice Vice President has seldom been realized and transitions are frequently a jolt. The classic illustration would be the case of Harry S Truman. An industrious Senator from Missouri and a reliable party stalwart, Truman was tapped in 1944 to replace the more radical Henry A. Wallace as the Democratic Vice Presidential nominee. This proved to be a decision of considerable significance. President Franklin Roosevelt, seeking an unprecedented fourth term, was not in good health. Within four months after being sworn in for the fourth time, the President was dead. The short time available for Truman, and the President's reluctance to involve his Vice President in key decisions, precluded adequate preparation of Truman to succeed Roosevelt. By his own admission, Truman came into the Presidency inadequately briefed, being unaware even of the secret project for developing the atomic bomb. Consequently, President Truman underwent an intensive period of on-the-job training as he was confronted with one monumental decision after another, including the use of the atomic bomb to end World War II, development of the Marshall Plan to assist Europe, and formulation of an American response to the Russian blockade of Berlin.

Status of Office

Among recent Presidents, Eisenhower and Carter have done the most to elevate the office of Vice President. In addition to being utilized actively in a partisan role, Vice President Nixon was assigned extensive campaign and ceremonial responsibilities and permitted to preside over Cabinet and National Security Council meetings in the President's absence.[26] The Vice President was also included in the six-man commission that supervised the administration after President Eisenhower's heart attack. Nixon's active partisan role as Vice President undoubtedly contributed to his successful campaign for the Republican Presidential nomination in 1960.

President Kennedy attempted, at the start, to provide his Vice President with meaningful work as an understudy. In addition to appointing Lyndon Johnson as Chairman of the President's Committee on Equal Employment Opportunity and Chairman of the

26. Corwin, *The President*, p. 60.

National Aeronautics and Space Council, the President also invited him to attend Cabinet meetings and staff briefings. Johnson was asked to represent the President at numerous functions at home and abroad, and, occasionally, the President sought Johnson's opinion on speeches and strategy.[27] As an outsider, Johnson was never really a part of the Kennedy team, nor very influential in White House decision making. Within a short time, Johnson, like numerous other Vice Presidents, found himself stifled by the office and reduced, for the most part, to the role of a spectator rather than a participant. Despite being frustrated as Vice President, Johnson was loyal and deferential, and when he became President, demanded the same from Vice President Humphrey.

Modern Vice Presidents have increasingly been expected to assume an active partisan role, emphasizing fund-raising as well as defense of the President's policies. In addition to increased public visibility for the Vice President, partisan activities help build up credit with the party which can pay dividends in a future campaign for the Presidential nomination. Delegating the partisan infighting to the Vice President permits the administration to assume a "Presidential posture," defending the President and challenging the critics by proxy. By taking the high road, the President emphasizes his role as statesman and leader, looking on comfortably from the Rose Garden as the Vice President confronts the opposition head on.

President Nixon used Vice President Agnew extensively as a partisan fighter. Agnew became a success as fund-raiser on the Republican banquet circuit, partly because of his speeches leveling partisan broadsides at critics of administration policy. In addition to occasional consultation with President Carter on policy and legislative matters, Vice President Mondale was very active in a partisan and ceremonial capacity.

As appropriate as the role of Presidential understudy would seem to be for Vice Presidents, there are a number of factors mitigating against it. Primary among these is the understandable preference among Presidents for delegating authority only to those they trust. There is, however, little inherent either in the relationship between President and Vice President, or in the manner in which Presidents select their running mates, that is especially likely to promote trust. The calculus determining the selection of Vice Presidential candidates

27. Doris Kearns, *Lyndon Johnson and the American Dream.* New York: New American Library (Signet), 1977, p. 169.

emphasizes political, geographical, and ideological balance. In order to maximize the appeal of the party's national ticket, leading contenders for the Presidential nomination sometimes end up as running mates. For the sake of balance and party unity, the Presidential and Vice Presidential nominations may go to members of different factions of the party. In either event, considerable potential for rivalry and resentment is an inevitable part of the process. Presidential nominees willing to share the ticket with a rival are likely to be less enthusiastic about sharing the reins of government.

Vice Presidents bent on exercising influence in government policy making as close advisers to the President are likely to end up frustrated. Few politicians are willing to give power to those they cannot control. The Vice President, unlike White House assistants and Cabinet secretaries, cannot be fired by the President. The independence of the office, combined with its lack of significant formal powers, means that the Vice President will exercise only as much influence as the President's confidence and trust permit.

CONCLUSION

Periods of Presidential disability are shrouded in uncertainty. The lengthy disabilities of Presidents Woodrow Wilson and Dwight Eisenhower, as well as the final days of Richard Nixon's administration, raised a number of serious questions, not the least of which was "Who is in charge here?" In this century the deaths in office of Presidents Warren Harding and Franklin Roosevelt, the assassinations of William McKinley and John Kennedy, and the wounding of Ronald Reagan have provided grim reminders of the transitory nature of Presidential leadership.

The experiences of recent administrations suggest that the modern Presidency has evolved institutions and procedures capable of managing the executive branch when the President is temporarily incapacitated. The untested provisions of the Twenty-Fifth Amendment are available if necessary.

FURTHER READING

Benedict, Michael Les. *The Impeachment and Trial of Andrew Johnson.* New York: W. W. Norton and Co., 1973. A concise account of the struggle between Andrew Johnson, the only President to be impeached, and the Radical Republicans in Congress.

Hansen, Richard. *The Year We Had No President.* Lincoln, Neb.: University of Nebraska Press, 1962. A thorough treatment of the question of Presidential disability.

Knebel, Fletcher. *Night of Camp David.* New York: Bantam Books, Inc., 1966. One of America's leading authors of political fiction attempts to answer the question: "What would happen if the President of the U.S.A. went stark-raving mad?"

Moses, John B., and Cross, Wilbur. *Presidential Courage.* New York: W.W. Norton and Co., 1980. An historical investigation into the health, medical symptoms, and disabilities of American Presidents.

Submission of Recorded Conversations to the Committee on the Judiciary of the House of Representatives by President Richard Nixon. Washington, D.C.: U.S. Government Printing Office, 1974. These transcripts of the actual conversations between President Nixon and his aides in the Oval Office make fascinating reading. (Also available from Dell Publishing Company, Inc., under the title *The Presidential Transcripts.*)

White, Theodore H. *Breach of Faith: The Fall of Richard Nixon.* New York: Dell Publishing Co., Inc., 1976. The decline and fall of a President as detailed by one of America's leading political historians. Considered by many to be one of White's best books.

Woodward, Bob, and Bernstein, Carl. *The Final Days.* New York: Avon Books, 1977. The *Washington Post* reporters who broke the Watergate story interviewed 394 people in pulling together this extraordinary account of President Nixon's final days in office.

Chapter 6

The White House

THE PRESIDENCY

One of the most significant developments in Presidential politics during this century has been the transformation of the Presidency into a large institution. The President and the Presidency are now quite distinct. Presidents come and go; the Presidency goes on, however, and has developed some perplexing qualities that persist from one President to another. Presidents find themselves in an ironic situation—the institutions created since 1939 to make the President's job more manageable have become one of his biggest problems. These structures, designed to make his job easier, seem, on occasion to make it harder. Understanding how and why this has happened requires a brief description of the institutions comprising the Presidential apparatus.

The Executive Office

The Executive Office of the President is the formal apparatus of the Presidency. Each succeeding President has reorganized some, or all, of its components. The basic assumption behind this institution is that the complexities of modern executive government are too much for an individual to handle. Consequently, the President has been given, by law, a number of agencies to assist him by providing information, analysis, advice, recommendations, and follow-up. Presidents are obliged to figure out an effective way to manage these agencies in order to benefit from their services. Each President has had problems doing this. As shown in Fig. 6.1, the major agencies in the Executive Office are at present:

The White House Office (WHO) This is the President's personal staff. It is important because the top echelon of senior staff is composed of people the President trusts. They have offices in the White House and are the only people other than family to see the President every day. Through screening of incoming communications, and scheduling of Presidential appointments and agenda, they heavily influence whom the President does and does not see. The WHO is composed of the President's personal aides and advisers, accountable only to him and serving at his pleasure. The President hires them and organizes them the way he wants. Staffers have no formal authority; their power comes from being able to speak to, and speak for, the President. Only the senior staffers are in direct contact with the President. Consequently, the staff system may be characterized by a struggle for access to the President.

There may, or may not, be a chief-of-staff, depending on the President's style. Some Presidents have preferred to be their own chiefs-of-staff, while others, notably Eisenhower and Nixon, have delegated significant power and responsibilities to their chiefs-of-staff. The President's Assistant for National Security Affairs has become a position of increasing importance. In addition to advising the President about foreign affairs and national security matters, this individual runs the National Security Council staff. A skillful tactician in this position can become more important than the Secretary of State.

Others on the senior staff include an assortment of aides and advisers, including the Press Secretary, assistants for Congressional relations and domestic affairs, and one or more special assistants and counsels to the President. Neither the duties nor the power of staff aides are clearly defined by their titles because their responsibilities depend on the President's needs. Both Theodore Sorensen and John Dean, for example, held the title of Counsel to the President. Sorensen enjoyed an intimate relationship with President Kennedy, serving as a speech writer and policy adviser. Dean's relationship with Presi-

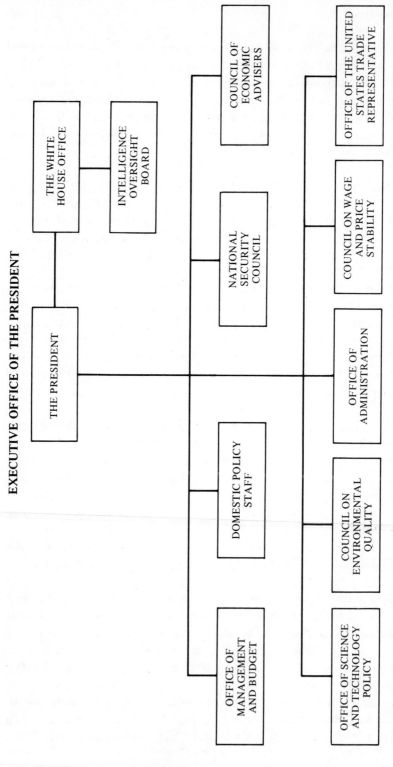

EXECUTIVE OFFICE OF THE PRESIDENT

THE WHITE HOUSE OFFICE

INTELLIGENCE OVERSIGHT BOARD

THE PRESIDENT

COUNCIL OF ECONOMIC ADVISERS

NATIONAL SECURITY COUNCIL

DOMESTIC POLICY STAFF

OFFICE OF MANAGEMENT AND BUDGET

OFFICE OF THE UNITED STATES TRADE REPRESENTATIVE

COUNCIL ON WAGE AND PRICE STABILITY

OFFICE OF ADMINISTRATION

COUNCIL ON ENVIRONMENTAL QUALITY

OFFICE OF SCIENCE AND TECHNOLOGY POLICY

Figure 6.1 The Executive Office of the President. Source: *United States Government Manual 1980–1981.* Washington, D.C.: Office of the Federal Register, National Archives and Records Service, 1980, p. 98.

dent Nixon was more remote, revolving around attempts to cover up the Watergate scandal.

These aides, of course, have assistants of their own, so that, including support staff, the WHO has numbered from 450 to nearly 600 during recent administrations. The size of this agency, while undoubtedly sufficient to cause difficulties, is only one of the problems Presidents face in trying to manage it.

The Office of Management and Budget (OMB) The primary duty of this agency, second in importance to the White House staff, is to assist the President in annual preparation of the Federal budget for presentation to Congress. This is a complex task, resulting in a budget document the size of a large telephone book. In the course of compiling it, the OMB screens agency requests for appropriations of money, and it requires executive officials to defend their requests. OMB is, therefore, a key tool in Presidential attempts to control the bureaucracy and bring departmental budgets in line with Presidential guidelines. This is a process of considerable importance, since the Federal government is now spending well over half a trillion dollars a year. Another OMB responsibility is the screening of agency proposals for legislation. This is known as central clearance, and it attempts to insure that executive departments will not propose legislation to Congress that conflicts with the President's legislative program. The director of OMB must be approved by the Senate.

The National Security Council (NSC) This Council was established to promote coordination between foreign and military policy in national security matters. It consists of the President, Vice President, and Secretaries of State and Defense. Advisers to the NSC include the Director of the Central Intelligence Agency, the Chairman of the Joint-Chiefs-of-Staff (military), and any additional advisers and experts the President deems relevant. Although designed to increase the range of alternatives and information available to the President, this council is advisory, and the President cannot be compelled to make use of it, much less follow its recommendations. With the exception of Eisenhower, who met weekly with the Council, Presidents have tended to circumvent the NSC by relying on an inner circle in foreign policy decision making. The role of the NSC frequently has been to ratify and legitimize policies that were debated and decided elsewhere.

The Council of Economic Advisers (CEA)   This agency is a response to the sensible proposition that Presidents need expert economic advice.   It consists of three professional economists, or financial experts, and their staffs.   The CEA is only one of several competing sources of economic advice for Presidents, including OMB, the Treasury Department, and various special assistants.

The Domestic Policy Staff   Established in the Executive Office in 1977, the purpose of the staff is to formulate and coordinate domestic policy recommendations for the President.   The Domestic Policy Staff often operates through *ad hoc* projects, or interagency committees to deal with program areas and specific problems.

Regardless of how the Executive Office is organized, it is expected to do certain things, such as coordinating proposals and policies, managing public relations, and advising the President.   Much of modern Presidential government consists of guiding priority proposals through Congress and overseeing implementation of programs within the complex structure of the executive bureaucracy.   Some coordination is necessary, and the staff system attempts to provide it within the White House.   Coordination involves, basically, keeping the White House in touch with the Congress and the Federal bureaucracy.

Congressional relations (or "legislative liaison," as it is known in staff jargon) frequently requires a lengthy period of on-the-job training in order for staffers to master subtleties, courtesies, and traditions involved.   This process entails more than simply keeping tabs on legislative proposals and preparing status reports.   Close consultation with Congressional leaders on strategy, and with relevant committee members on the contents of proposals, is the order of the day.   Compromise and flexibility are the required modes of operation for dealing with Congress.   This process frequently requires significant modifications in the President's proposals.   An inflexible stand by Presidential spokesmen accomplishes nothing and exposes their ignorance of the legislative process to both Congress and the news media.   An impulsive action by a staffer can antagonize an influential senator at a key point in the process.   Impatience, while perhaps justified, will not bring about the accommodations necessary to secure passage of important legislation.   Presidential assistants who assume, in the words of John Ehrlichman, that "the President is the government"[1] operate from a false premise.   Far from having control of

1. Dan Rather and Gary Paul Gates, *The Palace Guard*.   New York: Harper and Row, 1974, p. 232.

the government, Presidents soon learn that they barely have control of the executive branch.

The executive departments (such as Defense, State, Treasury, Justice, etc.), and their subdivisions, constitute a gigantic and complex governmental structure. They employ 2.8 million civilians and spend in excess of $600 billion a year. They are responsible for operating government programs in society by enforcing regulations and distributing social benefits. This is the second major area (called policy implementation) where staff coordination is required. Congress is fond of dividing control of programs between several departments and agencies. Consequently, Presidential assistants may be called upon to referee conflicts between agency heads and settle jurisdictional disputes within the bureaucracy. Administrative follow-up, while necessary to oversee the successful implementation of government programs, is a task guaranteed to strain the patience of any Presidential aide.

Assigned to the Press Secretary and an assortment of assistants is the difficult task of presenting and defending the President's policies before the news media and the public. They must take the heat between the President's public appearances. They hold briefings and issue press releases and clarification statements, and they attempt to contain unfavorable reactions to Presidential initiatives. In their public statements, optimism reigns eternal, and even the most devastating revelation (after the initial denials) is repackaged in a favorable light. In addition to scheduling the President's agenda for maximum public exposure, full-time efforts of some assistants are devoted to packaging the President's image and selling symbols and concepts to the public.[2]

ADVISING THE PRESIDENT

Presidential assistants are playing an increasingly important role in policy formulation by serving as sources of ideas, information,

2. Some of the more unusual handiwork in this area recently includes Ronald Ziegler's famous "Sea Shot" of President Nixon's casual stroll in the California surf with his shoes on, and President Carter relaxing in a cardigan sweater while conversing beside his fireplace on national television. Apparently Carter's media staffers and pollsters (along with his wife) were behind his efforts to change his image with the Camp David summit. On Ziegler and Nixon, see Rather and Gates, *Palace Guard*, p. 284.

and proposals. Key concepts in recent administrations have been generated within the staff, including the "Great Society" programs (Joseph Califano) and "Detente" and the "New China Policy" (Henry Kissinger). As an advisory agency, the staff should function to insure the uninterrupted flow of information to the President. The nature and quality of information and analysis can significantly affect the President's perception of alternatives available to him. The major problem in this area has proven to be a tendency of the staff to define the range of alternatives too narrowly. This results partly from the selective filtering of information, and partly from an overemphasis on loyalty at the expense of critical analysis.

Presidential Role

Presidents have contributed significantly to the problem by the way they run their staffs. In particular, the expectation that senior advisers serve as part of the President's emotional support system can create a situation not altogether compatible with smooth performance in the other areas. While they should strive to maximize their alternatives, for the most part Presidents seem to enjoy having their biases reinforced. Consequently, advisers are tempted to limit their conception of alternatives to those already favored by the President. Since several Presidents have done little to discourage, and much to encourage, this behavior, the situation can quickly degenerate into a mutually reinforcing game of "let's please the President." It was the repetition of this pattern in Lyndon Johnson's administration that prompted George Reedy to describe the staff system as the President's most persistent problem in keeping in touch with reality.[3] Reedy was President Johnson's Press Secretary and has the benefit of an insider's perspective.

Events since the Johnson administration have served to confirm the accuracy of Reedy's analysis. Network news correspondent Dan Rather's prophetic book, *The Palace Guard,* painted an even more bizarre protrait of the power struggle within the Nixon staff during the pre-Watergate era.[4] By now, the details are familiar. President Nixon selected as chief-of-staff his campaign manager, former advertis-

3. George Reedy, *The Twilight of the Presidency.* New York: Mentor Books, 1970, p. 88.

4. Rather and Gates, *Palace Guard.* See, especially, pp. 148–216. The following discussion is based on their analysis.

ing executive H.R. Haldeman. To consolidate his power within the staff, Haldeman rid himself of potential rivals by replacing them with inexperienced and ambitious young men of unquestioned loyalty. Haldeman outflanked his rivals by using the time-tested strategy of easing them upstairs to positions of little, or no, influence. Press Secretary Herb Klein (regarded as untrustworthy because he was a former newsman) was promoted with the President's consent and replaced by Ronald Ziegler, a Haldeman protege. Another key position fell into Haldeman's hands after Nixon expressed dissatisfaction with Domestic Adviser Arthur Burns. Haldeman suggested as his replacement Seattle zoning lawyer John Ehrlichman. Advisers such as Patrick Moynihan, who could not easily be replaced, were isolated, boxed out, and discredited.

With the staff under control, and feeling increasingly bolder, Haldeman went after Cabinet secretaries he regarded as too independent, or too liberal. Controlling White House communications and appointments, he was able to deny access to his rivals. "The President's busy, put it in writing," became the bulwark of Haldeman's defense as he consistently outmaneuvered more experienced politicians. Soon Nixon became remote and inaccessible, even to former close friends such as Health, Education, and Welfare Secretary Robert Finch. Only National Security Adviser Henry Kissinger had the political skills and foreign policy expertise necessary to maintain direct access to the President.

Isolation of the President Using this kind of behind-the-scenes manipulation, Haldeman succeeded in weaving a cocoon around the President. The innermost chamber was the so-called "Berlin Wall," consisting of Haldeman and Ehrlichman in the key positions of chief-of-staff and domestic adviser. All incoming communications had to go through Haldeman. Outside the Berlin Wall, and doing the leg work, was the "Beaver Patrol," consisting of young, inexperienced, but ambitious, Haldeman proteges who would follow orders unquestionably. Many of them were personally recruited by Haldeman from California advertising associates and college chums. Loyalty was the paramount consideration in their selection, and several of them would figure prominently in the Watergate affair. Those closest to the President were characterized by an abundance of political inexperience and unfamiliarity with Washington politics.[5] Although

5. *Ibid.*, pp. 188–216.

they had worked on the President's election campaign, none had
ever run for public office. A similar situation developed in the Carter
administration, with inexperienced Washington outsiders controlling
senior staff positions.

As Haldeman has pointed out in his own defense, he did not
isolate Nixon; rather, the President chose to be isolated. Haldeman
was merely the instrument for implementing the President's preference for seclusion.[6] While Haldeman's defense may seem a bit self-
serving, it does put the ball back in the President's court, where it
belongs. The staff is a creation of the President, reflecting his personality. Within the White House, the President creates the kind of environment he wants, and ambitious staffers quickly pick up cues on
how they must behave. If the President desires seclusion, as Nixon
did, it can easily be arranged by placing a stern chief-of-staff between
the Oval Office and the outside world. A President with a fragile ego
desiring protection from criticism can surround himself with an entourage of yes-men, as Lyndon Johnson did.

The overly protective, highly supportive staff functions to distort
the picture of external reality by helping the President create a false
image more to his liking. While this is undoubtedly comforting to
the President's ego, it does little to promote the sound advice and
critical analysis necessary for a realistic perspective on decision making. To understand why this pattern persists, four factors must be
considered. Each of these is serious enough in its own right, but
since they interact and reinforce each other, the impact of the
whole may be greater than the sum of its parts.

Access to the President This is the name of the game for Presidential advisers. They have neither formal authority, nor independent
power bases, from which to operate. They wield power only through
the President and in his name, and they are literally the President's
men. Those closest to the President are most likely to shape decisions.
Consequently, to be influential, they must have access to the President. This is the genesis of the perpetual power struggles within the
White House, as well as a key reason why White House assistants are
sometimes not reliable sources of sound policy advice. Because their
ambitions are linked so closely to the President, they are seldom

6.   It is also evident from Haldeman's discussion that he felt a strong need to
     protect the President. See H. R. Haldeman, *The Ends of Power.* New York:
     Times Books, 1978, pp. 56–67.

able to be sufficiently independent to be critical. Their position is one of constant insecurity, with ambitious rivals waiting in the wings, maneuvering for position.[7] As staffers struggle to hang on, it is little wonder that they modify their opinions and presentations to please the boss.

Presidential Personality Joseph Califano, having served on Lyndon Johnson's staff and in Jimmy Carter's Cabinet, believes that there are personality traits common to most Presidents. These include ambition, the desire to exercise power, egocentricity, and, most basic of all, the need and demand for loyalty.[8] The President's intimate advisers frequently become the focus of all these needs. There are few better settings for the President to meet these needs and vent his frustrations than the White House. Subordinates offer perfect targets for Presidential abuse and whimsy, and staffers are expected to take it. This may be the price of access, and they can be replaced by others who consider no price too great to be close to a President. It is unlikely that many future Presidents will surpass Lyndon Johnson for sheer vindictiveness and abuse of assistants. Johnson operated on the principle of dealing with his own insecurities by ridiculing and degrading others. The price of intimacy came high, Presidential aides often being required to sacrifice their dignity.[9] Describing his conception of a loyal subordinate, Johnson is reported to have said, "I want him to kiss my ass in Macy's window at high noon and tell me it smells like roses."[10]

The tendency of Presidents to use their assistants as sources of emotional support is easily understandable. The Presidency is a high-pressure job and is inevitably frustrating. The key to the President's relationship with his assistants is balancing his demands for *loyalty* with *receptivity* to new information and ideas. This has proven particularly difficult for insecure personalities who, when threatened by having their ideas challenged, equate independent

7.   Reedy, *Twilight of the Presidency*, p. 95.

8.   Joseph A. Califano, Jr., *A Presidential Nation.* New York: W. W. Norton and Co., Inc., 1975, p. 189.

9.   Doris Kearns, *Lyndon Johnson and the American Dream.* New York: New American Library (Signet), 1977, pp. 251–252.

10. David Halberstam, *The Best and the Brightest.* New York: Random House Inc., 1972, p. 434. Quoted in Richard T. Johnson, *Managing the White House.* New York: Harper and Row, 1974, p. 178.

thinking with disloyalty. This eliminates the give-and-take necessary for the careful scrutiny of ideas in the decision making process.

John Kennedy and Lyndon Johnson were polar opposites in this respect. Kennedy was self assured and confident in his dealings with advisers. He enjoyed the give-and-take of critical discussions and even an occasional heated exchange of ideas. Johnson's approach was to overwhelm others as a means of assuring himself that he was in control. Advisers soon learned that the President sought not the critical exchange of ideas, but reaffirmation of his sense of self through support of his opinions.[11]

Presidents have a right to expect loyalty from their aides. Trust requires that confidences be kept, and loss of trust quickly eliminates an adviser from the inner circle. While admittedly a desirable attribute for advisers, loyalty can begin to undermine the President if it results in uncritical support for his position during the decision making process.

The White House Atmosphere The President's working situation is characterized by two potentially destructive features: excessive deference and secrecy.[12] As head of state, as well as head of government, the President inspires a degree of reverence and awe, even among his advisers. Presidents Ford and Carter went to some lengths (symbolically, at least) to debunk the imperial Presidency and reduce the trappings of royalty surrounding the office. It is fine for Presidents to cook their own breakfasts, or carry their own luggage, but as ceremonial head-of-state, a certain amount of pomp and spectacle is inevitable in the Presidential office. Used with taste and dignity, this can be a political asset. If taken too seriously, it leads to yet greater remoteness of the President from the people and the Congress.

An obsession with secrecy also limits the President's contacts and constricts the inner circle. This may even result in the undesirable situation wherein the more important the problem, the fewer the number of minds that can be consulted for advice.[13] A setting of excessive deference, combined with ambition and absence of

11. This opinion is shared by numerous commentators. See Doris Kearns, *Lyndon Johnson and the American Dream,* pp. 1–12, 324–350. See, also, James David Barber, *The Presidential Character.* Englewood Cliffs, N.J.: Prentice-Hall, Inc., 1972, pp. 78–95.

12. Reedy, *Twilight of the Presidency,* pp. 23 ff.

13. *Ibid.,* pp. 23.

public scrutiny, can permit ill-conceived ideas to be taken far more seriously than they otherwise would be.

Cronyism Catchy nicknames abound to describe the President's inner circle: "the Irish Mafia," "the Berlin Wall," and the "Georgia Mafia," for example. In Presidents Harding's and Truman's times it was described with a great deal more candor and accuracy as government by crony. Those closest to the President frequently comprise a circle of long-time friends who have been through the political wars with him. The selection of the White House assistants from the President's campaign organization and personal following usually assures loyalty, but it may have an adverse effect on the quality of the staff's performance, especially in the areas of policy advice and implementation.

Frequently those in a Presidential administration who have the most outstanding records of achievement in society are to be found not in the White House, but in the Cabinet. Individuals of repute, accomplishment, leadership, and power are invited to sit as heads of executive departments. While managing these large bureaucracies, they help shape departmental policy and influence the allocation of billions in Federal funds. Only a select few, however, become close advisers to the President. The nature of the modern executive office dictates otherwise. Cabinet secretaries, in fact, must sometimes battle staffers for access to the President. The decline of the Cabinet and ascendency of Presidential assistants as policy advisers has prompted Stephen Hess, Brookings Institute scholar, to suggest that a major problem with the staff system is that it places the wrong people close to the President.[14]

ORGANIZING THE WHITE HOUSE

Alternate methods of organizing Presidential assistants have been carefully analyzed.[15] Three generalizations are supported by the ex-

14. Stephen Hess, *Organizing the Presidency*. Washington, D.C.: The Brookings Institution, 1976, pp. 164–165. Hess is an advocate of greater consultation between the President and the Cabinet on policy matters.

15. In addition to Hess, *Organizing the Presidency*, see, also, Richard T. Johnson, *Managing the White House*. New York: Harper and Row, 1974, and Louis W. Koenig, *The Chief Executive* (revised ed.). New York: Harcourt Brace and World, Inc., 1968, Ch. 7.

periences of recent Presidents. First, no method is foolproof, but each system has some clear advantages and problems. Second, the quality and integrity of the people making up the staff are at least as important as how they are organized. Finally, the President himself is of overwhelming importance. No organizational system can compensate if a President does not listen to advice, or insists that it be packaged into a preexisting set of assumptions.

Presidential staff systems are variations on one of three basic organizational themes.

The Team Approach

One of John Kennedy's contributions to the modern Presidency was his development of an alternative style of managing the White House. Kennedy's approach was aimed at avoiding the high potential for isolation inherent in a formalistic system and the chaos associated with a highly personalized system. Kennedy's system has been described as a wheel, with himself as the hub. The spokes of the wheel connected with his assistants.[16] There was no chief-of-staff. Contact with several different sources of input is virtually assured by this structure. Kennedy utilized this diversity by encouraging his aides to speak frankly.

Another useful feature was the system's flexibility, permitting the President to utilize his assistants as circumstances required. The duties of aides were not limited by their formal titles; responsibilities were assigned, or redefined, as needed, to deal with changing situations. By remaining in the thick of things, by being accessible, and by personally supervising his aides, Kennedy was able to generate a sense of teamwork rather than of destructive competition.[17] He controlled which tasks were delegated, and to whom. The composition of the inner circle could easily be modified to incorporate relevant department heads, executive officials, and outside experts.

This structure was compatible with the man who ran it. Kennedy's personality, being receptive to open discussion, permitted the system to function properly most of the time. Naturally, difficulties did arise. Managing the team creatively required considerable time and attention to detail. Treating advisers as generalists, rather than as specialists, permitted them to offer advice in areas where their ex-

16. Johnson, *Managing the White House*, p. 125.

17. *Ibid.*, pp. 125–131

pertise was rather limited. This made it all the more important for the President to supplement their advice with that of experts. On occasion, failure to do this created a misleading impression. For example, as incredible as it may seem, Kennedy and his team did not involve any of the Cuban experts in the State Department in their decision to support the ill-conceived Bay of Pigs invasion of Cuba.[18]

A more serious defect in the team approach is the susceptibility of individuals to group pressures. Presidential decision making councils are small, insulated, cohesive groups with a predisposition toward like-mindedness. This tendency can be aggravated by group dynamics, as it was during the Bay of Pigs decision. This decision, sometimes described as the perfect fiasco, resulted, in part, from the eagerness of advisers to reach consensus and please the President. A serious breakdown in critical analysis resulted, caused by pressures within the group. Collective self-deception and rationalization were reinforced by direct pressure on anyone challenging the group's assumptions. The President was apparently an active participant in this process.[19]

After the distressing realization that his system had failed its first major test, Kennedy instituted new procedures to assure more systematic critical evaluation of ideas before they were implemented. These included innovations such as the decision of the President to leave the room from time to time so as not to inhibit free discussion, and to give his brother, the Attorney General, the responsibility of assuring that critical discussions actually took place. These procedures, and others, were instituted during the Cuban Missile Crisis and proved to be invaluable by discouraging impulsive over-reaction to the situation. The President's initial position (in favor of an American air strike on the missile bases) was modified in the course of deliberations with his advisers to the more moderate solution of a naval blockade.[20]

The Formalistic System

As the size of the Executive Office has grown, this management approach has become increasingly important. Eisenhower and Nixon

18. Irving L. Janis, *Victims of Groupthink*. Boston: Houghton Mifflin Co., 1972, p. 25.

19. *Ibid.*, Ch. 2.

20. *Ibid.*, pp. 144–162.

employed highly centralized staff systems.   Ford and Carter began
their administrations with something similar to the Kennedy model,
but modified their organizations in the direction of a more formalized
system. President Reagan also employs this type of system.

The two distinctive features of this system are broad delegation
of authority, combined with a hierarchical structure headed by a
chief-of-staff to coordinate it. Any President using this system must
be comfortable with delegating power to others. The chain-of-
command feature requires that the President deal directly with only
a few assistants. The senior aides have a great deal of discretion in
making assignments and in supervising subordinates. Therein lies
both the strength and weakness of this system. By assigning numerous
tasks to others, the President can free himself from attending routine
matters in order to deal with issues of real significance. Hence,
President Nixon decided to concentrate on the great issues of international relations and delegate handling of domestic politics to assistants.[21] Nixon's experience also shows that, by delegating duties
to others, the President runs the risk of losing control over how assignments are performed.

The system is designed to keep trivia off the President's desk, but
a key question on any issue is whether the matter is routine, or is
important enough to warrant Presidential attention. This decision is
basic to determining whether an issue reaches the President, or is
handled for him by assistants. Given the inexperience and impetu-
ousness characteristic of some recent Presidential staffs, this may
result in delicate political matters being handled with an abundance
of confidence, but an absence of poise and subtlety.

Even routine matters are frequently important enough to warrant
proper handling. Two brief examples will illustrate this point. In
the course of attempting leadership of Congress and his party, certain
courtesies are expected of the President. Insensitive handling of these
relatively routine matters by subordinates can be damaging. An
incident occurred in the 1976 Presidential campaign which may have
made it more difficult for the Republican party to close ranks and
unify behind President Ford. After losing his bid for the Republican
nomination, Ronald Reagan's early attempts to offer his services to
the Ford reelection campaign were rebuffed by the President's staff,
apparently without the President's knowledge.[22] During President

21. Rather and Gates, *Palace Guard*, pp. 206–216.

22. *Dayton Daily News*, September 22, 1979, p. 3.

Nixon's first term, a request came up through White House channels urging the President to extend the courtesy of a telephone call to a terminally ill Republican Senator. The President never saw the request. Chief-of-Staff Haldeman decided that a phone call to the Senator's widow would be more appropriate and sent the memo back down through channels with instructions to "wait until he dies."[23]

The most interesting feature of the formalistic system is the role played by the chief-of-staff. Positioned at the top of the chain of command, the chief is responsible for the day-to-day functioning of the staff and for the coordination of its various components. From this key vantage point, incoming information is screened, appointments cancelled or rescheduled, and matters referred to the President, or sent back down the chain of command for further processing. Based on the experiences of past Presidents, selection of a chief-of-staff may create as many problems as it solves. In addition to increasing the staff system's potential for information distortion, the chief plays a crucial role in deciding which issues reach the President for determination—decisions the President should perhaps be making for himself.

To be of real value to the President, the position of chief-of-staff requires an individual with political, as well as management, skills. It requires a grasp of political nuances and subtleties, and an understanding of the rules of the game, that comes with years of experience. The insistence by some Presidents of placing close personal friends, who are inexperienced Washington outsiders, in control of the Presidential staff continues to be one of the more intriguing mysteries of American politics.

Based on the experiences during the Eisenhower and Nixon administrations, the formalistic system would seem to be susceptible to scandal and corruption.[24] Presumably because so much power is delegated, assistants are tempted to abuse it, or go into business for themselves. Although Eisenhower's personal integrity was never questioned, he was embarrassed by several conflict-of-interest situations involving his subordinates. Eventually, he was obliged to remove Chief-of-Staff Sherman Adams. The abuses of power in the Nixon administration were so great that, as the staffers went under, they dragged the President down with them.

23. Rather and Gates, *Palace Guard*, p. 238.

24. Johnson, *Managing the White House*, pp. 233–234.

The Personalized System

Both Franklin Roosevelt and Lyndon Johnson employed loosely structured staff systems, designed to maximize the President's personal influence in White House decision making processes. Despite similarities in structure, the two systems frequently produced differing results. Roosevelt's method of encouraging creative competition functioned to increase the President's alternatives by promoting presentation of differing points of view by White House assistants and executive officials. President Johnson's relationship to his advisers was based on personal domination and loyalty as a means of generating support for the President's ideas.

The Roosevelt system rested on the energy and ability of the President to manage personally the rivalry he encouraged between subordinates. The President functioned as his own chief-of-staff, making assignments to assistants and requiring them to report directly to him. Competition was encouraged by giving assistants similar assignments and overlapping jurisdictions. The potential for destructive competition inherent in this arrangement was channeled in a more creative direction by the President's personal management. By encouraging diversity of ideas, selecting personnel with differing philosophical points of view, and utilizing a system of rewards based on access to the President to encourage creative thinking, Roosevelt was able to maximize his alternatives while assuring that the power of final decision remained in his hands.[25] Executive officials and department personnel were involved in the advisory system, with the result that the competition of ideas was not confined to a few White House assistants. As described by Professor Louis Koenig, the Roosevelt method is the surest one yet invented for maximizing the President's personal influence, but has only limited relevance to the modern Presidency because "Roosevelt enjoyed a luxury his successors are doomed never to know. He could create much of his own bureaucracy, first in the New Deal and then in the war. His successors must work with an inherited bureaucracy."[26]

For reasons of both organization and Presidential personality, the loosely structured personalized staff system functioned differently when resurrected by Lyndon Johnson. The size and com-

---

25. W. Koenig, *The Chief Executive* (revised ed.). New York: Harcourt Brace and World, Inc., 1968, pp. 163–166.

26. *Ibid.*, p. 166.

plexity of the White House and the executive bureaucracy had increased considerably. In addition, the President's personality dictated a different style of management. It was probably the risk of relying on a chief-of-staff, combined with his own reluctance to delegate power to others, that motivated Lyndon Johnson to become his own chief-of-staff. He came to terms with the institutionalized nature of the Presidency by placing himself at the apex of the staff hierarchy. Johnson ran his staff with a combination of accessability and domination. He was available to his aides, but not receptive to their opinions, unless they happened to coincide with his own. Access was used as a reward or punishment, being granted in exchange for cooperation and subservience.[27]

Always overshadowing the structure was his personality, dominating his subordinates and demanding unquestioned loyalty. This resulted in a growing conflict between Johnson's style of personally dominating his advisers and the realities of making complex decisions. Meetings with advisers were often little more than monologues on the part of the President. As the failure of his Vietnam policy became increasingly apparent, the inner circle was constricted to a faithful few who were in agreement with the policy.

CONCLUSION

The White House staff was the center of action during the Watergate cover-up. This indicates both the importance and potential dangers an institutionalized staff has for the President. The overriding problem with the staff system is that it can leave the President too dependent on a few senior advisers. Reliance on the staff has tended to restrict unnecessarily the President's sources of information and alternatives to a small circle of advisers, most of whom are likely to share an outlook similar to the President's.

This analysis began with the proposition that some of the difficulties confronting the modern Presidency are rooted in the institution itself. To begin to understand this, we need to look no further than the White House. There the pervasive environment of excessive deference, an entourage of subservient and protective cronies, and the personal insecurities of Presidents can combine to create an atmosphere of unreality, in which critical analysis and sound decision making are the unlikeliest of occurrences.

27. Kearns, *Lyndon Johnson and the American Dream*, p. 252.

FURTHER READING

Haldeman, H. R. with Joseph Di Mona. *The Ends of Power.* New York: Times Books, 1978. The way it was, according to President Nixon's chief of staff.

Hess, Stephen. *Organizing the Presidency.* Washington, D.C.: The Brookings Institution, 1976. An analysis of the organization of the Presidency from Franklin Roosevelt to Richard Nixon, including a strong argument for revitalizing the role of the Cabinet in Presidential policy-making.

Johnson, Richard Tanner. *Managing the White House.* New York: Harper and Row, 1974. Johnson was a White House Fellow, serving under two Presidents. His analysis is a thorough consideration of the relationship between Presidential style and the organization, functioning, and impact of the White House staff.

Nash, Bradley D., with Eisenhower, Milton S., Hoxie, R. Gordon, and Spragens, William C. *Organizing and Staffing the Presidency.* New York: Center for Study of the Presidency, Proceedings: Vol. III, No. 1, 1980. A symposium with a panel of distinguished Presidential scholars.

Rather, Dan, and Gates, Gary. *The Palace Guard.* New York: Harper and Row, 1974. The definitive study of the struggle for power within President Nixon's staff prior to the Watergate scandal.

Reedy, George. *The Twilight of the Presidency.* New York: Mentor Books, 1970. After serving as Lyndon Johnson's press secretary, Reedy became one of the first commentators to call attention to the problems inherent in the Presidential staff system.

Chapter 7

Executive Politics

THE EXECUTIVE BRANCH

As Chief Executive, the President must attempt to manage a gigantic governmental structure composed of two distinct components. At the top are several thousand *executive officials* who are subject to considerable Presidential control, but are not without some potential power bases from which to operate. Below them is the *permanent government,* consisting of nearly three million civil service officials relatively insulated from Presidential control.

As shown in Fig. 7.1, there are 50 or so government departments and agencies over which the President has varying degrees of control and supervision. The executive bureaucracies consist of *departments* which have Cabinet rank, *agencies* which do not have Cabinet rank, and *regulatory commissions* and *boards.* The distinction between these three types of government organizations is not altogether clear. All three perform administrative and regulatory functions, and, to varying degrees, all are somewhat autonomous. Generally, Cabinet departments are more prestigious and influential, and have greater diversity and scope of responsibilities than agencies and commissions. Cabinet departments and most agencies report to the President. Some

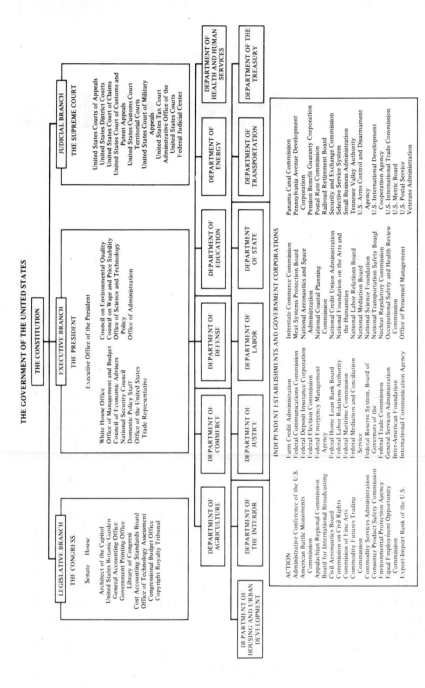

THE GOVERNMENT OF THE UNITED STATES

THE CONSTITUTION

LEGISLATIVE BRANCH

THE CONGRESS

Senate   House

Architect of the Capitol
United States Botanic Garden
General Accounting Office
Government Printing Office
Library of Congress
Cost Accounting Standards Board
Office of Technology Assessment
Congressional Budget Office
Copyright Royalty Tribunal

EXECUTIVE BRANCH

THE PRESIDENT

Executive Office of the President

White House Office
Office of Management and Budget
Council of Economic Advisers
National Security Council
Domestic Policy Staff
Office of the United States
  Trade Representative

Council on Environmental Quality
Council on Wage and Price Stability
Office of Science and Technology
  Policy
Office of Administration

JUDICIAL BRANCH

THE SUPREME COURT

United States Courts of Appeals
United States District Courts
United States Court of Claims
United States Court of Customs and
  Patent Appeals
United States Customs Court
Territorial Courts
United States Court of Military
  Appeals
United States Tax Court
Administrative Office of the
  United States Courts
Federal Judicial Center

DEPARTMENT OF AGRICULTURE

DEPARTMENT OF COMMERCE

DEPARTMENT OF DEFENSE

DEPARTMENT OF EDUCATION

DEPARTMENT OF ENERGY

DEPARTMENT OF HEALTH AND HUMAN SERVICES

DEPARTMENT OF HOUSING AND URBAN DEVELOPMENT

DEPARTMENT OF THE INTERIOR

DEPARTMENT OF JUSTICE

DEPARTMENT OF LABOR

DEPARTMENT OF STATE

DEPARTMENT OF TRANSPORTATION

DEPARTMENT OF THE TREASURY

INDEPENDENT ESTABLISHMENTS AND GOVERNMENT CORPORATIONS

ACTION
Administrative Conference of the U.S.
American Battle Monuments
  Commission
Appalachian Regional Commission
Board for International Broadcasting
Civil Aeronautics Board
Commission on Civil Rights
Commission of Fine Arts
Commodity Futures Trading
  Commission
Commodity Services Administration
Consumer Product Safety Commission
Environmental Protection Agency
Equal Employment Opportunity
  Commission
Export-Import Bank of the U.S.

Farm Credit Administration
Federal Communications Commission
Federal Deposit Insurance Corporation
Federal Election Commission
Federal Emergency Management
  Agency
Federal Home Loan Bank Board
Federal Labor Relations Authority
Federal Maritime Commission
Federal Mediation and Conciliation
  Service
Federal Reserve System, Board of
  Governors of the
Federal Trade Commission
General Services Administration
Inter-American Foundation
International Communication Agency

Interstate Commerce Commission
Meat Systems Protection Board
National Aeronautics and Space
  Administration
National Coastal Planning
  Commission
National Credit Union Administration
National Foundation on the Arts and
  the Humanities
National Labor Relations Board
National Mediation Board
National Science Foundation
National Transportation Safety Board
Nuclear Regulatory Commission
Occupational Safety and Health Review
  Commission
Office of Personnel Management

Panama Canal Commission
Pennsylvania Avenue Development
  Corporation
Pension Benefit Guaranty Corporation
Postal Rate Commission
Railroad Retirement Board
Security and Exchange Commission
Selective Service System
Small Business Administration
Tennesse Valley Authority
U.S. Arms Control and Disarmament
  Agency
U.S. International Development
  Cooperation Agency
U.S. International Trade Commission
U.S. Metric Board
U.S. Postal Service
Veterans Administration

Figure 7.1   The Organization of the Government of the United States.   (Source: *United States Government Manual* 1980–1981. Washington, D.C.: Office of the Federal Registrar, National Archives and Records Service, 1980, p. 32.

agencies are organized as government corporations and have greater autonomy. Federal regulatory bodies, responsible for oversight of aspects of commerce, communications, and finance are the most autonomous Federal bureaucratic organizations. They are headed by boards, or commissions, whose members are appointed to lengthy, staggered terms. Regulatory commissions function in a quasi-legislative and quasi-judicial fashion. They establish rules and regulations, enforce these regulations, and hold hearings regarding violations. The regulatory commissions are relatively autonomous; they do not report to the President, but are subject to Congressional oversight on matters of policy and budget.

The major executive departments having Cabinet rank are:

Justice
Defense
State
Treasury
Health and Human Services (formerly, Health, Education, and
    Welfare)
Housing and Urban Development
Agriculture
Transportation
Interior
Energy
Labor
Commerce
Education (created in October, 1979)

Executive departments are large bureaucracies subdivided into bureaus and services to handle administration of programs and enforcement of regulations. Each department allocates considerable resources and services, and has regulatory power to set and enforce guidelines for its programs. At present, two departments—Defense and Health and Human Services (HHS)—overshadow the others in size and budget. These two departments spend more than half the Federal budget, with HHS ahead of Defense. The 1981 Federal budget totals $662 billion with $143 billion going to Defense and $220 billion to Health and Human Services.[1]

1. The 1981 budget figures were reported in the *Dayton Daily News*, January
   28, 1980, p. 1, and May 13, 1980, p. 1.

The Cabinet

Collectively, the heads of the 13 departments comprise the President's Cabinet. Each of them has the title of Secretary, except for the Attorney General, who runs the department of Justice. Below them are nearly 3,000 executive officials serving as under-secretaries, assistant secretaries, and bureau chiefs. All of these officials, including the Cabinet, are appointed by the President and subject to approval by the Senate. The President has the formal authority to remove any of them for whatever reasons he chooses. When a new President takes office, these officials routinely offer their resignations.

The role of the Cabinet secretary is a difficult one, requiring a delicate tight-rope act. They have three primary areas of responsibility: advisory, representational, and managerial. Historically, the Cabinet has been an important source of *advisers* to Presidents. With the fairly recent development of a large institutionalized Presidential staff, the importance of the Cabinet as a source of Presidential advisers has diminished. Only a few modern-day Cabinet secretaries become close advisers to Presidents and, on occasion, they must out-maneuver White House assistants simply to gain access to the President. Conflict and mistrust between Presidential assistants and the Cabinet have been sources of friction within recent administrations, particularly President Nixon's and Carter's. The list of President Carter's Cabinet secretaries, fired at the urging of top White House assistants, is impressive, including Blumenthal (Treasury), Schlesinger (Energy), and Califano (Health, Education, and Welfare). In addition, Secretary of State Cyrus Vance's resignation was partly the result of serious disagreements with National Security Adviser Brzezinski over matters of policy, including the attempt to rescue the American hostages in Iran.

While Cabinet secretaries are usually consulted by the White House on matters falling within their departments' jurisdictions, the Cabinet does not advise the President, nor make policy as a group. Cabinet meetings are usually low-key affairs, used by the President to inform the Cabinet of White House policy. Recent Cabinet meetings have included individuals who are not members of the Cabinet, including White House assistants.

Policy Advisers Secretaries most likely to establish themselves as policy advisers to the President include the Attorney General and the Secretaries of State, Defense, and Treasury. The heads of

Defense and State are members of the National Security Council. This, along with the importance of their departments in international affairs, usually assures some involvement for them in national security matters. The Secretary of the Treasury may become an economic adviser, and the Attorney General is usually influential because he heads the Department of Justice, which is the Federal law enforcement agency. Given the importance of this position, Presidents frequently select friends (or even relatives) they trust to head the Justice Department. The few Cabinet secretaries able to crack the President's inner circle almost always come from this group. Consequently, these secretaries have come to be known as the "inner cabinet."[2] Secretaries from the outer cabinet (the other nine departments) are likely to exercise primarily managerial, rather than advisory, responsibilities.

One consequence of the relegation of the Cabinet to mostly managerial functions is the perpetuation of the myopic view of political reality encouraged by the Presidential staff system. Some of the most experienced and accomplished talent in an administration is excluded from the advisory system. Cabinet secretaries are generally individuals of considerable repute and accomplishment in private industry, management, finance, or education. Many of them enter the public service at considerable personal financial sacrifice and may be rewarded for their trouble by being relegated to limbo by White House assistants.

This development has another consequence for the public policy process. The decline of top executive officials as Presidential advisers leads increasingly to separation of policy making from policy implementation. As policy making has gravitated to the White House, executive officials responsible for administering policy find themselves increasingly remote from the decision making process. This increases the likelihood that impractical and unrealistic policies will be selected by those with little awareness of the difficulties of putting programs into effect.[3] When the policy proves impractical, the bureaucracy is blamed, while the problem may rest with the unrealistic approach of White House policy makers.

2. See, for example, Thomas E. Cronin, *The State of the Presidency*. New York: Little Brown and Co., 1975, pp. 191–192.

3. Stephen Hess, *Organizing the Presidency*. Washington, D.C.: The Brookings Institution, 1976, p. 9.

Not surprisingly, turnover is high among top-level executive officials. About half stay on their jobs for two years or less. These government executives find that they have developed a capacity for effective action just about the time they leave office, a situation that contributes to the independence of the bureaucracy from executive control.[4]

Representation   The department head's second major function is *representation*. The executive branch is more than an administrative structure; it is a configuration of political interests. Many of these relationships are long-standing and very durable, having withstood the best efforts of numerous Presidents to reorganize, or disrupt, them. Cabinet secretaries cannot be effective in their departments if they ignore established relationships and expectations. Although accountable to the President, department heads must also respond to pressures from within their own agencies, as well as from the private-interest groups that are the agencies' major clients, and the Congress, which must approve funding for the departmental budgets.

The relationships between a department, or one of its bureaus, and its Congressional and interest-group allies, are frequently so well established that they are described by graphic terms such as "the iron triangle," or the "triple alliance." A prudent administrator, rather than seeking to disrupt these relationships, attempts to use them to enhance and protect the agency's budget and programs. To do otherwise is likely to create morale problems within the department and suspicion among its client groups and powerful defenders in Congress.

Called upon to represent four different sets of interests (the White House, the department, the client groups, and Congress) the Cabinet secretary is frequently caught in the middle. Total compliance with the White House view results in accusations of selling out the department and its programs. Cooperation with Congress and the interest groups to protect the department's interests may result in charges by the White House that the Cabinet secretary is undermining the President's program and surrendering to the bureaucracy.

The manner in which top executives are selected, and departmental programs approved and funded, assures that this pattern will continue. Cabinet secretaries and other high-ranking executive officials are appointed by the President with the consent of the Senate.

4. Hugh Heclo, *A Government of Strangers: Executive Politics in Washington.* Washington, D.C.: The Brookings Institution, 1977, p. 110.

In practice, this means that the president is not so much choosing these officials as nominating someone likely to be acceptable to the Senate and the major organized interests the department represents. As a practical matter, the Secretary of Labor will likely be acceptable to organized labor and its friends in the Senate. Likewise, the Secretary of Defense should be acceptable to influential members of the Senate Armed Services Committee, just as the Attorney General must withstand the scrutiny of the Judiciary Committee. The Secretary of Agriculture is likely to be from a farm state and the Secretary of the Interior from the West. Careful choices to head Treasury and Commerce can retain the confidence and support of the business community, and so on.

The client groups being served by an agency's programs frequently come to regard it as "their department." They may have enough organized support in Congress to back up this claim, in which case the President takes a political risk in tampering with these established relationships. This is the same configuration of interests that can make it costly, in political terms, to fire an entrenched executive official, or slash an agency's budget. It makes enemies of potential allies, whose support will surely be needed at a later date to enact legislation.[5]

Management Management of a large organization is an additional responsibility of Cabinet secretaries. For that reason, in addition to the other criteria, Presidents often take into account the management experience of those being considered for top executive positions. A successful management track record in commerce, or government, is likely to prove especially useful to those attempting to run the really large departments such as Defense or Health and Human Services. The complexity of these agencies almost defies description and creates doubts about the ability of anyone to manage them effectively, given the political constraints involved.

As department managers, Cabinet secretaries can be an important link between the White House and the bureaucracy. Presidential decisions on policy and budgetary matters are conveyed through department heads to subordinates, and department budget estimates are monitored and brought more into line with Presidential guidelines. Conversely, secretaries who are really in touch with their departments can bring an element of realism into the President's

5. Malcom E. Jewell and Samuel C. Patterson, *The Legislative Process in the United States* (3rd ed.).   New York: Random House, Inc., 1977, pp. 273-274.

demands regarding policy and budgetary matters. There is, however, a fine line between astutely advocating the department's position and openly resisting Presidential initiatives. This suggests another reason why Cabinet secretaries are not usually trusted personal advisers to the President. Given the manner in which they are selected and must function, they are seldom totally committed to White House policy.

The Permanent Government

The development of large-scale bureaucratic structures in government has complicated executive politics immeasurably. To accomplish military, economic, and social tasks, the government has evolved large administrative agencies nominally under the control of the President. The advantages of the bureaucratic form of organization are well known and include division of labor, specialization, and hierarchical control. Bureaucracy permits complex problems to be broken down into more manageable segments which are assigned to specialists familiar with the subject matter. The chain of command permits policy makers at the top to utilize the skills and expertise of a vast array of subordinates for collection and analysis of information on which decisions may be based. Given the complexity of modern society, and the elaborate technology on which it rests, there may be no workable alternatives to bureaucratic organization.

Bureaucratic Momentum Probably the most frustrating aspect of bureaucracy for politicians is the tendency of large organizations to exercise a will of their own. This requires the President to spend considerable amounts of time and energy attempting to persuade government officials to do what he wants, or to stop doing something he opposes. The independence of government bureaucracy from its nominal superiors rests on three features, the first of which is bureaucratic momentum. This refers to the prior commitments that develop over time in a government agency. The activities and size of government have grown tremendously in this century, especially as a result of two world wars and the social-benefit and welfare programs of the postwar era. Decades of big government have created a policy momentum that is considerable in comparison with the limited opportunities for Presidents to provide fresh directions.[6] A

6. Heclo, *Government of Strangers*, pp. 15–16.

large share of the Federal government's total budgetary resources are already committed to existing programs. Literally hundreds of programs have been written into law as departmental policy. A great deal of the formal authority to run these programs flows directly from the Congress to the agency heads, or program directors, and not through the President.[7]

Bureaucratic momentum encompasses more than formal authority and budgets; at least as important are the loyalties of government workers. Given the manner of selection and the duties of government workers, their primary loyalties are most often reserved for their agencies, or the programs they operate, rather than the political leadership. Cabinet secretaries, as well as the White House, are viewed as outsiders, and not particularly well-informed outsiders at that. Political executives may come and go; the agency and its programs provide a more enduring focus for employee loyalties.

Specialization The second feature of bureaucracy which promotes independence from executive control is *specialization*. As government agencies have expanded, they have become more technically specialized. The growing reliance of politicians on the technical expertise of government agencies helps to perpetuate the dependence of policy makers upon their subordinates for information and analysis. The ability of bureaucrats to give, or withhold, information, expertise, or compliance is one of their greatest powers. This is increasingly important considering that the trend in government agencies is for top-level civil servants to become more, not less, specialized.[8]

Civil Service System The most familiar feature reducing the outside control of government agencies is the civil service system. The several thousand executive officials appointed by the President constitute only a handful of the approximately 2.8 million civilian Federal government employees. The remainder are selected and protected by the civil service system. In an effort to minimize the role of partisan politics, selection and promotion for civil service jobs is based primarily on merit considerations. Job security is high, and removal of a civil service employee for political reasons is both rare and difficult. (Transfers and reassignments are considerably more frequent.) Many civil service employees make a career out of govern-

7. *Ibid.,* p. 12.
8. *Ibid.,* p. 15.

ment employment, giving rise to the description of the bureaucracy as "the permanent government."

While the idea of a politically neutral government service to provide policy makers with expertise and analysis has considerable logical appeal, few Presidents have been very happy with it in practice. Complaints of bureaucratic intransigence, obstructionism, and red tape abound. The sheer size of the government would, by itself, create management difficulties. When combined with the emphasis on technical expertise and civil service, the momentum of bureaucracy has proved to be formidable.

Administrative Presidency Presidents naturally have been tempted to circumvent the bureaucracy. Given the complexities of modern government, this would seem to be impossible, but with this goal in mind, President Nixon attempted to create the administrative Presidency. Through his staff, Nixon tried to run a large number of government programs from the White House. Policy making was increasingly taken out of the hands of department personnel and relocated to groups dominated by White House assistants. By placing personal loyalists in departments and agencies (aiming at top-level career positions as well as executive officials), Nixon sought to monitor more effectively the activities of the executive branch.[9]

Even if the Watergate scandal had not intervened and destroyed his Presidency, it appears that President Nixon's attempts to institute direct management of key elements of the bureaucracy had mixed results at best. This is especially true regarding his attempts to create a super cabinet by regrouping domestic governmental responsibilities among Cabinet secretaries. Other aspects of his administrative Presidency (including attempts to control the budget through widespread impoundment of funds, and to limit bureaucratic discretion by formulating White House guidelines) failed because they generated substantial opposition in Congress. President Nixon's strategy, while meeting with only limited success, reflects the growing realization in the White House that day-to-day bureaucratic operations are *not* simply routine, but constitute key aspects of policy making.[10] Management of domestic programs includes decisions about regula-

9. Richard P. Nathan, *The Plot that Failed: Nixon and the Administrative Presidency.* New York: John Wiley and Sons, Inc., 1975, pp. 37-76.

10. *Ibid.,* p. 62.

tions, guidelines, grants, and budgets, which shape the essential nature of the program by defining and limiting eligibility and benefits.

The theory behind the civil service concept justifies awarding secure government positions on the basis of merit in exchange for a competent, politically neutral government service. It is misleading, however, to describe the government service as politically neutral. While not overtly partisan, civil servants are heavily invested in promoting and protecting established programs and procedures. For example, within two weeks after assuming office, President Reagan was involved in a conflict with the State Department bureaucracy. In an attempt to forestall reductions in foreign aid, State Department personnel prematurely leaked to the press the President's proposals for cuts in foreign aid. According to his aides, the President was angry about the leak, viewing it as proof that the Federal bureaucracy was trying to sabotage his policies before they could be developed fully. "He knew this would happen," said one Presidential adviser, "but he didn't think the guerrilla warfare would start so soon."[11]

In summary, bureaucratic momentum has serious implications for executive control of the administration. The powerful and well-established relationships and procedures within the permanent government define, to a considerable extent, the realities of executive power, limiting some alternatives and excluding others entirely. The permanent government controls much of the expertise and information that is the strength of the executive branch, and it runs the day-to-day affairs of the government. Given the frustrations inherent in attempting to manage a complex organization without adequate control, it is easily understandable if Presidents opt for a policy of open warfare with the permanent government. However, it is seldom advisable for a politician to adopt a policy that is likely to result in defeat. So far, the bureaucracy has seemed more than an equal match for the President and his assistants.

Although the reality of prior commitment of resources constitutes a serious limitation, it does not completely eliminate opportunities for executive leadership in new directions. Leadership of the executive branch is a long-term proposition requiring considerable patience and dogged persistence. A realistic view of what is possible in one Presidential term, combined with skillful use of executive authority, permits a gradual restructuring of governmental and budgetary priorities.

11. Reported in the *Dayton Daily News,* February 5, 1981, p. 4.

EXECUTIVE POWER

The essence of executive power is *discretion*. This is the basic distinction between actions that are ministerial (mandatory) and actions that are executive (discretionary) in nature.[12]   Discretion and judgment are executive prerogatives, permitting the President to impart a tenor, or sense of direction, to the executive branch. The broad limits on executive discretion consist primarily of the government's prior commitments, and the willingness of the Congress, bureaucracy, and courts to insist on compliance with them. Even then, there is still room for Presidential maneuvering.

Basic to Presidential discretion is the vague constitutional mandate that the President "take care that the laws be faithfully executed." (See Article II, Section 3, of the United States Constitution.) Left unresolved is the question of how vigorously the President must act in performance of this duty. Congress has found it impossible to write complex legislation without delegating discretionary authority to the executive branch. The courts have acknowledged that the nature of modern government requires Congress to pass general legislation, leaving to the executive officials the responsibility for detailed administration of laws and regulations.[13]   Implementation of government policy entails considerable freedom to choose among specifics, which, in turn, affects not only the nature of the policy, but the pace at which it is enforced.

Enforcement of Laws

These kinds of decisions about how an administration will enforce laws and regulations constitute much of the stakes of Presidential politics.   Political interests coalesce around Presidential candidates partially on this basis. Convention and electoral support, campaign contributions, and interest-group endorsements are delivered in exchange for commitments concerning the tenor and direction of a candidate's administration. At stake is the support of the President and the administration on matters such as desegregation guidelines, environmental and energy regulations, affirmative-action programs, and school bussing, to name only a few controversial issues. Other

12. Louis Fisher, *The Constitution Between Friends: Congress, the President, and the Law.* New York: St. Martin's Press, Inc., 1978, pp. 39–42.

13. *Ibid.*, pp. 27–29.

less publicized matters, such as antitrust enforcement and farm-price supports, are of considerable importance to organized interests.

A prerogative of the Chief Executive is the choice of pursuing a policy of vigorous enforcement, or one of moderation and accommodation. Regulations and guidelines may be enforced to the letter, or modified and delayed to lessen their impact. Legal action may be instituted, or discouraged, by the President and the Attorney General. What is at stake is nothing less than favorable treatment by the government's law-enforcement and administrative apparatus for various organized interests and social groups.

Southern Strategy Richard Nixon's famous Southern strategy for putting together convention support for his nomination in 1968 is a good illustration of the interplay of these forces. After defeating Ronald Reagan in the Oregon primary, Nixon decided to wrap up the Republican nomination by undercutting Reagan's Southern support. The Southern strategy began to take shape in a meeting in Atlanta with Southern leaders of the Republican party. As reconstructed by Theodore White, this meeting involved key Republican leaders, including Senators Thurmond of South Carolina and Tower of Texas. A significant amount of convention support (a maximum of 394 votes) was at stake. The philosophy of Nixon's administration was crucial to winning Southern support. Civil rights was the chief concern of the Southerners, including Supreme Court appointments and school desegregation guidelines. Nixon agreed with the Southerners that there were too many liberals on the Court; that compulsory school bussing, for the purpose of racial balance, was wrong; that Federal funds should be withheld from school districts only in clear cases of deliberate segregation; and that Southerners would be well represented in his administration. When Nixon left Atlanta his nomination was secure.[14]

Executive Discretion Nixon's skillful use of his potential resources as Chief Executive assured his nomination. His subsequent difficulty as President in implementing parts of his Southern strategy illustrates the limitations inherent in the role of Chief Executive. Enacting the Southern strategy into government policy required the cooperation of the executive branch, but cooperation was not forth-

14. Theodore H. White, *The Making of the President 1968.* New York: Pocket Books Division of Simon and Schuster, Inc., 1970, pp. 169–172.

coming. Not only the bureaucracy, but some members of the President's Cabinet, resisted. There was open conflict between Attorney General Mitchell and Health, Education, and Welfare Secretary Finch over school desegregation guidelines. The White House staff battled Housing and Urban Development Secretary Romney about Federal housing policy. (Romney was proposing the heresy of low-income integrated housing in the suburbs.) Even within the Justice Department there was some resistance to the policy by government lawyers.[15] Federal courts were generally more sympathetic to the pro-integration forces in litigation.

Executive discretion also encompasses the prerogative of no action, or even of obstructing action. A classic illustration of this is the infamous ITT affair. International Telephone and Telegraph, one of the world's largest corporations, became the subject of Federal antitrust action. President Nixon personally made the decision to encourage the Justice Department to drop the antitrust suit after

15. See Dan Rather and Gary Paul Gates, *The Palace Guard*. New York: Harper and Row, 1974, pp. 188–202.

ITT pledged $400,000 to underwrite the 1972 Republican national convention.[16]

There have recently been numerous instances of executive discretion in the area of environmental protection. For reasons of economic expediency, the Carter administration began to move away from vigorous enforcement of water- and air-pollution regulations. Because of a shortage of low-sulfur oil, President Carter decided to suspend the requirements of the Clean Air Act to permit utilities in some sections of the country to burn high-sulfur oil, despite the increase in air pollution. After concluding that the cost of pollution controls was inflationary, the White House asked the Environmental Protection Agency to consider postponing clean-water regulations mandated by the Congress in 1977. Shortly after President Reagan was inaugurated, American automobile manufacturers began seeking additional modifications in Federal air-pollution, safety, and fuel-economy requirements. The Chairman of General Motors Corporation, Roger B. Smith, met personally with Secretary of Transportation Drew Lewis for four hours. According to Smith, he received assurances from Lewis that "the administration definitely is going to ease back on auto industry standards."[17]

Management of the Executive Branch

As chief executive, the President has a number of formal powers to aid in managing the administration. If the President is to be responsible for executing the laws, some control is required over subordinates charged with implementing decisions. An important resource in this respect is the President's power to appoint and remove executive officials. However, of the more than 2.8 million civilian government employees, less than 3000 are subject to direct Presidential control. These executive officials are appointed by the President (subject to Senate confirmation) and can be removed at the President's order without Senate approval. Included are executive officials in the Cabinet departments and other agencies (such as the Food and Drug Administration and the Environmental Protection Agency) that do not have Cabinet rank. The Senate is especially attentive regarding

16. Barry Sussman, *The Great Cover-Up: Nixon and the Scandal of Watergate.* New York: New American Library (Signet), 1974, p. 226.

17. *Dayton Daily News*, February 22, 1981, p. 6.

Presidential nominations to the Federal courts, but is generally more permissive for executive appointments, so long as the interests of major social and economic groupings are taken into account. Presidential success with executive appointments is largely a matter of anticipating Senate reaction by selecting nominees acceptable to the Senate and major client groups of the agencies.

Executive officials may become sufficiently entrenched so that the political costs of removing them outweigh the potential benefits. The classic example would be J. Edgar Hoover, who ran the Federal Bureau of Investigation as his personal fief for nearly 50 years. Generally speaking, however, any executive official can be removed if the President is willing to take the political heat that results. Aside from political considerations, the civil service system constitutes the major restriction of the removal power. Most top-level executive policy makers are not protected by civil service since their jobs are considered clearly political in nature.

Some significant administrative policy makers are exempt from Presidential removal. There are 10 administrative units, known as Independent Regulatory Commissions (see Fig. 7.1), responsible for regulating aspects of commerce, communication, and finance. These include, among others, the Securities and Exchange Commission (which regulates the stock market), and the Federal Communications Commission (which licenses television and radio stations). Another important independent agency is the Federal Reserve Board, because its policies regulate the nation's banking system and significantly affect interest rates. Each of these agencies is headed by a board with several members, rather than a single department head. The President's power is limited to filling vacancies as they occur. By law, the commissioners serve overlapping, fixed terms of office (some as long as 14 years), making it difficult for one President to select a majority of commissioners. They can be removed only for malfeasance and not for overtly political reasons. [18]

Executive Orders Another significant Presidential power is the executive order. These administrative decrees have had far-reaching consequences within the government and outside of it. Within the

18. A principle established in the famous case of *Humphrey's Executor v. United States*, 295 U.S. 602 (1935). For a consideration of the constitutional ramifications of this case, see Edward S. Corwin, *The President: Office and Powers 1787–1957* (4th ed.). New York: New York University Press, 1957, pp. 86–93.

executive branch Presidents have issued executive orders requiring racial integration of the armed forces and establishing loyalty programs for government employees. Presidents since Franklin Roosevelt have used executive orders to enforce anti-discrimination policies in companies receiving government contracts. President Carter used this tool effectively in bargaining with Congress on the Alaskan lands bill. When the Congress failed to approve this measure in 1979, President Carter used his authority to block development of most of the land by executive order. During the 1980 session, after nine years of legislative fighting, the Senate and the House finally agreed on a bill preserving 104 million acres of land in Alaska.

It is unclear how many executive orders have been issued because a numbering system was not employed until 1907. Constitutional scholar Louis Fisher cites estimates as high as 50,000.[19] Executive orders are legal only when based upon the President's constitutional authority, or powers delegated by Congress. Some executive orders have been successfully challenged in the courts, most notably President Truman's order for a government seizure of private steel mills after a labor dispute during the Korean conflict.[20] On the other hand, the Supreme Court upheld Franklin Roosevelt's infamous executive order requiring relocation of 70,000 American citizens of Japanese ancestry from the West Coast after the outbreak of hostilities with Japan.[21] Since the inherent powers the President has as Chief Executive and Commander-in-Chief are not clearly specified, the limits and legality of executive orders will inevitably remain partly a question of legal interpretation.

Emergency Powers   Equally intriguing is the matter of the President's emergency powers. Numerous statutes, especially those designed to enable the government to cope with economic crises, permit the President to proclaim a state of national emergency. The vagueness and uncertainty surrounding Presidential emergency powers were indicated in a Senate hearing in 1971. It came as a

19. Fisher, *Constitution Between Friends,* p. 128. The preceding discussion of executive orders is based on Fisher's analysis on pp. 128–132.

20. *Youngstown Sheet and Tube Company v. Sawyer,* 343 U.S. 579 (1952).

21. *Korematsu v. United States,* 323 U.S. 214 (1944). Concise discussion of both the Youngstown and Korematsu cases is available in Carl B. Swisher, *Historic Decisions of the Supreme Court* (2nd ed.). New York: Van Nostrand Reinhold Co., 1969, pp. 142–150.

surprise, even to members of Congress, to learn that the United States had been in a declared state of emergency since 1933, when President Roosevelt proclaimed an emergency because of the banking crisis. Further investigation by a Senate committee disclosed that three other national emergencies were still in effect, one proclaimed by President Truman, and two by President Nixon.[22]

The seriousness of this situation is indicated by the fact that, among other things, Federal emergency legislation permits the President to order the seizure of property, to control production, transportation and communications, restrict travel, and institute martial law. To deal with this confusion, Congress enacted the National Emergencies Act of 1976. In addition to terminating the existing emergencies, this law requires the President to publicize any declaration of national emergency, and instructs the Congress to consider, at six-month intervals, the question of whether the emergency should be ended by Congressional resolution.

Federal Force   One decision the President must make when confronting a crisis is whether Federal force is necessary to manage the situation. Overt defiance of Federal law by state officials will almost certainly provoke a coercive reaction by the President, if persuasive efforts fail. As chief executive and Commander-in-Chief, the President is backed up by the Federal Bureau of Investigation, Federal marshals, the Justice Department, and, if necessary, the National Guard and armed forces of the United States. Federal troops have been used in the South to control disorders and state resistance associated with public school desegregation, and in all parts of the country to control riots and civil disorders.

Reorganization   A series of laws passed by Congress since 1939 has given the President some authority to reorganize aspects of the executive branch of government. It would be easy to overestimate the importance of this, however, since the legislation merely permits the President to submit reorganization proposals to Congress. The plans go into effect only if not vetoed by either house of Congress. Under this authority, President Carter succeeded in persuading Congress to establish a separate Department of Education out of the Department of Health, Education, and Welfare, and a new Department of Energy. President Carter was also successful in persuading

22. Fisher, *Constitution Between Friends*, p. 221.

the Congress to pass the Civil Service Reform Act of 1978. This law established a senior executive service that provides a pool of high-level Federal officials who may more easily be rewarded, reassigned, or dismissed by the President.

The Executive Budget

Perhaps the President's foremost administrative management tool, budget preparation permits some control over departmental budgets, and allows Presidential initiatives to reorder national budgetary priorities as well. A glance at Table 7.1 shows a significant reordering of priorities since 1960. During the Korean conflict, and the Cold War that followed, the Defense budget never constituted less than 59% of Federal spending.[23] In 1960, for the first time since the Korean war, Defense received less than half of the Federal budget. This trend continued even in the Vietnam War era. After that conflict was terminated, Defense's share of the budget continually declined, so that in the 1981 budget, it constituted less than 25%. The $143 billion proposed for Defense is a large budget by any standard, but it is considerably less than the $220 billion proposed for Health and Human Services. Table 7.1 also shows that a significant portion of the increase in the Federal budget since 1960 has come in the form of direct payments to individuals. These payments, which include Social Security, veterans' benefits, and Medicare, totaled $23 billion in 1960. By 1979, they had swelled to $213 billion and constituted 43% of the total budget. This reordering of budgetary priorities, while significant, took nearly 20 years.

The President's influence in this area rests primarily on a grant of authority from Congress—the Budget and Accounting Act of 1921. In addition to establishing the Bureau of the Budget (since renamed the Office of Management and Budget) to assist the President with budget preparation, this act also prohibits individual executive departments from independently transmitting budget requests to Congress. In putting the budget together, the President consults with the Council of Economic Advisers, the Office of Management and Budget, and the Treasury Department. Work begins about 18 months in advance of when the money will be spent, a time lag that

---

23. Figures for 1950–1959 are available in Nelson Polsby, *Congress and the Presidency* (3rd ed.). Englewood Cliffs, N.J.: Prentice-Hall, Inc., 1976, p. 158.

Table 7.1   Federal Budget Outlays in Current Dollars: 1960 to 1979

	Outlays (Billions of Dollars)					
Year	Total	National Defense	Total Non-defense	Payments for Individuals	Net Interest	Aid to State and Local Government
1960	92.2	45.2	47.0	22.9	6.9	7.0
1965	118.4	47.5	71.0	30.4	8.6	10.9
1969	184.5	79.4	105.1	52.8	12.7	20.3
1970	196.6	78.6	118.0	59.8	14.4	24.0
1971	211.4	75.8	135.6	74.5	14.8	28.1
1972	232.0	76.6	155.5	85.3	15.5	34.4
1973	247.1	74.5	172.5	95.9	17.4	41.8
1974	269.6	77.7	191.9	111.1	21.5	43.3
1975	326.1	85.6	240.5	142.7	23.3	49.7
1976	366.4	89.4	277.0	167.0	26.7	59.0
*TQ	94.7	22.3	72.4	42.7	7.0	15.9
1977	402.7	97.5	305.2	182.6	29.9	68.3
1978	450.8	105.2	345.6	195.4	35.4	77.9
1979	493.4	114.5	378.9	213.2	43.0	82.1

	Percent of Total Outlays					
Year						
1960	49.0	51.0	24.8	7.5	7.6	
1965	40.0	60.0	25.7	7.3	9.2	
1969	43.0	57.0	28.6	6.9	11.0	
1970	40.0	60.0	30.4	7.3	12.2	
1971	35.9	64.1	35.2	7.0	13.3	
1972	33.0	67.0	36.8	6.7	14.8	
1973	30.1	69.8	38.8	7.0	16.9	
1974	28.8	71.2	41.2	8.0	16.1	
1975	26.3	73.7	43.8	7.1	15.2	
1976	24.4	75.6	45.7	7.3	16.1	
*TQ	23.5	76.5	45.1	7.4	16.8	
1977	24.2	75.8	45.3	7.4	17.0	
1978	23.3	76.7	43.3	7.9	17.3	
1979	23.2	76.8	43.2	8.7	16.6	

*TQ = Transition Quarter. Until 1977, the fiscal year ended on June 30. Thereafter, the fiscal year ends on September 30.

Source: *Statistical Abstract of the United States.* (100th ed.), 1979. United States Department of Commerce, Bureau of the Census. Table No. 424, p. 255.

complicates the budgetary process because forecasts must be continually updated as the economic situation changes. Generally, the President makes the major decisions and leaves the details of compilation, preparation, and administration of the budget to the Office of Management and Budget. Several difficult decisions confront the President, including how much money to spend (the *size* of the budget), how to allocate the money (budgetary *priorities*), and whether to propose any new programs.

Prior Commitments of Budgeting Resources A significant constraint on the President's budgetary authority is the fact that, in any given year, most of the budget is already committed to existing programs. Table 7.2 reports the percentage of the Federal budget that is considered by the Office of Management and Budget to be relatively uncontrollable. Outlays considered relatively uncontrollable are those that can neither be increased nor decreased by Presidential decisions without a change in existing Federal laws, or are beyond administrative control, such as benefit payments, or contractual agreements. This portion of the budget consists mostly of direct payments to individuals or commitments for civilian or defense contracts, and has increased in 10 years from 65% to 75% of the total. The growth of uncontrollables is attributable partly to the proliferation of indexed programs and entitlements. Indexed programs are those, such as Social Security, in which benefits increase automatically with the cost of living. Entitlements are programs providing services and benefits to which citizens have a legal right, such as Medicare, or veterans' benefits. These programs are not literally beyond the control of the government, but are, in the short run, beyond the scope of the President's budgetary authority. To reduce significantly entitlements and indexed programs, the President must persuade Congress to change the law and redefine benefits. Since most of these programs have considerable support among organized interests and in the Congress, this is a formidable task.

The extensive network of prior commitments and the amount of income available are two key realities influencing the size of the budget. Another consideration is the overall condition of the economy. Budgetary decisions can be made realistically only by considering the relationship between the budget and the economy as a whole. When the economy is in a period of little, or no, growth and high unemployment (a recession), the President is likely to recommend

Table 7.2   Executive/Legislative Controllability of Federal Budget Outlays: 1970 to 1979.

Outlays (in billions of dollars, except %)

	1970	1972	1973	1974	1975	1976	1977	1978	1979
Total outlays	196.6	232.0	247.1	269.6	326.1	366.4	402.7	450.8	493.4
Relatively uncontrollable outlays	125.8	153.5	173.1	196.6	237.6	267.8	294.4	333.9	370.2
% of total outlays	64.0	66.2	70.0	72.2	72.9	73.1	73.1	74.1	75.0
Payments for individuals.	62.3	88.5	99.6	115.4	148.9	174.5	190.4	203.8	223.1
Net interest	14.4	15.5	17.4	21.5	23.3	26.8	30.0	35.4	43.0
Prior-year contracts and									
obligations.	41.5	39.2	39.6	43.8	50.7	50.9	55.3	72.3	82.1
National defense	24.1	19.4	17.7	20.4	22.3	17.9	18.5	28.2	32.4
Civilian programs.	17.4	19.9	21.9	23.4	28.4	33.0	36.8	44.1	49.6
Other*	7.6	10.4	16.5	13.9	14.7	15.6	19.0	22.3	22.0
Relatively controllable outlays . . .	73.3	81.2	76.9	78.4	92.5	102.8	112.9	121.9	128.6
National defense	51.6	53.2	52.5	52.2	57.0	64.2	70.8	67.8	71.7
Civilian programs.	21.7	28.0	24.5	26.2	35.5	38.7	42.1	54.1	56.9

Until 1977 fiscal year ended June 30; thereafter, September 30. Transition quarter July-September 1976, omitted.

*Other includes: Farm-price supports, revenue-sharing, and miscellaneous.

SOURCE: *Statistical Abstract of the United States* (100th ed.), 1979. United States Department of Commerce, Bureau of the Census. Table No. 427, p. 256.

a policy of deficit spending to stimulate economic growth. In order to spend more money than it has in income, the government must borrow money, financing this deficit through the sale of government securities. The cost of government bonds, and their interest rates, increase the national debt (presently about $1 trillion) while permitting short-term stimulation of the economy. In inflationary times, the President's economic advisers are likely to recommend a tax increase and/or cuts in government spending. For reasons discussed below, the use of budgetary tools as a means of fighting inflation has not proved especially effective.

Once the President and his advisers have adjusted the size of the budget in accordance with income and economic conditions, they must develop guidelines for allocating the money among the various departments. Here OMB plays a key role in collecting department estimates and enforcing Presidential guidelines by requiring department and agency representatives to defend their budget estimates. At this stage, budgeting becomes a complex bargaining process, with the President and his advisers attempting to impose ceilings, and departmental personnel attempting to defend, or enhance, their budgets.[24]

Considerable negotiation and compromise are required to bring agency estimates into line with Presidential ceilings, the bargaining process being characterized by flexibility on both sides. In the course of persuading department and agency heads to get along with less money than they want, the President permits appeals and may modify guidelines. By permitting OMB to play a more hard-line enforcer role, the President can enhance his bargaining position. While overall changes in agency budgets tend to be marginal, the President can, through a policy of gradual modification, begin the difficult process of reordering budgetary priorities.

The President must also decide if the time is right to move ahead with a new program. Any significant Presidential proposal (for a mass-transit system, or medical-care program, for example) carries with it the liability of justification. Specifically, from where will the money come to pay for it? In election years, (which, in the American Congressional system is *every other year)* a tax increase is probably out of the question. One alternative is to propose that existing funds be redistributed, thereby disrupting established programs and expectations. While this might prove less unpopular with

24. *Ibid.,* pp. 153–165.

voters, it is likely to be very unpopular with members of Congress, bureaucrats, and interest groups whose pet programs are cut. The feasibility of establishing the program now and paying for it later (deficit spending) depends on the state of the economy as well as the mood of Congress. If there is budgetary deficit (as there has been in all but 2 of the last 22 years), Presidential proposals for a significant increase will encounter resistance in the powerful Budget and Appropriations Committees in Congress. The only realistic strategy may be to fight for a more modest version of the program with hopes of expanding it later.

When these difficult choices have been made, priorities established, and bargaining concluded, the President transmits the annual budget message to Congress. This is followed by the Economic Report of the President, prepared by the Council of Economic Advisers. This report consists of further explanation and justification for the fiscal policies advocated by the President.

Congressional Approval From the perspective of executive management, the budgetary process is complicated immeasurably by the fact that the entire budget must be approved by the Congress. In the course of Congressional deliberations, some modifications in the President's proposals are inevitable. Before appropriating money from the Federal treasury, Congress, through its Budget and Appropriations Committees, scrutinizes the proposed budget in great detail. In the House of Representatives, for example, the 50 or so members of the Appropriations Committee devote full time consideration to budgetary matters. Most are senior representatives from safe districts who are not easily intimidated, either by their colleagues or the President. The Appropriations Committee operates through specialized subcommittees, each corresponding to a major department of the executive branch. The subcommittees guard their jurisdiction and prerogatives carefully and expect mutual support in this area from the other subcommittees. Perhaps most important, the Congress has generally been very supportive of the Appropriations Committees, approving their recommendations with only small deviations.[25]

25. Richard F. Fenno, Jr., "The House Appropriations Committee as a Political System: The Problem of Integration," *American Political Science Review,* 56, June 1962, pp. 310–324. See, also, Lance T. LeLoup, *Budgetary Politics: Dollars, Deficits, Decisions.* Brunswick, O.: Kings Court Communications, 1977, p. 172.

Economic Management

The budget is one aspect of a larger responsibility the President has for providing direction in the government's attempts at management of the economy. The Employment Act of 1946 established for the Federal government the general responsibility of maintaining a stable and prosperous economy, and for fostering conditions which will afford employment opportunities for those willing and able to work. The Council of Economic Advisers was established to assist the President in monitoring the economy, diagnosing problems, and recommending measures as needed.

This is a classic case of responsibility without power. The tools available to the President for managing the economy are woefully inadequate compared with the scope of that assignment. This is true partly because of the increasingly complex nature of economic problems. It is also true because the manner in which American monetary and fiscal policy is formulated is both uncoordinated and highly political. For these reasons, the responsibility for providing leadership in the area of economic management has proven to be one of the President's most challenging assignments.

The uncoordinated nature of this process results from the fact that different government agencies are responsible for various aspects of economic and budgetary policy. *Monetary policy* involves interest rates, or how much it costs to borrow money. The rate of economic expansion and the availability of credit are influenced by decisions in this area. *Fiscal policy* involves the combination of taxes and spending. Within the limits of prior commitments and Congressional approval, the President has a considerable say about government spending. Tax increases or decreases, however, directly affect the government's income and, therefore, the size of the deficit. Tax policy is largely in the hands of the Congress, particularly the House Ways and Means and Senate Finance committees. The President may recommend a change in tax policy, but Congress determines the final details, including the timing of any change.

The lack of coordination inherent in this system is even more apparent when it is recalled that monetary policy is largely in the hands of the Federal Reserve Board (Fed). This agency is an independent agency, relatively insulated from the President's control, which tends to take a conservative position (high interest rates) on monetary policy. Conflict between the President (especially Democratic Presidents) and the Fed is not unusual. Whether the government's monetary and fiscal policies are coordinated, or competing, depends largely upon the economic philosophies of the individuals involved and not upon the President's preferences.

Because of the uncoordinated and political nature of this process, government policy has proved to be more effective in dealing with unemployment than inflation.[26]   The economic prescriptions for unemployment are usually acceptable to Congress. Involving either a tax cut, or job programs, or both, these recommendations are likely to be popular with politicians, especially in an election year.

Inflation Presidential attempts to deal with inflation are likely to prove less effective for several reasons, but primarily because they are politically unpopular.   Recommendations by the President's economic advisers for dealing with inflation are likely to include cuts in government spending, higher interest rates, and a tax increase. For reasons already outlined, it is difficult to reduce significantly government spending once programs are established. High interest rates, as is by now obvious, will not control inflation in the absence of effective energy- and oil-import policies. Tax increases, regardless of how necessary they may be, are not politically feasible in an election year. For approximately half the time Congress is in session, income tax increases are virtually out of the question because of possible repercussions at the polls as representatives seek reelection. At the very least, the highly political nature of this process disrupts the timing of a change in tax policy. This situation is complicated further by the tendency of the Federal government to pursue policies that are inflationary.[27]   This includes not only full-employment policies, which are politically popular, but indiscriminate deficit financing as well.

Presidential Persuasion Presidential attempts to use persuasion as an economic tool have met with some success, especially in labor disputes. For example, in April, 1962, President Kennedy used a

26. Dorothy B. James, *The Contemporary Presidency* (2nd ed.). New York: (Pegasus Bobbs-Merrill Co., Inc.), 1974, pp. 95–96. Chapter IV of James' book is an excellent discussion of the President's economic responsibilities.

27. Numerous writers have made this argument. A particularly forceful and concise analysis can be found in Reo M. Christenson, *Challenge and Decision: Political Issues of Our Time* (5th ed.). New York: Harper and Row, 1976, pp. 46–50.

combination of threats and persuasion to convince Roger Blough, the president of United States Steel, to reconsider a price increase after Blough had publicly announced the price rise. The proposed price increase was four times the size necessary to cover the costs of a labor contract that President Kennedy had persuaded the unions to accept only days before.[28]   Likewise, President Johnson was reasonably successful with jaw boning tactics.   The deficiency of persuasion as an economic management technique is that it relies on voluntary compliance.   President Carter, for example, found it easier to modify his wage and price guidelines than to persuade business and labor to comply with them.   President Nixon resorted to the un-orthodox step of peacetime wage and price controlls in an attempt to control inflation. Mandatory wage and price controls, while an option, are considered only as a last resort since they are strongly opposed by both labor and business and are difficult to administer as well. Both Democratic and Republican Presidents are ideologically predisposed to avoid them except in a wartime economy.

These political considerations, combined with changing economic circumstances, place limitations on the capacity of government to manage an inflationary economy. Since the outlook for the 1980's is for more inflation fueled by shortages of raw materials and energy, the President's responsibility for providing leadership in this area is shaping up as one of the major challenges of executive leadership.

CONCLUSION

The proliferation of impressive titles associated with the Presidency has created a misleading impression about the extent of the President's powers. Descriptions of the President as Chief Executive and chief administrator create the illusion that the President is in control of the government when he is not. The realities of executive power are defined by the extensive network of prior commitments of govern-mental and budgetary resources, reinforced by bureaucratic momen-tum.   These realities rest on the highly technical and specialized nature of the executive departments, as well as the important role played by the Federal bureaucracy in implementing, and the Congress in defining, and funding, the policies and programs of the govern-

28. For a detailed account of this incident by one of President Kennedy's top advisers, see, also, Theodore C. Sorensen, *Kennedy*. New York: Harper and Row, 1965, pp. 449–452.

ment. In the area of economic management, the President's role is important, especially in initiation of the budget. Like other tools of economic management, budgetary power is shared with the Congress. Moreover, effectiveness of government policies in this area depends partly on the voluntary compliance of powerful private institutions.

Executive leadership is a long-term proposition requiring a realistic view of what is possible in one Presidential term. The President's tools as chief executive, if used with diligence and patience, permit a gradual restructuring of governmental and budgetary priorities.

FURTHER READING

Califano, Joseph A. *A Presidential Nation.* New York: W.W. Norton and Co., Inc., 1975. An interpretation of the modern Presidency by a Washington insider. Califano was a member of President Carter's Cabinet and President Johnson's White House staff.

Fisher, Louis. *The Constitution Between Friends: Congress, the President, and the Law.* New York: St. Martin's Press, Inc., 1978. One of America's leading Constitutional and Presidential scholars sheds some light on the confusing tangle of legal relationships between the President and Congress.

Heclo, Hugh. *A Government of Strangers: Executive Politics in Washington.* Washington, D.C.: The Brookings Institution, 1977. A study of life at the top of the Federal bureaucracy. Relationships between appointed political executives and top-level career civil servants are analyzed in this excellent study.

LeLoup, Lance T. *Budgetary Politics: Dollars, Deficits, Decisions.* Brunswick, O.: King's Court Communications, 1977. A readable and up-to-date discussion of the politics of the budgetary process.

Pechman, Joseph A. (ed.). *Setting National Priorities: The 1980 Budget.* Washington, D.C.: The Brookings Institution, 1979. Several scholars collaborate to discuss how more than half a trillion dollars in Federal funds will be spent.

Pious, Richard M. *The American Presidency.* New York: Basic Books, Inc., 1979. An up-to-date and detailed treatment of the powers of the Presidency.

Nachmias, David, and Rosenbloom, David H. *Bureaucratic Government USA.* New York: St. Martin's Press, Inc., 1980. An analysis of the consequences of the bureaucratization of American government.

Seidman, Harold. *Politics, Position, and Power: The Dynamics of Federal Organization* (3rd ed.). New York: Oxford University Press, Inc., 1980. The dynamics and politics of the executive branch described by a scholar who was also a member of the Federal service for 25 years.

Shull, Steven A. *Presidential Policy Making: An Analysis.* Brunswick, O.: King's Court Communications, Inc., 1979. A detailed analysis of the President's role in shaping public policy.

Chapter 8

The Politics of Compromise

THE HILL

At the opposite end of Pennsylvania Avenue from the White House is Capitol Hill. The Hill is not an impressive summit, but few Presidents have been able to conquer it. Atop the Hill is the Capitol, seat of the most formidable and independent legislative body in the world. Rich in tradition, the United States Congress guards its powers and prerogatives jealously. The most prized of all Congressional traditions is independence of executive control. The Congress has evolved procedures and an organization admirably suited to maintaining its independence as a legislative body.

While some Presidents and various commentators consider the Congress at best a nuisance, if not an obstruction to effective government, this is not a realistic view. The powers of Congress are impressive. In addition to being able to remove a President from office, Congress has the formal authority to enact into law programs which distribute social and economic benefits, modify the tax structure, and promulgate regulations. Each year the Congress appropriates billions in tax money and oversees the implementation of programs which spend these Federal funds. While the executive branch is a major source of legislative proposals, Congress itself initiates and debates many significant proposals and modifies virtually every Presidential proposal sent up to the Hill.

The independence of Congress from the President is one of the most distinctive features of American politics. From the beginning of the American Republic, Congress was envisioned not only as a legislative body, but as the key restraint on the power of the Presidency. The President's relations with Congress begin to make sense only when understood in this context. By reasserting its authority in response to Presidential abuses of power, the Congress has reaffirmed its traditional role in the American constitutional system.

Congressional Committees

The independence of the Congress from President and party depends not only on its formal powers of authorization, appropriation, and oversight. Equally important is the organization and functioning of Congress, its traditions and procedures, and the manner in which members of Congress are selected. One of the most important characteristics of Congressional organization is the committee system. The manner in which Congressional committees (and their subcommittees) have evolved assures not only that they will play a key role in shaping the contents of legislation, but also that committees will continue to constitute a primary source of Congressional independence from the executive. This is true because the President can neither control the selection of members, nor the choice of chairpersons of Congressional committees.

There are several types of legislative committees, but by far the most important in Congress are the standing (or permanent) committees. There are 15 in the Senate and 22 in the House of Representatives. Each committee has a specialized area of jurisdiction, which is protected by the rules of Congress. Except in unusual circumstances, bills within the jurisdiction of a committee are routinely assigned to it. This system of writing legislation through specialized committees permits members of Congress to develop expertise in particular policy areas. Specialization is mandated not only by the heavy work load of Congress, but also because of the highly specialized and complex nature of the executive branch. If the Congress is seriously expected to oversee the performance of the executive branch in enforcing laws, implementing policy, and spending Federal money, specialization is the only feasible approach.

The most prestigious and influential of the standing committees in Congress (and their jurisdiction) include:

House and Senate Appropriations (Federal spending)
House Ways and Means and Senate Finance (revenue and taxes)
House and Senate Armed Services (defense policy)
House and Senate Judiciary (questions of constitutional law,
    civil rights, and impeachment)
House Rules (controls agenda in the House)
House International Relations and Senate Foreign Relations
    (foreign policy, international affairs, and treaties)
House and Senate Budget (recommends spending ceilings)

These committees are considered choice assignments and nearly
every member of Congress will eventually want a seat on one of them.
Other committees deal with a wide range of government policy, such
as agriculture, energy, commerce, banking, and public works. In addition to writing legislation, most standing committees have responsibilities to oversee performance of executive agencies within
their area of jurisdiction.

Legislative Role   Committees have a considerable say in shaping
legislation because members of Congress frequently defer to their
judgment, feeling that specialized members of committees are in the
best position to determine the contents of legislation in their area
of expertise. Committee versions of bills can be (and frequently are)
amended by members of Congress on the floor, but an unfavorable
committee report seriously undermines a bill's chances of passage.

Basis of Assignment   The individual member's seat on a committee is protected by custom and seniority and carries over from one
term of Congress to another. Many factors besides seniority (including the member's background, expertise and reputation for
reliability) influence assignment to committees,[1] but only defeat
at the polls, or a drastic change in the party balance in Congress,
constitutes a serious threat to a member's seat on a committee.

The member from the majority party with the most seniority on
the committee usually becomes chairperson, subject to approval of

1.   Nicholas A. Masters, "Committee Assignments in the House of Represen-
     tatives," *American Political Science Review,* 55 (June, 1961), pp. 345–357.

the party members meeting in caucus. The power of committee chairpersons is no longer what it once was, but still includes setting the agenda, scheduling and running the meetings, and, in the Senate, designating the subcommittees, choosing the floor manager of bills from the committee, and sitting on conference committees. White House consultation with these powerful legislators frequently provides a good gauge of how extensively the President must modify legislative proposals in order to gain a favorable report from key committees.

Independence The single most important aspect of the committee system for Presidents is that it is completely independent of executive control. Committee chairpersons and members are, of course, amenable to Presidential influence and persuasion, but they usually drive a hard bargain. The decentralized system of specialized committees with jurisdiction protected by Congressional rules and traditions, and members protected by seniority, constitutes the single greatest reality confronting Presidents in their attempts to influence the Congress.

The fate of President Carter's proposed tax on the windfall profits of oil companies once again demonstrated the power of Congressional committees. Late in 1979, his proposal emerged from the House of Representatives in reasonably good shape. The House version of the bill (endorsed by the President) would have collected an estimated $277 billion over an 11-year period. Oil interests are stronger in the Senate, however, particularly on the Finance Committee which has 9 members from the oil-producing states. Unfortunately for the President, tax bills are within the jurisdiction of the Finance Committee. By the time the Finance Committee and Chairman Russel Long (an oil millionaire from Louisiana) finished with the bill, the tax had been cut in half, reducing the estimated take to $138 billion. After this first-round victory over backers of the President's version of the bill, the oil-state Senators (led by Bentson of Texas) were successful in trimming an additional $10 billion off the tax by amending the bill on the floor of the Senate.[2] The committee succeeded in depriving the President temporarily of the initiative so that their bill became the focus of discussion and a crucial consideration in shaping the final compromise ($228 billion) between the two versions.

2. *Dayton Daily News,* November 27, 1979, p. 6.

Congessional Leadership

In addition to the informal leadership provided by committee chair-persons and ranking members, the Congress has a formal leadership structure as well. On one of the few occasions when members vote along strict party lines, the majority party selects the Speaker of the House and floor leaders and assistants in both houses. The minority party selects its own floor leaders and assistants. Congressional party leaders are influential because they have years of legislative experience and have the support of their colleagues, and because they are in key positions in the communication network of Congress.

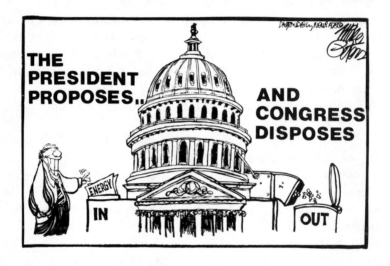

Regular channels of communication with party leaders are a hallmark of successful Presidential leadership in Congress. In the course of performing their difficult task of building the majority co-alitions necessary to pass legislation, Congressional leaders negotiate with the administration about the appropriate timing and strategy of the President's legislative program. One reason for the legislative difficulties of some recent Presidents was an unwillingness (in Nixon's case) and an inability (in Carter's case) to establish an amic-able working relationship with Congressional leadership. President Carter got off to a particularly bad start with House Speaker Tip O'Neill by firing one of O'Neill's long-time friends from a high-level position in General Services Administration.

Given the independent manner by which the leadership is chosen, most recent Presidents have found it inadvisable to attempt to influence the selection of Congressional leaders. A notable exception occurred during the Nixon administration when the President's Chief-of-Staff, H. R. Haldeman, informed Senate Republican leader Hugh Scott that the White House had decided Scott should be replaced as Senate minority leader. The ineffectiveness of the President in influencing selection of Congressional leadership was dramatized when Senate Republicans reelected Scott by a wide margin.[3]

Congressional Elections

The distribution of power in Congress is such that any member able to get reelected consistently will eventually be able to move up in the power structure. Committee chairpersonships and ranking memberships offer excellent power bases from which to protect and promote constituency interests. Access to these power bases, and to elective positions of party leadership, depend not on Presidential goodwill, but primarily upon the ability of members of Congress to accumulate seniority by getting reelected regularly. Some of the most influential people in American government are little known outside of Washington except in the states, or Congressional districts, which elect them.

The manner in which members of Congress are selected is another key reason for their independence of both political party and the President. Cohesive disciplined legislative parties are most likely when the party has a strong organization which controls the nomination of candidates. The trend in American politics, however, is in the direction of weaker party organization, less party unity in Congress, and greater independence of candidates from the organization. The strong committee system assures that the party will not be the focus of decision making in Congress. More importantly, the party organization has little impact on the nomination and election of members of Congress.[4]

Members of Congress are nominated and elected locally, usually with little input from the President or the national party. Candidates

3. Dan Rather and Gary Gates. *The Palace Guard*. New York: Harper and Row, 1974, pp. 302–303.

4. For further documentation of these recent trends, see, among others, Malcolm E. Jewell and Samuel C. Patterson, *The Legislative Process in the United States* (3rd ed.). New York: Random House, Inc., 1977. pp. 91–96, 263–264, and 391–399; and Larry M. Schwab, *Changing Patterns of Congressional Politics*. New York: D. Van Nostrand Company, 1980, pp. 80–99.

for Congress must win two elections: the primary, which decides the party's nomination, and a general election, pitting candidates of the two parties against each other.   For both types of Congressional elections, one striking generality stands out: Incumbents nearly always win.   In the last 25 years, upwards of 95% of incumbent Senators and Congresspersons won their primaries, and over 90% were reelected.[5]   (The figures are even higher if freshmen members of Congress, who are more likely to lose, are excluded.)   Although veteran members of Congress are rarely defeated, the number of competitive seats is declining, not only due to the power of incumbency, but also because state legislatures draw House districts in a manner that will protect incumbents of their party.[6]

When Presidents intervene in Congressional elections, it is most often to protect incumbents and win the goodwill of members of their party rather than to punish uncooperative legislators.[7]   Even Franklin Roosevelt was unable to oust Democratic Congresspersons he opposed, and President Nixon's efforts produced mixed results at best.

Generally speaking, members of Congress are nominated and elected locally.   They use their own organizations and finances, frequently from safe districts with excellent prospects for reelection. They are seldom obligated to the President or the party, and may justifiably consider an unpopular President a threat to their own reelection.   These considerations combine to create a situation wherein many of the incentives that motivate members of Congress are either local (constituency interests, campaign contributions, and votes), or personal (ideology and ambition).

Partisan Balance in Congress

The nature of Congressional elections also contributes to the high potential for the deadlock characteristic of Presidential/Congressional relations. The Congress and the President are not only elected from different constituencies (local as opposed to national), but they are chosen by differing electorates as well. Citizens who vote reg-

5.   Jewell and Patterson, *Legislative Process in the United States,* Chapter II, 12, pp. 88–92.

6.   Schwab, *Changing Patterns of Congressional Politics,* pp. 71–72.

7.   Jewell and Patterson, *Legislative Process in the United States,* p. 263.

ularly in Congressional elections are generally more partisan, as well as more interested in politics, than those who vote only in Presidential elections. Turnout in Congressional elections is low (usually around 40%), but generally reflects the underlying distribution of party identification among the electorate.[8] Consequently, Democrats, who presently outnumber Republican voters by a ratio of 3 to 2, have usually controlled the Congress during the postwar era. In 1978, for example, 70% of the Democrats in Congress were elected by victory margins of 60% or greater.[9] The Democratic dominance of Congress is reflected in the fact that Republicans have not controlled both houses of Congress since the Eisenhower landslide gave them a slim majority from 1953 to 1955. Democrats controlled both houses of Congress from 1955 until 1981, when the Republicans won a majority in the Senate.

Differing Electorates Differences between the Presidential and Congressional electorates have prevented similar Democratic dominance in Presidential elections. Since the end of World War II, control of the Presidency has been nearly evenly divided between Democrats and Republicans. The greater instance of Republican success in Presidential than in Congressional elections can be attributed primarily to the nature of the Presidential electorate. Presidential elections, being more important and better publicized, attract considerably more voters (between 55% and 60%), a significant portion of whom are less partisan, less interested, and more likely to vote on the basis of candidate and issue orientations.[10] This fact, combined with the increasing tendency of voters to split their tickets, means that Republicans, if they nominate an attractive candidate, have reasonably good prospects for winning the Presidency, but less chance of gaining, or maintaining, control of the Congress. Consequently, the already high potential for conflict between the President and Congress is increased by the prospect that a Republican President will likely face a Democratic Congress. Of Republican Presi-

8. Angus Campbell. "Surge and Decline: A Study of Electoral Change," in Angus Campbell et al. (eds.), *Elections and the Political Order*. New York: John Wiley and Sons, Inc., 1966, pp. 40–62.

9. *Congressional Quarterly Guide to Current American Government: Fall 1979*. Washington, D.C.: Congressional Quarterly, Inc., 1979, p. 88.

10. Campbell, "Surge and Decline" pp. 42–43.

dents since World War II, only Eisenhower enjoyed partisan majorities in both houses of Congress.

While Republican Presidents generally face considerable difficulties with a Democratic Congress, the presence of a numerical majority of Congressional Democrats does *not* assure that Democratic Presidents will have an easy time of it. In the Congress, party unity and cohesion are relatively weak, and coalitions frequently shift with different issues. For reasons already outlined, the President cannot compel members of the administration's party to follow his lead. Research on Congressional support for the President's position on roll-call votes in Congress since 1955 demonstrates that Presidents have been able to command only partial support from their party and have been forced to rely on the opposition party for some support on crucial issues. On the average, the President's party in Congress has supported the administration's position between one-half and three-quarters of the time, while Presidential support in the opposition party is usually less than 50%, but still great enough to be significant on controversial issues.[11] The President is generally more successful in persuading members of Congress, particularly the opposition party, to follow his lead on foreign policy issues than on domestic matters. On domestic issues, members of Congress are more likely to follow their own predispositions and their perceptions of constituency preferences.

The fact that the partisan balance of Congress in the last 50 years has usually favored the Democrats is a major reason that Democratic Presidents have had greater legislative success than Republican's. Generally, the larger the administration's majorities in Congress, the greater the President's opportunities for legislative success. Presumably, one reason for President Johnson's astounding success in Congress was the two-to-one Democratic majority he enjoyed in Congress from 1965 to 1967. President Kennedy, not commanding such large majorities, was unable to overcome the conservative coalition to pass key legislation, including the civil rights bills and medicare program, that President Johnson eventually signed into law.

The partisan balance is only a partial explanation of Presidential success with Congress. During his first two years in office, President Carter's majority in the House of Representatives was virtually identical with Johnson's and only slightly less in the Senate.[12] While

11. Jewell and Patterson, *Legislative Process in the United States,* pp. 396-399.

Carter enjoyed some legislative success amidst generally rough sledding, his performance was in no way comparable to Johnson's.

One obvious difference between Johnson and Carter was their level of political skills and experience in Congress. Beyond that, however, was a more subtle difference in Congress itself. The large Congressional majorities that President Johnson enjoyed were piled up as a result of his landslide Presidential victory in 1964 when the Democrats gained 38 seats in the House. There were a substantial number of freshman Democrats swept into Congress on the President's coattails.

President Carter's victory in 1976, on the other hand, produced no coattails, and his percentage of the popular vote was less than that of the Congressional Democrats. The large Democratic majorities in Congress were not due to Carter's Presidential victory, but resulted, instead, from the disastrous Republican Congressional defeat in the 1974 mid-term elections when the party suffered the negative effects of the Watergate scandal, including President Nixon's resignation and President Ford's unpopular decision to pardon Nixon. Three months after President Nixon resigned, the Republicans lost 43 seats in the House and 3 in the Senate.[13] Subsequently, in the Presidential election of 1976, the Democrats, already having huge majorities in Congress, gained only 1 seat in each house. Despite the substantial majorities in both houses, there were few Democratic members of Congress who felt obliged to President Carter for their election.

Ideological Balance in Congress

On domestic issues, the traditional nemesis of Democratic Presidents has been the conservative coalition of Southern Democrats in alliance with Republicans, which frequently undermines Democratic majorities in Congress by voting in opposition to Northern Democrats. This

12. The party balance for Kennedy from 1961 to 1963 was 263 Democrats to 174 Republicans in the House, and 64 Democrats to 36 Republicans in the Senate. Johnson's 1965–1967 majorities were: House: 295 (D) to 140 (R), and Senate: 67 (D) to 33 (R). Carter's 1977–1979 majorities were: House: 292 (D) to 143 (R), and Senate: 62 (D) to 38 (R). The figures for Kennedy and Johnson are from *Congressional Quarterly Weekly Report* 32 (November 9, 1974), p. 3105. The figures for Carter are from *Congressional Quarterly Guide to Current American Government: Fall 1979*, p. 90.

13. *Congressional Quarterly Guide to Current American Government: Fall, 1979*, p. 90

coalition appears on about only one-fourth of Congressional roll calls, but it usually wins about half of those.[14] This traditional pattern of conservative opposition to domestic innovations proposed by liberal Presidents has been complicated recently by an increasing tendency of more liberal and metropolitan Republicans (mostly from the East) to align with Northern Democrats in opposition to conservative Republicans and Southern Democrats. This tendency, along with greater numbers of Northern Democrats being elected since 1974, moved the Congress in a more liberal direction. The liberals in Congress not only initiated much of the social policy during the Nixon administration, but significantly modified President Ford's budget proposals as well, by increasing funding for social programs.[15] The ideological balance in Congress shifted in a more conservative direction as a result of the 1980 elections. The Republicans won a majority in the Senate, and the conservative coalition gained strength in the House of Representatives.

SELLING THE PRESIDENT'S PROGRAM

As the previous discussion indicates, there are numerous factors affecting Presidential success in Congress, such as partisan balance and ideological composition, that are beyond the control of the administration. These factors, along with the independence of Congress, define the realities of the legislative situation confronting the President. Whether the President successfully maximizes the potential of this situation depends on a combination of organization, personal skills, persuasion, and compromise.

Liaison Organization

As foreign relations consume an increasingly larger share of the President's time, the responsibility for monitoring the progress of the administration's legislative program has been, of necessity, delegated to White House assistants. Like several other features of the institutionalized Presidency, this approach was first formalized as a staff

---

14. Jewell and Patterson, *Legislative Process in the United States,* pp. 392–393. The conservative coalition first appeared during, or shortly after, World War II.

15. Schwab, *Changing Patterns in Congressional Politics,* pp. 139–150.

function during the Eisenhower administration. The importance of this responsibility was expanded by President Kennedy when he designated Lawrence F. O'Brien as Special Assistant for Congressional Relations and Personnel, a position of equal rank with other top-level White House staffers. O'Brien, empowered to speak and act for the President, was able to coordinate departmental liaison efforts with those of the White House.[16] Subsequent administrations have attempted, with varying degrees of success, to emulate this approach. Two of the least successful and most amateurish Congressional liaison operations were those of the Nixon and Carter administrations. Their inexperienced liaison teams violated some of the basic ground rules of good Congressional relations.

Consultation   Since the Congressional-Presidential relationship is basically adversary in nature, with a high potential for conflict, some cooperation is required in order to avoid a stalemate. Consultation between the administration and Congressional leaders not only promotes the communication necessary for planning legislative strategy and timing; it also provides the symbols of cooperation and deference that the Congress expects. The elected leadership of Congress can be a valuable source of intelligence for the President. Its estimates of vote counts is usually accurate, and it knows which legislators are favorable, opposed, or undecided about a bill—indispensable information for a successful lobbying effort. Committee chairpersons and ranking members can indicate which provisions of a bill will meet the most opposition in their committees. One reason President Carter's energy package took nearly two years to be enacted was that the administration drafted it with no Congressional consultation.[17]

The liaison operation of the Carter administration during its first year and a half has been described as a comedy of errors. Disorganization and inexperience contributed to lapses ranging from failure to return telephone calls of influential members of Congress to total breakdowns in communication with Congressional leadership. Eventually the operation was reorganized along lines suggested by Vice President Mondale, the only member of the Carter team with

16. Abraham Holtzman, *Legislative Liaison: Executive Leadership in Congress.* Chicago: Rand McNally and Co., Inc., 1970, pp. 15–16.

17. *Congressional Quarterly Guide to Current American Government: Fall, 1979,* p. 54

Congressional experience.[18]   Congressional relations during the
Nixon administration suffered from similar deficiencies, but, in addition, were characterized by an arrogant and contemptuous style
on the part of the White House assistants.

Compromise   Consultation is important partly as an indicator
of the President's willingness to compromise. Congress regards itself
as an equal to the executive branch and has the independent sources
of power to back up that claim. The necessity for accommodation
dictates that the administration be willing to accept modifications in
its proposals. From a realistic perspective, the question facing the
President is not if he should compromise, but rather when and how
to compromise in order to strike the best bargain.

Careful liaison work is required because the fragile coalitions,
painstakingly pieced together by Congressional leaders can easily
be disrupted by a poorly timed public statement, or an insensitive
remark in private by administration spokespersons. President Carter's
much publicized disdain for the "wheeling-and-dealing" style of
Washington politics, while perhaps an asset in the Presidential election, proved to be of little value in dealing with Congress.

Clear Priorities   One of the President's legislative responsibilities
is to make choices. Legislative leadership consists partly of clearly
communicating administration priorities to Congress in matters of
policy and budget. Presidents unclear about their priorities create
problems for themselves because Congress is unwilling to regard every
proposal as having Presidential priority. Hard choices must be made
about which proposals merit commitment of Presidential prestige
and influence. One of President Carter's early difficulties with Congress was his failure to clearly specify legislative priorities. At one
point in 1978, 60 bills (far too many) had been given Presidential
priority.[19]

Coordination   A major responsibility of the Congressional liaison
staff is to provide the coordination necessary to clearly communicate
Presidential priorities, and then to follow up with effective lobbying
for these proposals. Much of the coordination effort is aimed at
minimizing competition with the President's program from within

18. *Ibid.*, pp. 49–53.

19. *Ibid.*, p. 49.

the executive branch. The major executive departments have their own liaison operations, which, if not coordinated by the White House, may work against the President's proposals rather than for them. In addition to coordinating lobbying efforts with White House policy, the departments are expected to clear any proposed legislation with the Office of Management and Budget to prevent conflicts. Coordination and central clearance frequently work to the advantage of both the White House and the departments. The administration gains access to the manpower and expertise of the departments which may be mobilized to defend the program in Congress, and the departments gain White House support for some of their proposals.[20]

Services An extensive service operation is an essential part of a successful Congressional liaison organization. Many of the legislators' personal and constituent needs can best be met with help from the executive departments or the White House. The executive branch can cultivate the goodwill of members of Congress by providing them with information, expertise, assistance with bureaucratic red tape, and jobs. Legislators rely on departments to keep them informed of decisions about grants, contracts, and projects in their districts.[21] Executive departments are able to use their expertise and chain-of-command to expedite Congressional inquiries and assist constituents having problems with the bureaucracy.

Government appointed jobs are among the most prized political plums the executive branch has to offer. The administration benefits by pleasing an influential legislator, who benefits, in turn, from having successfully sponsored a constituent for a government job. However, since the demand for patronage jobs considerably exceeds the supply, there are inevitably many members of Congress whose requests cannot be granted. From this perspective, patronage can be an asset only if properly handled. President Carter again handicapped himself unnecessarily by permitting chief assistant Hamilton Jordan to dispense patronage haphazardly. Eventually, this responsibility was turned over to the Congressional relations staff.[22]

20. Holtzman, *Legislative Liaison*, pp. 232–236.

21. *Ibid.*, pp. 234–236.

22. *Congressional Quarterly Guide to Current American Government: Fall, 1979*, p. 50.

Direct Lobbying   Organization is crucial for providing the attention to detail and follow-up needed to maintain the momentum of the legislative program.   Departmental lobbyists usually handle routine matters so that the White House liaison staff is free to concentrate on important legislation.   Two or three administration lobbyists are assigned to the Senate and several to the House.   A major responsibility is to identify legislators who are undecided and contact them personally.   Techniques of influence emphasize the soft sell, consisting of reasoned arguments supporting the merits of the proposal, as well as more direct pressure, including personal appeals from party leaders, the White House, and influential constituents, or interest groups that have been mobilized by departmental lobbyists.[23]

The Presidency itself is a resource, especially when the President is popular with Congress and the public.   In addition to promises of campaign assistance and support for legislation of friendly Congresspersons, the White House can grant access to its vast resources of free publicity.   Exposure in the form of public support and recognition of legislators by the President, and invitations to White House social and ceremonial functions, are useful devices for cultivating goodwill and building up credit with Congress.

Presidential Skills and Experience

Although much Congressional lobbying is now delegated to White House assistants, there are inevitably situations when the President's personal intervention can make a difference.   When there is a great deal at stake, the President may make a personal appeal to legislators for their support.   A carefully timed telephone call can be effective, but an invitation to the White House provides a more imposing setting for the President to maximize his success at personal persuasion.   Most attention is paid to members of Congress who are undecided on the issue, although, on rare occasions, the President may be persuasive enough to change some key votes.

There is a general understanding, shared by nearly everyone, that legislators are not expected to jeopardize their chances for reelection by alienating large blocs of voters, or powerful organized interests, in their constituency.   The President's task is to convince people that

23. Holtzman, *Legislative Liaison*, pp. 232–236.

what he wants is in their own interests as well.[24]   To this end, a variety of arguments, based on party loyalty, patriotism, and national interest, or the welfare of constituent groups, as well as moral suasion, may be effective.   Sometimes all that the President requires is that key legislators refrain from opposing a bill. At other times, the President may appeal directly for active support: "We've got to have your vote or we lose." This "indispensable vote" argument has proved effective on occasion, perhaps because of the flattery implicit in the suggestion that the whole issue will stand, or fall, on a single legislator's decision.

In the intimate setting of the Oval Office, persuasion is partly a matter of logical argument, and partly a matter of personal skills and the way in which the argument is made. The medium is the message in the sense that the style of the presentation may be as important as its content. Among recent Presidents, Lyndon Johnson was clearly in a class by himself in both Congressional experience (he first went to Congress as an administrative assistant in 1931) and personal persuasive skills. Much has been made of his persuasive ability, especially the famous "Johnson treatment," involving an energetic combination of pleading, flattery, argument, and sincere conviction, supplemented by dynamic physical gestures—arm flailing, and glad-handing.[25] Johnson's impressive physical size and domineering mannerisms, combined with his extensive network of contacts and obligations for past services, made the President an imposing figure in an intimate setting. Underlying Johnson's success was more than energetic antics. His persuasive skills were partly a result of an innate ability to assess shrewdly the motivations and needs of his target.[26]

This kind of personal attention, while useful, has its limits not only because it is costly in terms of the President's time and energy, but because it loses its effectiveness if used too frequently. Some Presidents play down this technique, simply because it is not their style. President Nixon preferred to devote most of his energy to foreign relations. Neither Eisenhower nor Carter enjoyed this kind

24. Richard Neustadt, *Presidential Power: The Politics of Leadership.* New York: John Wiley and Sons, Inc., 1960, pp. 58–62.

25. There are numerous accounts of "the treatment." One of the most entertaining and concise is found in Barber, *The Presidential Character.* Englewood Cliffs, N.J.: Prentice Hall, Inc., 1972, pp. 79–83.

26. For an elaboration of this idea, see Kearns, *Lyndon Johnson and the American Dream.* New York: New American Library (Signet), 1977, pp. 125–132.

of wheeling and dealing, and neither had cultivated the extensive network of contacts necessary to make it work. Consequently, they, along with Kennedy, made extensive use of the Congressional liaison staff, reserving their personal intervention for key situations.

Public Appeals

It is easy to overestimate the importance of public opinion in American politics. Most political decisions are made by a small number of decision makers with considerable inattention and lack of interest on the part of the public.[27] Attempts to find links between the behavior of legislators and the political opinions of their constituents have been only partially successful.[28] Research suggests that the relationship between the President's public standing and his success in Congress is indirect at best. In statistical terms, there is a modest association between the President's public prestige and Congressional support in the area of foreign policy, and no relationship between Presidential popularity and Congressional support in domestic matters.[29] A Presidential appeal for general public support on any legislative issue may fail for two reasons: widespread public apathy and ignorance about political issues, and the absence of a strong association between Congressional behavior and public support of the President.

There is, however, a significant relationship between the President's popularity with Democratic voters and support for him among Democratic legislators. Likewise, the President's popularity among Republican voters contributes to Presidential support among Re-

27. The most elegant and well-documented defense of this thesis is found in Thomas R. Dye and Harmon Zeigler, *The Irony of Democracy* (4th ed.). North Scituate, Ma.: Duxbury Press, 1978, Chs. 4, 5, and 6.

28. The classic study is Warren E. Miller and Donald E. Stokes, "Constituency Influence in Congress," *American Political Science Review,* 57 (March, 1963), pp. 45–56. More recent investigations include two by George C. Edwards III, "Presidential Influence in the House: Presidential Prestige as a Source of Presidential Power," *American Political Science Review,* 70, (March, 1976) pp. 101–113, and "Presidential Influence in the Senate: Presidential Prestige as a Source of Presidential Power," *American Politics Quarterly,* 4 (October, 1977), pp. 481–500.

29. Edwards, "Presidential Influence in the House," pp. 101–106.

publican legislators.[30]   This suggests that Presidential addresses, speaking tours, and appearances directed at mobilizing support among partisans, activists, opinion leaders, and particular interest groups may be considerably more useful than an address to the general public in generating legislative support on key issues.[31]

Presidential addresses to the general public are perhaps more useful for broader goals such as building public confidence and dramatizing events. The confidence the public has in the President may not be directly related to Congressional support on specific issues, but it is relevant in two ways. When the President's standing in the polls is low, his bargaining position is weakened and opponents are less restrained about attacking his policies. More importantly, Presidential popularity is a key factor in how well the President's party does in the Congressional mid-term elections. In every mid-term election in this century, except one (1934), the President's party has lost seats in Congress. Losses in the House of Representatives have ranged from a low of 4 seats for the Democrats (in 1962) when Kennedy was President, to staggering losses such as 55 seats (in 1946) and 47 seats (in 1966) for the Democrats, and 48 seats (in 1958) and 43 seats (in 1974) for the Republicans. Other factors, particularly the state of the economy and fluctuations in voter turn-out, are important in explaining these losses, but Presidental popularity is strongly related to how many seats in Congress the President's party loses in the off-year elections.[32]

If the President has skill, timing, and a flair for the dramatic, he can use events to seize the initiative by focusing public and media attention on the need for specific legislation. President Johnson, for example, was able to use the events in and around Selma, Alabama,

---

30. *Ibid.,* pp. 105–113.

31. Holtzman reported that half the executive departments he surveyed utilized the technique of mobilizing interest-groups for legislative support. See Holtzman, *Legislative Liaison,* pp. 232–236.

32. Research by Edward R. Tufte showed that from 1944 to 1970 the correlation (r) between Presidential popularity and seats lost in Congress by the President's party was r=– .75. Tufte's regression equations indicate that for every percentage point the President drops in popularity, his party stands to lose about 1.2 seats in Congress in the upcoming mid-term election. See Edward R. Tufte, *Data Analysis for Politics and Policy.* Englewood Cliffs, N. J.: Prentice-Hall, Inc., 1974, pp. 74–77.

in 1964 to dramatize the need for a Federal voting rights law. After network television coverage captured the brutality of the Alabama state police in handling peaceful civil rights demonstrators, the President addressed a joint session of Congress that was televised nationwide during prime time. The President launched into one of his best addresses, outlining the needs for voting rights legislation. Speaking "for the dignity of man and the destiny of democracy," the President concluded to a thunderous ovation as he vowed, "we shall overcome."[33]   These events, and the President's skillful exploitation of them, undoubtedly contributed to the approval by Congress of the Voting Rights Act of 1965, a significant piece of Federal legislation since it resulted in dramatic increases in black voter registration and participation in the South.

Initiative and Veto

Although there are only a few constitutional powers granted to the President in the legislative arena, they are significant. Chief among them are the prerogatives to initiate legislation and budgets, and to veto acts of Congress. Less significant, and rarely used, is the power to call Congress into special session to consider proposals for dealing with specific problems. The Constitution, laws, and public expectations all provide sources of legislative initiative for the President. The Constitution permits the President to recommend legislation to Congress and requires him (Article II, Section 3) to address the Congress on the state of the Union. Other addresses and reports to the Congress are required by law, including the Economic Report and the Budget Message. In addition to clearly establishing the President's prerogative to make legislative proposals, these provisions permit the White House to create media events. Extensive television coverage is given to the State of the Union Address, as well as an assortment of speeches and special messages to Congress, and occasionally even a veto messge. The budget and economic reports help to set the legislative agenda and, consequently, receive detailed scrutiny by the printed media. Probably at least as important as these provisions is the now universal expectation on the part of the Congress, the media, and the public that the President will submit a legislative program to the Congress.

33. Kearns, *Lyndon Johnson and the American Dream*, pp. 238–240.

Initiative is strategically important because it assures that Presidential proposals will receive a hearing. Beyond that, however, it is easy to overestimate the importance of executive initiative in the legislative process. Congress itself is a significant source of legislation in domestic matters, especially when the minority party controls the Presidency.[34] In addition, the Congress frequently makes major modifications in executive proposals, as the fate of President Carter's energy and tax proposals amply demonstrated. Legislative initiative is not dominated by the President; it is shared not only with the Congress, but with the bureaucracy and major organized interests as well. Significant legislation is sometimes passed only after a long incubation period in Congress during which the proposal is kept alive until the public, the President, and a majority of Congress are ready to accept it.

After a bill is passed by Congress, the Constitution (Article I, Section 7) gives the President 10 working days to decide whether to sign it, let it become law without his signature, or veto it and return it, with his objections, to the house in which it originated. The Presidential veto may be used to stop objectionable legislation, but it is more frequently used as a threat to support the President's persuasive efforts in bargaining for an acceptable version of a bill. Backing up this threat is the fact that, on the average, Congress has been able to muster the two-thirds majority required to override Presidential vetoes only 3% of the time.[35] Presidents Kennedy and Johnson, in fact, had no vetoes overridden. A more realistic limitation on the veto is the fact that Presidents are usually reluctant to veto an entire bill to stop one or two objectionable provisions. The absence of an item veto strengthens the bargaining position of the Congress by requiring the President to accept, or reject, a bill in its entirety. Objectionable, and even extraneous, provisions (known as riders) are occasionally added by the Congress to legislation, particularly appropriations bills, to take advantage of this situation.

A survey of the veto records of Presidents since Franklin Roosevelt showed that Presidential use of the veto has decreased significantly,

34. Steven A. Shull, *Presidential Policy Making: An Analysis.* Brunswick, O.: King's Court Communication, 1979, pp. 68–69. Recent areas of Congressional leadership in domestic policy include water pollution, banking and commerce, campaign finance, women's rights, and taxation.

35. Jewell and Patterson, *Legislative Process in the United States,* pp. 253–254.

and that about 40% of Presidential vetoes were pocket vetoes.[36] These occur when Congress adjourns before the President has had the constitutionally required 10 working days to consider a bill. In that case, the President is free simply to put the bill "in his pocket" and ignore it. This happens on occasion because much legislation is passed in the last few days of a Congressional session during the last minute rush toward adjournment. If a bill is really significant, Congress can prevent a pocket veto simply by remaining in session a few days longer, as they did to prevent President Truman from utilizing the pocket veto to stop the Taft-Hartley Act.

CONGRESSIONAL OVERSIGHT OF THE EXECUTIVE BRANCH

The government's elected representatives have at their disposal three different means of overseeing and supervising the performance of the executive branch. These include authorization, appropriation, and investigation. While these are imperfect tools for monitoring behavior of an institution as complex as the executive branch, they are, nonetheless, significant sources of power in the perpetual struggle between Congress and the executive branch.

Authorization

In 1946, Congress passed the Legislative Reorganization Act, which empowered its standing committees with broad jurisdiction in executive oversight activities. Since that time, the acts of Congress prescribing the organization, authority, and programs of Federal agencies have become increasingly detailed.[37] These developments, in combination with its traditional budgetary powers and the constitutional authority to approve executive appointments, have given Congress even greater potential to influence or significantly modify, the direction of policy in executive agencies.

Congressional Vetoes   The growing reluctance of Congress to delegate broad authority without attaching strings to it has been manifested by an increasing reliance on the legislative veto. There

36. Shull, *Presidential Policy Making,* pp. 84–86.

37. Jewell and Patterson, *Legislative Process in the United States,* pp. 450–454.

are differing versions of Congressional vetoes, but all are directed at disallowing, overriding, or prohibiting actions of executive agencies. A common method is the one-house veto, which permits *either* house of Congress to reject an executive decision, as in the case of Presidential proposals to reorganize aspects of the Federal government. Congressional authority permitting President Carter to propose a gasoline-rationing plan contained this type of legislative veto. Some legislative vetoes are even more rigorous, requiring *both* houses of Congress to vote affirmatively on an executive action (the War Powers Resolution, for example). Others may even permit Congressional committees to veto programs of executive agencies before they are implemented.[38]

In addition to the increasing use of the legislative veto, Congressional authorization authority includes the power to modify, redefine, or terminate existing programs. In response to pressure from an assortment of commercial, manufacturing, and advertising interests Congress has, on occasion, changed both the jurisdiction and the regulatory authority of Federal agencies.[39]

Investigation

Detailed investigations of the activities of administrative agencies by legislative committees combine authorization (the power to recommend a change in the agency's authority) with the threat of bad publicity for the agency, since committee investigations receive extensive media coverage. A wide range of executive activities have been investigated, but undoubtedly the most spectacular committee

38. Louis Fisher, *The Constitution Among Friends: Congress, the President, and the Law.* New York: Saint Martin's Press, Inc., 1978, pp. 102–103.

39. For example: In 1963, Congress eliminated the Area Redevelopment Administration. See Randall B. Ripley, *Congress: Process and Policy* (2nd ed.) New York: W. W. Norton and Co., Inc., 1978, pp. 339–340. Another interesting case involves the Federal Trade Commission (FTC), one of the most consumer oriented of the Federal agencies. From 1965 to 1969, Congress prohibited the FTC from restricting the tobacco industry's cigarette advertisements on television. More recently, in response to growing pressure from commercial and advertising interests, the House passed legislation in 1979 (HR 2313) to restrict the authority of the FTC to regulate advertisers, and instituted a legislative veto over FTC actions. See *Congressional Quarterly Weekly Report,* December 8, 1979, p. 2278. The Environmental Protection Agency (EPA) has increasingly come under attack by corporate interests and utilities attempting to use the same tactics to curb the agency's regulatory power in the area of pollution control.

investigations were those during the Nixon administration. The Senate Select Committee on Presidential Campaign Activities (better known as the Watergate Committee) conducted televised hearings which included John Dean's remarkable performance and Alexander Butterfield's devastating revelation of the taping system in the White House. This was followed by an investigation by the Judiciary Committee of the House of Representatives that resulted in approval by the committee of articles of impeachment against President Nixon for obstruction of justice and violation of the constitutional rights of citizens. Within a few days, Richard Nixon became the first President to resign from office.

Executive Privilege The investigations of the Watergate affair and the subsequent impeachment hearings helped bring the issue of executive privilege sharply into focus. Executive privilege, while not formally articulated as a doctrine until the Eisenhower administration, refers to a traditional and long standing executive prerogative which permits the President to withhold sensitive information, including executive branch documents and communications, from Congress and Congressional committees. The considerable advantages already enjoyed by the executive branch in struggles with the Congress over control of information is enchanced by this doctrine.

Historically, executive privilege has been primarily a political, rather than a legal, question. Conflicts between Congress and the executive in this area have most often been resolved by a process of compromise and accommodation, with the executive providing at least part of the requested information.[40] Because the boundaries of executive privilege had not been clearly defined, it became a legal and constitutional issue, as well as a political question, during the Nixon administration when the President's bold claims of privilege pushed the doctrine to new heights. In addition to his refusal to permit White House assistants to testify before Congress, the President claimed that executive privilege could permit the withholding of information concerning a criminal investigation.

40. Three of the better and more concise accounts of the development and ramifications of the doctrine of executive privilege are: Robert G. Dixon, "Congress, Shared Administration, and Executive Privilege," in Harvey C. Mansfield (ed.), *Congress Against the President*. New York: Praeger Publishers, 1975, pp. 125–140; Richard M. Pious, *The American Presidency*. New York: Basic Books, Inc., 1979, pp. 351–354; and Arthur M. Schlesinger, Jr., *The Imperial Presidency*. Boston: Houghton Mifflin Co., 1973, pp. 156 ff.

The issue was clarified somewhat by the Supreme Court's decision in the case of *United States v. Nixon*.[41] The special prosecutor in the Watergate investigation subpoenaed several tapes of conversations between Nixon and his aides in the Oval Office. While the President claimed that the tapes, consisting of private conversations between the Chief Executive and his aides, were privileged information, the prosecutor insisted that the tapes were evidence in a criminal prosecution. The Supreme Court was unanimous in rendering a decision that, because of the damaging contents of the tapes, would ultimately force the President to resign. In addition to requiring the President to surrender the tapes, the Court maintained that executive privilege, while not absolute, did have a legitimate basis in the constitutional system because of the need for confidentiality in foreign relations and military matters.

In essence, the Court upheld the validity of executive privilege by defining some of its limits in the area of criminal law. For this reason, the decision has been described as a defeat for Nixon, but a victory for the Presidency.[42] Left largely unanswered were questions about conflict between the President's prerogative to keep information privileged and the responsibility of the Congress for oversight and investigation of executive activities. Presumably these questions remain largely a political matter to be resolved by a process of mutual accommodation between Congress and the President.[43]

Appropriation

Congressional prerogatives in the areas of raising revenue and spending Federal funds are protected by both constitutional provisions and tradition. A significant development in this area occurred in 1974 when Congress passed the Budget and Impoundment Control Act, which modified Congressional budgetary procedures. The President

41. 418 U.S. 683 (1974).

42. Dixon, "Congress, Shared Administration, and Executive Privilege," p. 183.

43. This is true for several reasons. First of all, the executive's prerogative to define the nature of privileged information is supported by law as well as by court decisions. The Freedom of Information Act, as amended in 1974 permits the President, by executive order, to exempt national security matters from disclosure. Likewise, the executive has at his disposal an elaborate classification system by which many government matters are classified as "secret," or even "top secret," at the discretion of executive officials. *Ibid.*, pp. 130–136.

retains the initiative in budgetary matters, but Congress, after detailed work by the Budget Committees, must pass resolutions establishing its own targets and ceilings for Federal spending. The Appropriations committees cannot exceed the ceilings unless Congress votes to change them. Political scientist, Larry Schwab, after studying the Federal budgetary process from 1975 to 1979, concluded that the new process has strengthened the position of Congress by mandating better coordination, encouraging more debate on national priorities, and permitting Congress to develop budgetary proposals significantly different from the President's in the area of social programs.[44] The Congress was able to use its budgetary power to force President Carter to make substantial cuts (in excess of $16 billion) in the proposed 1981 budget.

Another major provision in this law came in direct response to President Nixon's widespread use of impoundment of funds as a *de facto* item veto in appropriations matters. Impoundment refers to the refusal by the President to permit Federal agencies to spend funds that have been appropriated by Congress. In yet another use of the legislative veto, the 1974 budget law permits *either* house of Congress to override a deferral of program funds, and requires *both* houses to approve any Presidential cancellation (recision) of appropriated funds.

Despite these efforts by Congress, there inevitably remains a certain amount of slack in a budget as large as the Federal government's. Louis Fisher has described in detail the discretionary spending power available to the executive branch in his book *Presidential Spending Power.* Using a bewildering array of confidential funding systems, accounts can be juggled and funds transferred and reprogrammed to pay for operations that the Congress does not know about, much less approve. Included in these processes are an indeterminate amount of secret funds (unknown even to Congress) used mostly for intelligence operations.[45]

44. Schwab, *Changing Patterns of Congressional Politics,* pp. 49–60.

45. See Louis Fisher, *Presidential Spending Power.* Princeton, N.J.: Princeton University Press, 1975, pp. 75–122, 202–228. Allowing for inflation since Fisher's 1975 investigation, the amount of money involved probably exceeds $20 billion, not a large percentage of the total Federal budget, but certainly a significant amount of funds.

CONCLUSION

The 20th century has seen the Presidency increase in importance and power as the national government has expanded in scope and as international relations have become increasingly important. In response to the challenge posed by a stronger Presidency and a larger and more complex executive branch, the Congress has moved to reassert its traditional role as an independent and equal partner in the American constitutional system. By modernizing its budgetary procedures, Congress has increased its potential for developing budgetary proposals significantly different from the President's. Through increasing reliance on the legislative veto and detailed administrative guidelines in legislation, Congress now has greater capacity for executive oversight. Perhaps most importantly, in the midst of a constitutional crisis, the Congress demonstrated an apparent willingness to impeach the President, if necessary. These recent developments, combined with more traditional sources of Congressional power and independence, such as the system of decentralized committees and local nominations and elections, assure that the Congress will not be dominated by the President.

The independence of Congress is not without its price. In recent years, Presidential-Congressional relations have more frequently been characterized by deadlock than by Presidential domination.[46] A key question for American politics and society in the 1980's is not if the Congress can restrain the President, but rather if a political stalemate can be avoided on controversial issues. Energy policy and economic management are complex and interrelated issues that are likely to prove especially challenging for government decision makers. Policy alternatives in these areas are likely to be politically unpopular, requiring sacrifices by the public and reduction of energy consumption. Whether the President and Congress can muster the commitment and cooperation necessary to produce effective policies in these areas remains to be seen.

46. See Jewell and Patterson, *The Legislative Process in the United States,* Ch. II, especially pp. 259–275.

FURTHER READING

Fisher, Louis. *President and Congress: Power and Policy.* New York: The Free Press, 1973. An examination of how Congress and the President share four types of power: legislative, spending, taxing, and war-making.

Holtzman, Abraham. *Legislative Liaison: Executive Leadership in Congress.* Chicago: Rand McNally and Company, Inc., 1970. A thorough study of the organization and strategy of Congressional liaison at both the departmental and White House level.

Jewell, Malcolm E., and Patterson, Samuel C. *The Legislative Process in the United States* (3rd ed.). New York: Random House, Inc., 1977. The authoritative text on the organization and functioning of American legislatures.

Ripley, Randal B., and Franklin, Grace A. *Congress, the Bureaucracy, and Public Policy.* Homewood, Ill.: Dorsey Press. An analysis of the complex interactions between Congress and the Federal bureaucracy in the policy making process.

Schwab, Larry M. *Changing Patterns of Congressional Politics.* New York: D. Van Nostrand Company, 1980. An up-to-date, concise, and readable analysis of the politics of the Congress.

Chapter 9

The Pinnacle:
National Security Policy

It is a fundamental axiom of international politics that nations seek security rather than peace. This is necessitated by the organization of the international political system. Nation-states, which constitute the basic units of international politics, interact with one another under conditions of anarchy. The international political system potentially approximates Thomas Hobbes' state of nature—the war of all against all. Since there is no sovereign to impose stability amidst the chaos, any order that develops within the international system results fortuitously as states pursue policies of perceived self-interest. In this system, peace is simply the temporary absence of conflict. Peace is not a primary objective, but it is occasionally a by-product of attempts by nation-states to maximize their power and enhance their security.

In the threatening environment of international anarchy, nation-states have sought security through creation and maintenance of a system of countervailing powers. By following balance-of-power strategies in foreign policy, nation-states are able to resist attempts by other states to dominate the international system. Nation-states seek security by maximizing their military power and by participating in networks of alliances to balance the power of other states and alliance systems.

Pursuit of balance-of-power policies does not totally explain the behavior of states in international politics. Although nations engage

in power-politics out of necessity, their behavior is frequently justified ideologically. In an era of mass mobilization and potential total
war, ideological crusades can assist leaders in generating popular support by providing a moral basis for the exercise of power. Throughout
the Cold War era, the role of anti-Communist ideology in American
policy was primarily to mobilize Congressional and public support
for policies once they had been decided upon. Ideology is, however,
more than simply a means for justifying power-politics.   Over a period
of time, ideological assumptions affect the content and direction of
policy by limiting the options available to decision makers. In the
United States during the Cold War period, certain policy alternatives
were politically risky and others unacceptable because national
security policy makers had been so successful in cultivating fervent
anti-Communist beliefs among Congressmen and the public. Moreover, it is apparent that some policy makers, including the President,
eventually came to believe their own rhetoric. President Lyndon
Johnson, for example, was genuinely sincere in his attempts to "save
South Vietnam" from the Communists, although it is questionable
whether such a massive commitment was in any way necessitated by
American security interests. In an institutional setting as personalized
as the Presidency, the personality of the President inevitably affects
which alternatives are considered, or rejected, in national security
policy making.

In brief, the necessity in international politics for each nation-
state to pursue its own security interests through diplomacy, alliances,
and military strength results in a scramble for power. The pursuit
of international power is justified ideologically as a means of generating political support. It is in the interests of each state that no single
nation, or alliance, dominates the international political system. For
these reasons, states seek to protect their security interests by adopting foreign policies which contribute to the establishment and maintenance of a balance of power in international politics. As the
distribution of international power changes, states modify their
foreign policies in an attempt to restore a balance. Due to considerations of domestic politics, political ideology, and the personalities of
leaders, the conduct of American foreign policy has, on occasion,
contrasted sharply with the conduct required by the state system.[1]

1.   A highly regarded power politics interpretation of American foreign policy
     is John Spanier's *American Foreign Policy since World War II* (8th ed.).
     New York: Holt Rinehart and Winston, 1980. See pp. 1–49.

PRESIDENTIAL PRIMACY IN NATIONAL SECURITY AFFAIRS

Presidential primacy in American national security policy is a matter of historical record. The Chief Executive generally does not dominate foreign policy to the total exclusion of other political actors, but the President is the most influential individual in American foreign policy-making. The President has the largest share of formal powers in national security affairs, including control of diplomacy and military policy. In addition, the conduct of foreign relations within the state system has requirements that are most compatible with features of executive power. Successful implementation of foreign policy requires speed, unity, and, on occasion, secrecy. None of these traits is characteristic of legislative deliberation. National security planning requires detailed information, expertise, and analysis—again attributes of the executive branch. Rapid changes in technology, particularly in nuclear weapons systems, have heightened the advantages of the executive by increasing the importance of a speedy and unified response. Long before the development of systems of rapid communication and sophisticated nuclear weapons, the framers of the Constitution recognized the primacy of the executive in foreign affairs. Although creating a system of shared powers, the Constitution grants the most significant diplomatic and military powers to the President. The tendency toward Presidential primacy has been continually reinforced by statute, tradition, and popular expectations.

The President has generally faced considerably fewer constraints in national security decision making than in domestic politics. This may be explained partly by the dependence of Congress on the executive for information about national security affairs, but it seems mainly to be part of an historical pattern of Congressional deference to executive judgment in national security matters. Presidential primacy has been the rule rather than the exception in national security policy. Under the leadership of Theodore Roosevelt and Woodrow Wilson, the United States emerged as a significant power in world politics. This period of strong Presidential leadership in national security policy lasted from the turn of the century until 1919. With the rejection by the Senate of American entry into the League of Nations, the United States entered a period of relative isolation which lasted from 1920 until about 1939. During this period, American foreign policy was directed mainly at influencing events in the Western Hemisphere, particularly the Caribbean.

Eventually, conflicts among European powers forced the United States, for reasons of its own security, to abandon isolationism. Policies opposing the expansion of Nazi Germany began to take shape under the leadership of President Franklin Roosevelt. Inextricably, the United States was drawn into another world war. The totality of the conflict and the American determination to batter the Germans and the Japanese into unconditional surrender placed the President at the head of another moral crusade. Executive authority was pushed to new heights as the Congress delegated vast emergency powers which brought everything from agricultural commodities to transportation and communications under Federal control. The civilian labor force was integrated into the war effort. Sweeping authority was granted to executive agencies for preventive detention and control of internal security, seizure of private property, stockpiling of strategic materials, and suppression of information. Most, but not all, of Franklin Roosevelt's wartime proclamations rested on statutory authority. Congress had been more than willing to grant the President adequate emergency powers.

Although World War II ended, the emergency did not. What ensued was a Cold War—a war of nerves—between the United States and the Soviet Union. The loss of Eastern Europe and China to Communist control created, in the view of the national political leadership, a continuing national security emergency. A permanent state of confrontation with monolithic Communism became the dominant paradigm of American national security policy. Delegation of statutory authority to the executive continued in an atmosphere of perpetual crisis. For example, the President was empowered, under Title II of the Internal Security Act of 1950, to authorize, during time of internal security emergency, the apprehension and detention of persons likely to engage in, or *conspire* to engage in, espionage and sabotage.[2]

In brief, the postwar era has been, until recently, a period of Presidential domination of national security affairs. This period of executive dominance, lasting from the end of World War II until roughly 1973, was characterized by little Congressional initiative

2. John Malcolm Smith and Cornelius P. Cotter, *Powers of the President during Crisis*. Washington, D.C.: Public Affairs Press, 1960, p. 34.

in foreign policy and the near absence of Congressional participation in decisions regarding the use of American military force. The paramount role of the executive in the initiation of national security policy was institutionalized by the creation, since 1947, of machinery for that purpose. The practice of large-scale Presidential war making was supported, or tolerated, by the Congress as a means for implementing national security objectives.

The President's Powers in National Security Affairs

The Constitution permits the President to conduct diplomatic relations. The President is empowered to deal with representatives of foreign governments by sending and receiving ambassadors. Implicit in this, and reinforced by custom, is the President's power to grant diplomatic recognition of foreign governments by receiving their ambassadors. The President can terminate diplomatic relations with a foreign government by withdrawing American diplomatic personnel. Equally as significant is the President's power to appoint and remove policy makers within the executive branch, including not only diplomats and ambassadors, but important national security personnel as well. Included among Presidential appointees are the Adviser for National Security Affairs, the head of the Central Intelligence Agency, military advisers, and top-level personnel in the Departments of State and Defense.

The President's control of top-level diplomatic, military, and national security positions is reinforced by the executive's advantages in having access to classified information and intelligence and having the expertise required to interpret it. An elaborate intelligence and communications network, computer storage and retrieval of data, and detailed analysis by Defense and State Department personnel are at the President's fingertips. As events unfold rapidly during a crisis, access to the resources of the executive and military bureaucracies contributes to the President's ability to determine government policy.

Fundamental to executive primacy in national security policy is the President's constitutional position as Commander in Chief of the armed forces. Article II, section 2, of the Constitution states simply:

The President shall be Commander in Chief of the Army

and Navy of the United States, and the Militia of the several States, when called into the actual Service of the United States ....

The Commander in Chief clause is at least as significant for what it does not say as for what it does say. While constitutional scholars disagree on the exact meaning of this clause, it has most frequently been interpreted, partcularly by executive officials, as a grant of inherent power to the President. Stated differently, the Constitution has created an office—the Commander in Chief—but has not clearly defined, or limited, the duties and powers of that office. This constitutional ambiguity adds considerable flexibility to government policymaking by permitting the President freedom to act in national security matters, particularly during a crisis. The potential for expansion of the President's powers as Commander in Chief, in the absence of clearly defined limits, has raised serious constitutional questions about the proper limits of executive authority.

The Constitution attempts to maintain some balance between the President and Congress by requiring the President's appointments to be approved by majority vote of the Senate. Likewise, treaties negotiated by executive department personnel require consent of two-thirds of the Senate. Executive agreements between the President and another head of state do not require Senate approval and are, therefore, being used with increasing frequency. Most executive agreements encompass relatively routine matters, but some are of considerable significance for national security policy, such as the agreement President Franklin Roosevelt made with England in 1940. In what became known as the Destroyer Deal, the President traded 50 American ships in exchange for leases of British naval bases in the Caribbean. This represented another step in an American commitment to Britain's defense and possible American involvement in World War II. President Nixon used executive agreements to end American participation in the Vietnam War and to implement a 5-year freeze on offensive nuclear weapons as part of his negotiating strategy to obtain a Strategic Arms Limitation Treaty (SALT I).[3]

Although the President is designated as Commander in Chief, the Congress is given the authority to declare war and to appropriate

3. John Spanier and Eric M. Uslaner, *How American Foreign Policy Is Made.* New York: Praeger Publishers, 1974, p. 45. Constitutional scholar Louis Fisher reported that well over 5,000 executive agreements were negotiated between 1940 and 1970. See Louis Fisher, *President and Congress.* New York: The Free Press, 1972, pp. 44–47.

public funds for maintenance of the armed forces. However, the ability of the Commander in Chief to *initiate* war has undermined Congressional authority to declare war. The prerogative of the President to initiate war was established as early as 1846 when President James K. Polk ordered General Zachary Taylor's troops into disputed territory along the Rio Grande. Not surprisingly, the Mexican government took offense at the presence of foreign soldiers and responded militarily. President Polk then asked the Congress to recognize the *existence* of war by virtue of Mexico's attack. The Congress responded overwhelmingly as the President asked, declaring war for only the second time in American history. Former President John Quincy Adams, then serving in Congress, warned that "the President of the United States has but to declare that war exists, with any nation upon Earth, by the act of that Nation's government, and the war is essentially declared."[4]

Although the Congress has declared war only 5 times (1812, 1846, 1898, 1917, and 1941), the President has dispatched American combat forces into action well over 100 times. In this century alone, American Presidents have sent United States combat forces into action, without a declaration of war, in China, Siberia, Mexico, the Caribbean, Korea, Lebanon, the Dominican Republic, Vietnam, Cambodia, and Iran. Included in these interventions were two major wars in Korea and Vietnam.

In the course of protecting American security interests, Presidents have frequently taken action as Commander in Chief which increased the likelihood of military conflicts with foreign governments. When, for example, the Germans adopted a policy of unrestricted submarine warfare in an attempt to strangle England, President Wilson's response was to arm American merchant ships. Before the United States became a combatant in World War II, President Roosevelt began to provide British ships with escorts by American naval vessels, ordering Navy commanders to attack German submarines on sight. In response to the Russian blockade of Berlin in 1948, President Truman ordered an American airlift of supplies into West Berlin until the blockade was lifted. In October, 1962, in what was potentially a nuclear confrontation, President Kennedy ordered a naval blockade of the island of Cuba to force the Soviet Union to remove medium-range ballistic missiles they had installed.

4. Cited in R. Gordon Hoxie, *Command Decision and the Presidency: A Study in National Security Policy and Organization.* New York: Reader's Digest Press, 1977, p. 9.

National Security Policy Making

In many respects, the foundations of present-day national security policies, and the institutions for their implementation, were essentially the work of the Truman and Eisenhower administrations. The modern executive national security apparatus began to take shape in 1947. With the passage of the National Security Act (as amended in 1949 and 1953), the formulation and virtual authorization of military programs passed to the national security agencies. The machinery established by the Congress was intended to provide a framework for essential decisions on designing, building, and maintaining a modern nuclear retaliatory force, updating the continental defense system, and formulating national strategy.[5] For the next 20 years, Congress seldom challenged executive primacy in national security affairs.

The National Security Act, as amended, was aimed at unifying the defense establishment and creating machinery to advise the President in national security matters. The Department of Defense was created, bringing the separate branches of the military services within a single administrative department. The Air Force was established as a separate military branch distinct from the Army, and the Central Intelligence Agency was created. In an effort to provide some coordination between the foreign, military, and defense policies, the National Security Council (NSC) was established. It consists of the President, the Vice President, the Secretary of State, and the Secretary of Defense. The head of the CIA and the Chairman of the Joint Chiefs of Staff are advisers to the NSC, along with any other individuals whose advice the President may require. A major objective of Congress in establishing the National Security Council was to ensure that the relevant officials and agencies would be included, or, at least, consulted, in national security decision making. During World War II, Franklin Roosevelt had employed a freewheeling style of decision making, wherein the choice of which officials to incorporate into decisions was a matter of Presidential discretion.

Except for the President, Vice President, and Secretary of State, all of this national security machinery has been created since 1947. This is not to suggest that each of these components is equally significant in formulating policy; only that Congress considered national security problems of sufficient importance to create the machinery. In practice, the NSC has seldom been as influential as its name would imply. Except for Eisenhower, Presidents have frequently circum-

5.   *Ibid.,* pp. 11–32.

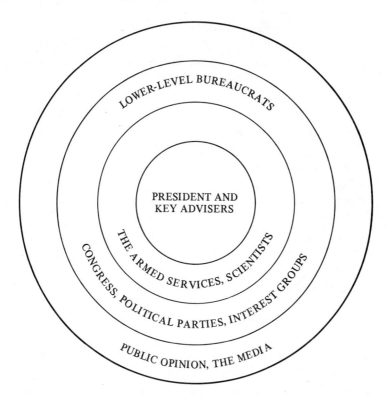

Figure 9.1 The concentric circles of power in foreign policy decision making.
Source: John Spanier and Eric M. Uslaner, *How American Foreign Policy Is Made*. New York: Praeger Publishers, 1974, p. 55. Used with the permission of the publisher.

vented the Council by excluding some members from the inner circle and by including advisers who are not members of the NSC, particularly the increasingly important Adviser for National Security Affairs.

The decision making process in foreign policy has been described as a set of four concentric circles.[6] As depicted in Fig. 9.1, the innermost circle includes those who make the major decisions about American foreign policy—the President and his closest advisers. Each of the three remaining circles has successively less impact on national security policy. The second circle is composed of the foreign policy and military bureaucracies, and Presidential advisers and Cabinet secretaries who are not in the inner circle, but who may be consulted. The bureaucracies function to provide information and

6. Spanier and Uslaner, *How American Foreign Policy Is Made*, pp. 54–97.

analysis, and to implement decisions made by the inner circle. Possessing the expertise to collect and analyze intelligence, the bureaucracies make policy recommendations to the inner circle. In the opinion of some analysts, the inner circle has more often given serious consideration to the recommendations of the Defense Department than to those of the State Department.[7] In addition to providing information and policy recommendations, the bureaucracies handle the day-to-day implementation of decisions in foreign and military policy, exercising discretion in routine matters.

The Congress, in addition to delegating considerable discretionary authority to the executive, has, until recently, generally accepted Presidential leadership in defining national security goals and policies. The Congress rarely initiated policy in national security matters, was frequently not consulted, and seldom complained about this arrangement. From 1959 until 1968, Congress never cut Presidential requests for the Department of Defense budget by more than 4%, occasionally, as in 1961, appropriating more than the President requested. On the average, between 1948 and 1964, Presidents were successful in gaining Congressional approval 70% of the time for proposals in the area of foreign relations. Presidential proposals for domestic legislation were approved by Congress only about 40% of the time.[8] By and large, the role of Congress in postwar national security policy has been that of accepting, modifying, or rejecting Presidential proposals. In the wake of the imperial Presidency, the Congress has demonstrated renewed interest in participating in national security policy, enacting measures aimed at assuring consultation between Congress and the executive. This has caused concern among some analysts that this Congressional reaction, discussed below, will hamper the President's ability to formulate and implement effective national security policy.

Farthest removed from foreign policy decision making is public opinion, regarded by many analysts primarily as a result, rather than a cause, of policy. Public opinion on foreign policy questions is notoriously unstable. Many citizens have no opinions on numerous issues, while others have different views on the same issue at various times. As the rally-round-the-flag effect has demonstrated repeatedly,

7. *Ibid.*, p. 64.

8. Aaron Wildavsky, "The Two Presidencies," in Aaron Wildavsky (ed.), *The Presidency*. Boston: Little Brown and Co., 1969, pp. 230–243. See, especially, Table 1, p. 231.

public opinion responds to international conflict and crisis in a manner generally favorable to the President. The President can usually count on public and Congressional support during a crisis. Support for military intervention will likely be initially high, but may decline as the costs and casualties begin to mount. This was particularly true of America's first televised war, the Vietnam conflict. The effect of nightly nationwide media exposure of the escalating conflict was to increase the polarization of opinion about the war and to activate opposition to it.

The size and composition of the President's inner circle fluctuate considerably, depending upon the President's decision-making style. Generally, some, but not all, of the members of the National Security Council will be incorporated, the Vice President being the most likely to be excluded. Since the NSC was established, the influence of the Secretary of State has declined relative to the Secretary of Defense, and especially the Adviser for National Security Affairs. This is attributable partly to the preference of some Presidents to be their own Secretary of State, and partly to the increasing importance of the National Security Adviser. Enjoying the advantage of proximity and access to the President and total commitment to White House policy, this key adviser has played an increasingly important role in formulating policy.

Presidents Truman and Eisenhower permitted their Secretaries of State (Dean Acheson and John Foster Dulles) major roles in national security policy. In an effort to bring policy making under White House control, Presidents Kennedy, Johnson, and Nixon deliberately selected less forceful personalties as Secretary of State (Dean Rusk and William Rogers), enchancing the status of the National Security Adviser. During the Nixon years, Henry Kissinger was an especially forceful adviser in national security matters, Secretary of State Rogers' role being confined mostly to management of the State Department. When Kissinger was eventually elevated to the position of Secretary of State, he then occupied both positions, affirming his preeminence as the President's major national security adviser.

Because of President Carter's inexperience in foreign relations, Secretary of State Cyrus Vance was relatively influential early in the administration. An advocate of restraint and patience in international relations, Vance's influence diminished as a result of the Iranian crisis and the Soviet invasion of Afghanistan. At the time of the administration's approval of the attempt to rescue the American hostages in Iran, Secretary of State Vance, an opponent of the

plan, was not present. The National Security Council was convened to approve the plan while Vance was out of town. Not surprisingly, the Secretary resigned a short time later.

Crisis Decision Making, 1962: The Cuban Missile Crisis

The decisions made by the Kennedy administration during the
13 days of the Cuban missile crisis illustrate the primacy of the
President's inner circle during a national security crisis. On October 16, 1962, President Kennedy was informed by the Central
Intelligence Agency that Air Force photo reconnaissance had clearly
established the presence in Cuba of Soviet intermediate-range ballistic
missile launching facilities. It was estimated that the missile system
would be operational within a short time and have the capability of
delivering nuclear warheads to targets as far away as Chicago.

The President promptly convened a group of advisers to devise
a plan that would get the missiles out of Cuba before they were
operational. This group of advisers came to be known as the Executive
Committee of the National Security Council—the Ex Comm for short.

(Reproduced from the Collections of the Library of Congress)

In addition to the President and his brother, the Attorney General, prominent members included Secretary of Defense Robert McNamara, Secretary of State Dean Rusk, Treasury Secretary Douglas Dillon, and Foreign Policy Coordinator McGeorge Bundy. Each of these men had been involved in the Bay of Pigs fiasco a year and a half earlier. Other members of the Ex Comm included General Maxwell Taylor, CIA Director John McCone, White House staffer Theodore Sorensen, Soviet expert Llewellyn Thompson, Vice President Lyndon Johnson, and several high-ranking members of the State and Defense Departments.[9]

A diplomatic solution to this problem might have been possible. Removing obsolete American missiles from Turkey in exchange for withdrawal of the Soviet missiles in Cuba was one suggestion, but the President rejected this approach. Time was short, and once the system was operational, it would be considerably more difficult to persuade the Russians to dismantle it. Moreover, the President had a point to make with Soviet leader Khrushchev. The fact that the Russians had been so bold as to move their missiles 90 miles from the American mainland, apparently expecting no response beyond ineffective diplomatic protests, was regarded by the President as a dangerous sign. Perhaps Khrushchev was beginning to believe that the United States would no longer fight to protect its interests. Such a belief was dangerous because it increased the possibility of war by miscalculation. Failure to respond forcefully, the President concluded, would only increase Soviet pressure on Europe, especially in Berlin.[10]

Kennedy decided to proceed deliberately, hoping to find a way for Khrushchev to back down gracefully. There would be no compromise, no diplomatic shenanigans by the Russians—only a clear message that the United States would not tolerate offensive missiles in Cuba. This fundamental decision to force the Russians to remove their missiles rather than to negotiate a compromise was exclusively the President's, as was the responsibility for the consequences. Critics have contended that Kennedy unnecessarily escalated the situation into a crisis. From the President's perspective, however, America's resolve was being tested, and the outcome would have worldwide ramifications.

9. Irving L. Janis, *Victims of Groupthink: A Psychological Study of Foreign Policy Decisions and Fiascoes.* Boston: Houghton Mifflin Co., 1972, p. 140.

10. Spanier, *American Foreign Policy since World War II,* p. 23.

For 5 days, the Ex Comm met continuously. According to participants' accounts of the meetings, the committee proceeded carefully
and deliberately, canvassing a wide range of alternatives. The President was careful to avoid dominating the meetings, encouraging the
frank exchange of ideas and debate of alternatives. The President
went so far as to institute "leaderless sessions"—meetings of the Ex
Comm at which the President was absent—to encourage more give
and take. Special attention was given to examining the risks and
benefits of various alternatives, and to anticipating the Russian
response.

Although numerous alternatives were discussed (including a
military conquest of Cuba), the most serious consideration was given
to a naval blockade of Cuba to prevent Russian ships from bringing
in missiles and equipment, or an air strike to destroy the missile
sites. The air strike option had a considerable disadvantage in that
Russian technicians might be killed. Enthusiasm for this option
diminished further when the Air Force was unable to assure the
President that a surgical air strike could knock out all the missiles.
To be completely effective, the air strike would require a follow-up
invasion by Marines. An air strike was nevertheless the preference of
two influential Senators with whom the President consulted.

The naval blockade had the advantage of forcefully communicating American concern to the Russians without inevitably pre-
cipitating a military confrontation. It had the additional benefit
of permitting the Russians time to resolve the difficulty they had
initiated. If moderation failed, the level of American force could
easily be escalated.

On October 22, President Kennedy announced to the world
that the island of Cuba had been "quarantined" and that no ships
carrying missiles, or related equipment, would be permitted in the
quarantine zone, which extended to a radius of 800 miles from the
island. The Congress was informed of this decision only a short time
before the public. After the President announced the blockade, he
continued his efforts to avoid putting Khrushchev into a box. In
order to give the Russian leader more time, the President reduced
the radius of the blockade from 800 to 500 miles. On October 25,
several Russian ships turned around and headed back out to sea
before entering the quarantine zone.

Although the blockade was a military success in the sense that the
Russians elected not to challenge the United States Navy in its own
backyard, the missiles were still in Cuba. Before escalating the con-

frontation, the President sent additional warnings to the Soviet Union, reiterating that the only way to end the crisis was to remove the missiles. Khrushchev indicated that he was favorably disposed if the United States was willing to make some concessions.[11] The crisis was resolved on October 28, when Kennedy and Khrushchev agreed that if the Soviet Union would dismantle and remove its missiles, the United States would agree not to invade Cuba.

CONTAINMENT AND PRESIDENTIAL WAR

In addition to Presidential primacy, a second distinguishing feature of American postwar national security policy has been a tenacious commitment to containment of Communism. The total defeat of Germany during World War II fundamentally changed the balance of power in Europe. The most powerful European country had been eliminated, temporarily, as a political and military force. Much of the remainder of Europe was in ruins after 6 years of total war. The geographic insulation of the United States from this massive destruction, along with American development of the atomic bomb, elevated the United States to the status of a great power. For domestic political reasons, the United States elected to demobilize its armed forces immediately following World War II and was not in an optimum position for the postwar confrontation with the Soviet Union. In May 1945, the United States had an army of 3.5 million men in Europe. Within a year, the United States had withdrawn all but 400,000 troops and had reduced personnel in the Air Corps and Navy as well.[12]

The Soviet Union, which emerged from World War II as the world's other great power, began a policy of postwar expansionism. Much of Eastern Europe was already occupied by the Red Army as a result of the conflict with Germany. In the nations they controlled militarily, the Russians proceeded to establish pro-Soviet governments.

When the Soviet policy of "defensive expansionsim" (the creation of satellite governments) was transformed into expansionist pressure on Greece and Turkey, the United States was obliged to respond. This situation was compounded by the inability of Britain to meet its traditional obligations in that area. American policy-

11. Janis, *Victims of Groupthink*, p. 145.

12. Spanier, *American Foreign Policy since World War II*, p. 23.

makers belatedly came to the realization that the United States was the only nation with military strength capable of balancing Soviet power. The realities of Soviet postwar foreign policy necessitated the development of a new American strategy.

Soviet expert George Kennan's analysis suggested that the West was to be continually confronted by Soviet pressure. The appropriate response, Kennan suggested, was a policy of "long term, patient, but firm and vigilant, containment."[13]   The pattern of *ad hoc* response to crises was replaced by a more coherent and unified approach aimed at the containment of the Soviet Union. This assumption would dominate American national security policy for the next 25 years, in the process becoming distorted into knee-jerk anti-Communism that would involve the United States in conflicts having little to do with the containment of Soviet expansionism.

The Truman Doctrine

It was in this atmosphere of Cold War that President Harry Truman formulated what became known as the Truman Doctrine. Before a joint session of Congress on March 12, 1947, the President outlined the basis of the American response to post World War II realities. The Truman Doctrine emphasized that it must be the policy of the United States "to support free peoples who are resisting attempted subjugation by armed minorities or outside pressure," and that American help should be primarily economic aid which was essential to economic and political stability.[14]   The Truman Doctrine was implemented by massive economic aid to Europe and a system of military alliances for collective security. The President requested, and received, from the Congress a major commitment of American economic and military aid. Although this included $400 million in aid to Greece and Turkey, the primary focus of the containment policy was in Europe. National security planners shared the assumption that the security of the United States was closely linked to the economic and political independence of Western Europe. To permit Soviet domination of the Continent would disrupt the world balance of power and endanger American security. European economic recovery was critical to stabilizing the situation.

The centerpiece of the Truman administration's efforts to pro-

13. *Ibid.,* p. 26.

14. *Ibid.,* p. 28.

mote European economic recovery was the Marshall Plan, proposed by Secretary of State George C. Marshall in a commencement address at Harvard University in June, 1947. The plan to rebuild Europe's economies consisted, not of loans, but of direct grants of American aid. There was no other way to achieve rapidly the objective of restoration of European economic health essential to political stability and military strength. The Congress was generally supportive of the idea, and the Communist take over of Czechoslovakia in 1948 encouraged the United States to speed up economic aid for Europe. In the next 3 years, the European Recovery Program cost the United States more than $10 billion.[15] It is unlikely that the American government has ever made a better investment.

The Truman administration's efforts at containment were not confined to economic aid. An elaborate system of alliances was created during this period, which still constitutes the basis of American efforts at collective security. Early in 1948, President Truman began to encourage American membership in the North Atlantic Treaty Organization. With the aid of Republican Senator Arthur Vandenberg, the President began building bipartisan Senate support for the NATO alliance. The Communists again obliged the President by dramatizing the need for collective security. This time the pressure was in Berlin. The city, which is jointly administered by the Russians and the Western allies, is 110 miles inside the Soviet-controlled sector of Germany. On June 24, 1948, the Soviets initiated a blockade of Berlin in an effort to force the Western allies out of the city. As President Truman assessed it, the Berlin crisis was a test of strength with implications for all of Western Europe. Since the Russians had closed the land corridor to the Western zones of the city, the allies supplied West Berlin for more than 10 months by means of a massive airlift. With this added incentive of direct Soviet military pressure on Western Europe, the NATO alliance was signed on April 4, 1949. It was the first alliance between the United States and European powers in 170 years.[16]

Initially, the Truman administration's policy of containment proved successful. Europe was revived economically and militarily,

15. Hoxie, *Command Decision and the Presidency*, p. 74.

16. *Ibid.*, p. 75. The original members of NATO included the United States, Canada, Great Britain, France, the Netherlands, Belgium, Luxembourg, Denmark, Norway, Iceland, Italy, and Portugal. The Federal Republic of Germany became a member in 1954.

constituting a formidable barrier against further Western Soviet expansion. In the long run, containment would prove more workable in Europe than in Asia, especially as the emphasis shifted increasingly from economic to military assistance.

Korea

At the end of World War II, after the surrender of Japan, Korea was temporarily divided at the 38th parallel, a division which eventually became permanent when the United States and Russia were unable to agree on reunification. On June 25, 1950, the Communist government of North Korea, with Soviet encouragement and armaments, decided to reunify the country by military force. The invasion of South Korea took American national security planners by surprise. The Truman administration regarded this invasion by North Korea as an instance of *Soviet* aggression and decided to respond militarily, even though the United States had earlier indicated that Korea was outside of the American defense perimeter.[17]

The decisions made by the Truman administration, which involved the United States in the Korean conflict, are illustrative not only of the ability of the President to initiate and expand a war, but also of the acquiescence of the Congress in national security policy. Within 24 hours after the North Korean invasion, the U.N. Security Council had passed a resolution demanding the withdrawal of North Korean forces from South Korea. That same afternoon President Truman had dinner with his principal national security advisers. The President, who was not enthusiastic about the National Security Council, did not convene that body.[18]

Two days later, June 27, the President, for the first time, met with Congressional leaders to discuss the Korean situation. The United States intended to defend Korea, Truman said, and this action was in response to a U.N. Security Council resolution. In reality, this statement by the President was less than candid. The second Security Council resolution to which he referred, drafted by the United States, and calling for U.N. members to render assistance to South Korea to repel the armed attack, was still being debated in the U.N. at the time.

17. Spanier, *American Foreign Policy since World War II*, p. 60.

18. Those in attendance at this dinner were Secretary of State Acheson, Secretary of Defense Johnson, the Joint Chiefs of Staff, and several high-ranking State Department officials.   See Hoxie, *Command Decision and the Presidency*, p. 90.

It is apparent from the sequence of events that the decision to intervene was made first, and that the U.N. resolution subsequently became the excuse for the intervention. The same day, the President ordered American air and naval forces to provide air cover and support for South Korean troops. When this proved ineffective in turning the tide, the President decided, 4 days later, to commit American ground combat forces. Following this decision, the President met with a Congressional delegation, informed them of his decision, and found general support.[19]

Under the fiction of a U.N. police action, President Truman launched America's first great Presidential war. Far from being content to restore the peace by repelling aggression, the President soon expanded the conflict into a major war involving the Chinese. Within 3 months, the U.N. forces, composed largely of American soldiers, had pushed the North Korean forces out of South Korea. The status quo had been restored, and a negotiated settlement would conceivably have restored peace. At this point, the Truman administration fundamentally altered American policy and, by so doing, escalated the conflict into a major war, prolonging the conflict for two and a half more years.

Initially, the war had been fought to restore South Korea's independence. This goal was abandoned in light of the favorable military situation, and the United States decided to attempt to unify Korea by military force. The Truman administration was provided with a rare opportunity to overrun North Korea and put the entire country under the control of the pro-American South Korean government. Containment was abandoned; conquest of North Korea became the administration's new goal. This decision was destined, in the words of General Omar Bradley, to involve the United States in "the wrong war, at the wrong place, at the wrong time, and with the wrong enemy."[20]

United States forces crossed the 38th parallel and struck into North Korea. With the Communist forces in retreat, American troops advanced north through Korea in the direction of China. In retrospect, there appears to have been abundant evidence that this policy would provoke a reaction from China. Throughout the fall of 1950, the Chinese had repeatedly warned the United States, publicly and through private diplomatic channels, that they would not tolerate

19. *Ibid.*, pp. 90–92.

20. Cited in Janis, *Victims of Groupthink*, p. 57.

American intervention in North Korea. Truman's national security advisers, regarding China as militarily weak, concluded that the Chinese warnings were a bluff. Within a few weeks after the American entry into North Korea, the Chinese retaliated. On November 28, 1950, the Chinese Army attacked in massive numbers, routing the American forces. The Chinese, inflicting a major defeat on General Douglas MacArthur's forces, soon pushed the Americans out of North Korea and nearly off the Korean peninsula. After months of bitter fighting, the American forces again advanced to the 38th parallel. From this point on, the war became essentially a stalemate until a truce was finally negotiated.

The response by President Truman to the Korean situation established two significant precedents in American national security policy. First, the Truman administration had equated military action by a Soviet ally as tantamount to Soviet aggression, and, therefore, a threat to the containment policy and requiring a response. This was the genesis of a subtle shift in the containment policy, which would increasingly justify American military involvement worldwide in opposition to Communism. The assumption that Communism was a monolithic entity controlled from Moscow would continue to haunt American national security policy long after Communist unity had begun to break down. The second precedent established by Truman's Korean policy was the launching of a large-scale Presidential war justified by bold claims of inherent powers as Commander in Chief. In the President's judgment, American national security interests required a military response; therefore, he initiated one. The President, and the President alone, would decide when a military response was appropriate to assure the integrity of the containment policy. It had become an accepted premise of national security policy that the President was acting within his constitutional authority whenever he initiated a war. An equally important lesson of the Korean War—the limitations of American power and the inadvisability of American involvement in a land war in Asia—would have to be relearned through seven more years of fighting in Vietnam.

The lessons of Korea were not lost on President Dwight Eisenhower. During his two terms, the President was intent on "waging peace." The General, being more realistic about military power than many civilian national security planners, was determined to avoid becoming involved in another land war in Asia. No sooner was the Korean War concluded than pressure began to mount for American involvement in the Indochina War. In the spring of 1954, the French garrison at Dien Bien Phu came under siege by Communist forces. With the French on the brink of defeat, close advisers to the President, including Chairman of the Joint Chiefs of Staff Radford and Secretary of State Dulles, recommended American air strikes to assist the French. Strategic Air Command General Curtis Le May concurred. The President was more cautious and was not prepared to intervene in Southeast Asia without Congressional and allied support. Finding neither, the President did not commit American forces. [21]

President Eisenhower elected to plan national security policy on the basis of American strengths, which were air power and strategic nuclear superiority. The Eisenhower administration relied primarily on a policy of deterrence—discouraging Soviet aggression by threat of massive nuclear retaliation. The President, utilizing this nuclear umbrella to protect America and its allies, was able to avoid major military interventions. Essentially, Eisenhower had rejected the idea that there could be a military solution to the Cold War. [22]

Vietnam

National security planners during the Kennedy/Johnson era did not share Eisenhower's realistic assumptions about the limitations of American power. Deterrence of a Soviet attack on the United States or its European allies was seen as too modest a goal for the most powerful nation on earth. America, they felt, must have the capability to respond to the Communist challenge anywhere in the world. Mas-

21. David Halberstam, *The Best and the Brightest*. Greenwich, Conn.: Fawcett Publications, Inc., 1972, pp. 169–180. In the spring of 1954, Gen. Matthew Ridgway made a detailed inquiry into the logistical and manpower costs of an American commitment in Indochina. His conclusion: between 500,000 and 1,000,000 men, plus enormous construction and engineering costs, and draft calls approaching 100,000 men per month. In addition, Ridgway's report emphasized the political nature of the war—especially that much of the population would likely side with the Communist insurgents. In May, 1954, shortly after the fall of Dien Bien Phu, Ridgway briefed President Eisenhower. According to Ridgway, "The idea of intervening was abandoned." Halberstam, p. 178.

22. See Stephen E. Ambrose's evaluation of Eisenhower in *Rise to Globalism: American Foreign Policy, 1938–1976*. New York: Penguin Books, 1976, pp. 217–271. The threat of massive retaliation was supplemented by economic and military aid, and by covert operations by the Central Intelligence Agency, which included the toppling of pro-Soviet governments in Iran (1953) and Guatemala (1954). See also Hoxie, pp. 293–294.

sive retaliation was out; "globalism," counter-insurgency, and anti-guerrilla warfare were in.

National security advisers of the Kennedy/Johnson era prided themselves on being a tough new breed, ready, even eager, to meet the challenges of the Cold War around the world. The reality was far different. The best and the brightest were academic strategists and systems-management experts who grossly overestimated American military capabilities. While President Eisenhower's goal had been to avoid war, the new breed determined that America must be able to fight two and a half wars at once: a major war in Europe, one in Asia, and a small brush war to boot.[23] With Europe reasonably secure, they believed that the showdown with Communism would come in the Third World, probably in Southeast Asia. An area of secondary importance to the United States' security interests had come to be seen symbolically as vital—as worth fighting for.

The choice of Vietnam as the theater of combat in which to confront Asian Communism proved to be a mistake. Far from demonstrating the superiority of American mechanized warfare over guerrilla tactics, this conflict proved just the opposite—that a mechanized Western army without popular support could not prevent a successful war of national liberation. South Vietnam was almost ideal for guerrilla warfare. The central government was not in control of the countryside and had little popular support. There was a substantial, and well-trained cadre of Vietcong guerrillas operating in the countryside. South Vietnam, which had been created by the 1954 Geneva agreement concluding the Indochina War, was essentially an artificial society in a state of civil war. The Geneva agreement called for an election to be held in 1956, the likely result of which would have been the unification of Vietnam under nationalist leader Ho Chi Minh. The newly established government of Ngo Dinh Diem in South Vietnam did not permit the election to take place, thus destroying prospects for the peaceful reunification of Vietnam. The United States elected to recognize South Vietnam as an independent nation, propping up the Diem regime in the hopes of maintaining a foothold in Southeast Asia.

The American buildup in Vietnam began gradually: a few hundred technicians during the Eisenhower administration, 16,500 advisers by the time President Kennedy died, and, incredibly, more than 550,000 American military personnel during Lyndon Johnson's

---

23. See Hoxie, *Command Decision and the Presidency*, p. 295.

administration. For Dwight Eisenhower, a professional soldier familiar with logistical problems, the implications of military involvement in Vietnam had been obvious: huge costs for little gain. President Kennedy's national security advisers failed to come to similar conclusions for two reasons. They had great faith in the superiority of mechanized warfare over guerrilla tactics, and they never fully comprehended the political nature of the war, regarding it primarily as a military problem. Consequently, they assumed, because of new developments in mechanized warfare, that great gains could be made with little cost.[24]

One of the most striking features of the American commitment in Vietnam was its piecemeal nature. Long-range policy was shaped by a series of short-range decisions. Each succeeding escalation increased the importance of the commitment, making it more difficult for the United States to extricate itself from the quagmire. According to foreign policy expert John Spanier, "at no point did policy-makers in Washington sit down, take time, and ask themselves some fundamental questions about Vietnam: Was it vital to American security interests and, if so, how vital?"[25]

During the Johnson administration major policy decisions about Vietnam were made by a small group of executive officials who came to be known as "the Tuesday Lunch Group." This group, meeting at noon on Tuesdays to deliberate Vietnam policy, usually included less than a dozen individuals. Until 1968, the Tuesday Lunch Group was characterized by the prevalence of shared assumptions and camaraderie. Membership in the inner circle fluctuated with the passage of time, but the core of the Tuesday Lunch Group consisted of Secretary of Defense Robert McNamara, eventually replaced by Clark Clifford; White House Assistant McGeorge Bundy, replaced by Walt Rostow; Secretary of State Dean Rusk; General Earl Wheeler, Chairman of the Joint Chiefs of Staff; and CIA Director Richard Helms. Undersecretary of State George Ball participated in the meetings for several years as a token Dove. From time to time various White House aides were in attendance.[26]

The criterion for remaining in the inner circle was loyalty to the President and to the policy of escalating military involvement in

24. Halberstam, *Best and Brightest,* pp. 150–154.

25. Spanier, *American Foreign Policy since World War II,* p. 144.

26. Janis, *Victims of Groupthink,* pp. 103–105.

Vietnam. By weeding out dissidents who questioned the policy, the President created an environment in which the decision makers who met to deliberate were essentially in agreement with the policy, assuring that their decisions were a foregone conclusion. This shared assumption regarding the necessity of a military response in Vietnam, and the intense emotional commitment to the policy on the part of the President, resulted in a failure to canvass the full range of alternatives. Key assumptions were not thoroughly examined, or reconsidered, with the result that the extent of the eventual commitment was seriously underestimated.

THE CONSTITUTIONAL DILEMMA

The Cuban missile crisis and the undeclared wars in Korea and Vietnam are indicative of a larger constitutional difficulty. The American system of government continually confronts a basic dilemma. From the standpoint of the conduct of foreign policy, the American system suffers from a number of "congenital deficiencies."[27] The system of shared powers between executive and Congress, while fundamental to the American conception of limited government, can intrude on the privacy, flexibility, promptness, and incisiveness of

27. In the words of George F. Kennan, *The Cloud of Danger: Current Realities of American Foreign Policy.* Boston, Ma.: Little Brown and Co., 1977, p. 3.

action generally considered necessary to the effective conduct of foreign policy by a great nation. The American constitutional system requires the restraint of executive power. The effective conduct of foreign relations within the international/state system is most compatible with a strong executive capable of decisive, unified action. Providing the President with the necessary authority to act with secrecy and dispatch in foreign relations, while preserving the balance of the constitutional system, is a fundamental problem of American government. The increasing importance of a national security policy in the nuclear age has heightened this dilemma.

Presidential Imperialism

During the postwar era, the tradition of Presidential primacy in national security affairs was supplanted by a period of Presidential domination, or imperialism, leading to increased tensions between the President and the Congress. The roots of the imperial Presidency are anchored in the Cold War ideology that dominated American politics from the end of World War II until the era of detente. The Cold War era was characterized by a pervasive fear of Communism and a belief in permanent crisis which justified global intervention by the United States. From this situation ensued the aggrandizement of Presidential power in national security matters. These developments have been carefully documented by Pulitzer Prize-winning historian Arthur M. Schlesinger, Jr., in his meticulous book *The Imperial Presidency*.[28] Chief among the distinguishing features of Presidential imperialism was a willingness to push inherent powers beyond previous limits.

Presidential imperialism was manifested in two ways. The first of these was large-scale Presidential war making, justified by sweeping claims of inherent powers as chief executive and Commander in Chief. President Truman's decision to involve the United States in the Korean conflict, the first Presidential war, was a significant step in the development of the imperial Presidency. President Kennedy's decision to blockade Cuba, while not leading to a military conflict with the Soviet Union, served to illustrate the tension between the right of Congress to be consulted and the need for secrecy and dispatch during a crisis.

28. Arthur M. Schlesinger, Jr., *The Imperial Presidency*. Boston, Ma.: Houghton Mifflin Co., 1973, pp. 177–277.

The escalation and conduct of the Vietnam War was characterized by widespread deception on the part of the White House. President Johnson deliberately concealed the monetary costs of the war, and President Nixon approved secret military operations, including the bombing of Cambodia.[29] When Congress repealed the Gulf of Tonkin Resolution, Nixon simply replied that he did not need it and would conduct the war by relying on inherent powers as chief executive and Commander in Chief. When Congress threatened to cut off the money to pay for the bombing of Cambodia, the administration's reply was that it would find the money elsewhere in the defense budget. In addition to the cost in loss of life and destruction, this futile attempt to enforce the American world view in Asia had unfortunate consequences for the American economy and national political unity. This was accomplished without a declaration of war, or even much consultation with the Congress. By approving appropriations for these wars, and supporting the Tonkin Gulf Resolution, Congress acquiesced to Presidential policy. Congress did not, however, decide the basic question of peace and war, which is its constitutional responsibility.

Beyond the issue of Presidential war was the broader problem of disdain for the constitutional system of checks and balances, the Congress, and the civil rights of the press and individual citizens. A key distinction between Presidential imperialism and activism is the willingness to consult with the Congress and elicit its support. Past Presidents (even Lincoln, Wilson, and Franklin Roosevelt) most often sought approval of their policies in the form of ratification by act of Congress.[30] Presidents Johnson and Nixon attempted, in the name of national security, government actions that would be tolerated in American society only during a state of total war, or extreme national emergency. The conception of national security was expanded to encompass domestic matters, including covert surveillance, suppression of lawful dissent, and widespread limitations on access to government information. Eventually the legitimate political opposition became a target of these tactics. The singular distinguishing feature of Presidential imperialism was the insistence that inherent executive

29. Doris Kearns, *Lyndon Johnson and the American Dream.*   New York: New American Library (Signet Book), 1977, pp. 294–297.

30. On this point, see Louis Fisher, *The Constitution Between Friends: Congress, the President, and the Law.* New York: St. Martin's Press, 1978, pp. 46–49.

power exempted the President from the restraints of the American constitutional system. After his resignation, President Nixon summarized it this way in an interview with David Frost: "Well, when the President does it, that means it's not illegal."[31]

The Congressional Response

Congressional acquiescence aided and abetted the development of Presidential imperialism. Congressional passage of the Tonkin Gulf Resolution in 1964 provides one of numerous examples. This resolution was a response to an alleged attack by North Vietnamese torpedo boats on two American destroyers cruising in the Gulf of Tonkin. The resolution, passed overwhelmingly by the Congress, was a statement of support for the President "to take all necessary measures to repel any armed attack against the forces of the United States and to prevent further aggression."[32] The Tonkin Gulf Resolution also authorized the President to take all necessary steps, including armed force, to assist any member, or protocol state, of the Southeast Asia Collective Defense Treaty. The ease with which President Johnson won approval of this resolution is instructive. The resolution passed the House of Representatives unanimously and passed the Senate with only two dissenting votes. It is more than a little ironic that within 5 years substantial numbers of Congressmen and Senators were supporting legislation to curb Presidential initiatives in Southeast Asia.

As the conflict between Congress and the President heated up, the Congress was confronted with open defiance in the form of a flood of Presidential impoundments of funds and claims of executive privilege. These constituted a direct challenge to Congressional supremacy in the appropriation process and obstructed attempts by the Congress to investigate activities of the executive branch. These assaults on Congressional prerogatives inevitably provoked a reaction. In addition to nearly impeaching President Nixon for obstruction of justice and abuse of executive power, Congress imposed legal limitations on Presidential impoundment of funds, clarified the application of emergency powers, and attempted to require accountability in the exercise of war powers and secret executive agreements.

31. As reported by United Press International in the *Dayton Journal Herald,* June, 1977.

32. Cited in Spanier and Uslaner, *How American Foreign Policy Is Made,* pp. 47–48.

As opposition to large-scale American military involvement in Southeast Asia began to increase, the Senate attempted to use the power of the purse to influence government policy. In 1970, the Senate passed the Cooper–Church amendment prohibiting funds for the maintenance of American ground forces in Cambodia. This was followed by the McGovern–Hatfield amendment cutting off funds for American forces in Vietnam after December 31, 1971. In the face of strong administration opposition, neither of these restrictions was able to pass the House of Representatives. A modified version of the Cooper–Church amendment was eventually passed into law, but not until American forces were already out of Cambodia. In 1971, Congress passed the Mansfield amendment urging the President to set a date for the withdrawal of American forces from Indochina. This amendment was attached as a rider to a defense procurement bill. Rather than veto the entire bill, President Nixon reiterated that since the amendment was not the policy of his administration, he intended to ignore it.[33]

In addition to threats to eliminate funds, the Congress enacted several statutes aimed at clarifying and restraining Presidential authority in the areas of impoundment, national emergencies, executive agreements, and war powers. Because of the increasing importance of executive agreements in structuring America's international commitments, and because a number of executive agreements had been kept secret, the Congress enacted the Case Act.   This legislation, passed in 1972, was intended to keep the Congress better informed about executive agreements. It requires the Secretary of State to transmit to the Congress within 60 days the text of any international agreement other than a treaty, to which the United States government is a party. Compliance with the Case Act by the executive departments has been less than complete. A Senate study in 1977 revealed that 39% of executive agreements enacted in 1976 were reported to Congress after the 60-day deadline—some as much as a year late. It was also discovered that not all executive agreements were being disclosed.   By redefining a number of agreements as "arrangements," executive officials elected not to disclose them to the Congress, or, in some cases, even to the State Department. To improve compliance with the Case Act, the Congress enacted legislation in 1977 requiring any government agency entering into an inter-

33. *Ibid.,* p. 73.

national agreement to transmit the text of the agreement to the State Department within 20 days.[34]

Another major statute came in direct response to President Nixon's attempts to use impoundment of funds as a *de facto* item veto. Impoundment is the process by which the President, through the Office of Management and Budget, refuses to permit Federal agencies to spend funds that have been appropriated by the Congress. The first impoundment of appropriated funds during the modern era occurred in 1941, when President Franklin Roosevelt ordered impoundment of public works funds he deemed not to be of an essential defense nature.[35] The General Appropriations Act of 1951 specifically authorized impounding to prevent deficiencies and to effect economies in government operations. Presidents Truman, Kennedy, and Johnson impounded Federal funds, but it was Richard Nixon's extensive use of impoundment that motivated the Congress to enact legislation clarifying, and limiting, the President's power to impound funds. The President, abandoning the pretense of using impoundment for purposes of administrative efficiency, went after programs and policies with which he disagreed, going so far as to impound $3 billion which had been appropriated over his veto.[36] The Congress reasserted its prerogatives in the appropriation process by enacting the Budget and Impoundment Control Act of 1974, permitting either house of Congress to override a deferral of program funds, and requiring approval by both houses of Congress for a Presidential cancellation (recision) of appropriated funds.

The Congress attempted to clarify the President's emergency powers through enactment of the National Emergencies Act of 1976. This statute terminated existing states of emergency and required the President to publicize any declaration of national emergency. In the event of a Presidential declaration of a national emergency, the Congress is authorized to consider, at 6-month intervals, the question of whether the emergency should be ended by Congressional resolution.

34. Fisher, *Constitution Between Friends,* p. 209.

35. Robert E. Goostree, "The Power of the President to Impound Appropriated Funds: With Special Reference to Grants-in-Aid to Segregated Activities," in Aaron Wildavsky (ed.), *The Presidency,* p. 729.

36. Robert E. DiClerico, *The American President.* Englewood Cliffs, N.J.: Prentice-Hall Inc., 1979, p. 91. Nixon impounded a total of $18 billion.

Of the several statutes enacted during the 1970's, the War Powers Resolution has perhaps the greatest implications for national security policy. Passed in 1973 over President Nixon's veto, this legislation attempts to specify situations and procedures under which it is appropriate for the President to commit American military forces to combat. Without a prior declaration of war, the President is authorized to commit American forces in order to repel an attack upon the United States, its territories or possessions, or its armed forces. The President is expected to consult with the Congress "in every possible instance" before committing American forces to combat. When the President uses this emergency power, he is to report in writing to the Congress within 48 hours, explaining his actions. A key provision of the resolution specifies that within 60 days after this report is submitted, the President must terminate the military intervention unless Congress has (1) declared war; (2) granted an extension of the 60-day limit; or (3) cannot meet because of an attack on the United States. At anytime American military forces are engaged in hostilities without a declaration of war, the Congress may direct the President to remove these forces by passing a concurrent resolution not subject to Presidential veto.

Crisis Decision Making, 1975: The Mayaguez Incident

Less than one year after assuming the Presidency, Gerald Ford was confronted with an incident of piracy at sea. President Ford responded by ordering American military forces to rescue the crew of the S.S. Mayaguez, recapture the ship, and to attack the Cambodian mainland. President Ford's decisions during the 3 days of the crisis, as well as the aftermath of this incident, are instructive regarding the viability and pitfalls of the War Powers Resolution.

On May 12, 1975, the American merchant vessel Mayaguez, en route from Hong Kong to Thailand, was fired upon, boarded, and seized by Cambodian naval forces. Even though the Mayaguez was 60 miles off the Cambodian coast, had a civilian crew and a cargo of containerized freight, the Cambodians apparently assumed it was a spy ship and proceeded to tow the American vessel toward a Cambodian port. Nine hours after this seizure, President Ford convened the National Security Council (NSC) for the first of 4 meetings to deal with the matter. Present at the first meeting were Vice President Nelson Rockefeller, Secretary of State Henry A. Kissinger, CIA Director William E. Colby, Secretary of Defense James R. Schlesinger,

(Reproduced from the Collections of the Library of Congress)

Air Force General David C. Jones (acting Chairman of the Joint Chiefs of Staff), two White House assistants, and several deputy Secretaries of State and Defense.[37]

The President had decided to handle this crisis personally because he wanted to take decisive action. Confidence in the American Presidency had been shaken by Richard Nixon's resignation 9 months earlier. Since Nixon's downfall, the Congress had repeatedly attempted to seize the initiative in national security policy. Particularly distressing to American allies was the Congressional decision to stop aid to Turkey, a NATO ally, and the intensive Congressional investigation of the American intelligence community.

The President and his national security advisers quickly agreed on two objectives: to recover the ship and its crew, and to do so in a manner which would demonstrate to the international community

37. Richard G. Head, Frisco W. Short, and Robert C. McFarlane, *Crisis Resolution: Presidential Decision Making in the Mayaguez and Korean Confrontations.* Boulder, Col.: Westview Press, 1978, p. 109. The synopsis of the *Mayaguez* incident is based on the detailed analysis by Head, Short, and McFarlane, pp. 101–148.

that the United States was prepared to act decisively to protect its interests.   The decision makers shared an assumption that a swift response was important, not only to demonstrate America's resolve, but to recover the ship and its crew, which would be considerably more difficult once the *Mayaguez* was secured in a Cambodian port. The President ordered that a strong diplomatic protest be delivered to the Cambodian authorities, and that efforts be intensified for gathering more intelligence and for planning diplomatic and military alternatives.

Not the least of the President's problems was ascertaining the location of the *Mayaguez* and its crew. The movements of the ship were continually monitored by Navy reconnaissance aircraft, several of which were fired on by Cambodian naval vessels. During the course of the rescue operation there would seldom be certainty about the location of the crew of the *Mayaguez*

A second NSC meeting was held on the morning of May 13, 1975. Those in attendance were the same as at the first meeting, with the addition of two White House aides and the absence of Secretary of State Kissinger, who was out of town.   After it was reported that no response to American diplomatic protests had been received from the Cambodians, serious consideration was begun of a variety of options. Alternatives discussed ranged from diplomatic measures and various rescue plans to retaliatory attacks on Cambodian facilities and large-scale bombing of the port of Kom Pong Som. Shortly after this meeting, American diplomats delivered a message to the Cambodian Embassy in Peking. The message, reiterating American demands for return of the *Mayaguez* and her crew, was rejected by Cambodian authorities.

At this stage, President Ford initiated consultation with members of Congress, as required by Section 3 of the War Powers Resolution, as he interpreted it. Efforts at consultation consisted of formal and informal briefings of various members of Congress on four different occasions by the President, his staff, representatives of the Departments of State and Defense, and the Central Intelligence Agency. The initial consultation on May 13 involved 10 Congressmen and 11 Senators.[38]

At the third meeting of the National Security Council, held the evening of May 13, opinion began to gravitate toward military options, including recovering the ship and its crew and retaliatory

38. *Ibid.*, pp. 114–115.

bombing of Cambodian facilities. Secretary of State Kissinger was emphatic about the use of force, feeling that a decisive American response would serve as a much-needed example to the rest of Asia, particularly North Korea. According to the reports of participants, this NSC meeting, like the others, was characterized by lively debate and a consideration of a wide range of alternatives. At the conclusion of this meeting, the President ordered detailed preparations for operations to recapture the ship and rescue the crew. The details of the plan, developed by the Joint Chiefs, called for a boarding party of American Marines to recapture the *Mayaguez,* and an assault by Marines on the island of Koh Tang. Air strikes on ports and military facilities on the mainland of Cambodia were authorized. The Senate Foreign Relations Committee, the House International Relations Committee, and the Committee on Armed Services, as well as the House Appropriations Defense Subcommittee, were briefed by various executive officials.[39]

The final NSC meeting was held the afternoon of May 14 to review details of the operation. There was by now considerable agreement that the military option was in order because diplomatic efforts had produced no results. At the conclusion of the meeting, President Ford approved the plan and issued orders to execute it. The rescue operation began within an hour and a half.

The Marine assault force encountered substantial resistance from the Cambodians. Although nearly all of the assault helicopters were hit by antiaircraft fire, they were able to land the Marines successfully. Naval air cover prevented Cambodian reinforcements from hampering the operation. Within little more than an hour American forces had recaptured the *Mayaguez* and occupied the island of Koh Tang. The crew was not on board the *Mayaguez,* apparently having been removed to the Cambodian mainland. The President issued a statement, broadcast nationwide, that the United States would cease military operations when the crew was released. Meanwhile, American air strikes on the mainland continued. Due to difficulties in communicating with the Cambodian government, Washington was unaware that the crew had already been released, but was not yet in American hands. In less than 3 hours after the operation began, the crew was returned to the *Mayaguez,* which was now under American control. When this information was relayed to Washington, the President ordered offensive military operations to cease. The fighting

39. *Ibid.,* p. 122.

between Cambodian forces and American Marines continued sporadically 8 more hours before all American military personnel were successfully disengaged.[40]   Fifteen Americans were killed in action, two were missing, and several aircraft were shot down, or badly damaged.   An additional 23 Americans had died earlier when an Air Force helicopter crashed en route to the staging area for the assault.

A short time later, President Ford submitted a written report to the Congress.   Reaction to the President's decisions was generally favorable.   Numerous domestic and foreign newspapers, including the *New York Times*, endorsed the operation as a triumph.   The President's approval rating climbed 12 percentage points in the Gallup poll.   Within a few weeks, however, the reactions of some Democrats in the Congress began to assume aspects of a partisan witch-hunt. Part of this negative Congressional reaction was related to ambiguities in the War Powers Resolution, especially regarding the precise meaning of the word "consultation."   The resolution does not absolutely require the President to consult with the Congress in advance of military operations.   The President is directed to consult in "every possible instance," leaving an option for a rapid, or secret, response prior to consultation.   Even more ambiguously, consultation is mandated, but not defined, by the resolution.   Despite diligent efforts at consultation on the part of the President, the Congress is free after the fact to claim that consultation was inadequate, particularly if there are partisan gains to be made by such a strategy.

Given President Ford's extensive efforts at keeping numerous members of Congress informed during the course of the *Mayaguez* incident, Congressional claims of inadequate consultation would seem preposterous.   However, as the election year unfolded, the clamor from Democratic Congressmen grew louder.   Despite the near-total diplomatic isolation of the young Cambodian government and its refusal to respond to Washington's attempts to communicate, a subsequent Congressional report denounced the administration for not pursuing diplomatic alternatives more vigorously.   The timing for the release of this report was especially suspect, coming as it did just one day before the foreign policy debate between President Ford and Democratic candidate Jimmy Carter.[41]

In brief, the *Mayaguez* incident suggests that the War Powers

40. *Ibid.,* pp. 122–141.

41. *Ibid.,* p. 146.

Resolution does not unduly encroach on the President's military power. The Commander in Chief was able to react swiftly and decisively within the provisions of the resolution. Far from limiting Presidential power, the resolution authorizes the President to commit American forces to combat without prior Congressional authorization, if necessary. In this respect, the resolution simply acknowledges present-day realities. It is also apparent that, at least for short-run military interventions, the War Powers Resolution can constitute a convenient escape mechanism for the Congress. If the military operation is successful, Congress can bask in the glory along with the President. If an intervention is a failure, or proves to be controversial, Congress can subsequently disavow it through claims of inadequate consultation.

Moreover, a major assumption shared by proponents of the War Powers Resolution—that a warlike President must be restrained by a more moderate Congress—is not in accordance with American history. In the past, the Congress has demonstrated an enthusiasm for militarism generally equal to that of the President.[42] In various ways, including funding, the Congress approved American participation in both Presidential wars since the last declaration of war in 1941. Given the remarkable ease with which President Lyndon Johnson won approval for his Tonkin Gulf Resolution, it appears questionable whether the War Powers Resolution would have prevented American involvement in Vietnam. Only after the war became protracted and unpopular did Congressional opposition become significant. It is possible that the provisions of the resolution could have shortened the conflict by influencing the President to seek a negotiated solution at an earlier stage. It is possible, however, that sustained Congressional pressure to end the conflict could have produced an even more massive escalation designed to pound North Vietnam rapidly into submission.

A more basic limitation inherent in the War Powers Resolution relates to the nature of modern warfare. The procedures in the resolution will likely prove irrelevant in the event of a nuclear war. Should world leaders lose control of the machinery of modern warfare, or elect to use it for a preemptory strike, retaliation will be immediate and automatic. "To all intents and purposes, Congress will not declare World War III."[43]

42. Spanier and Uslaner, *How American Foreign Policy Is Made*, p. 135.
43. *Ibid.*, p. 138

Table 9.1 Congressional Support for Administration Budget Requests

Year	Defense[a]	% Change Per Year	% Change From Request	Aid[a]	% Change Previous Year	% Change From Request	Labor-HEW[a]	% Change Per Year	% Change From Request
1954	34.4	−26	−3.9	4.5			2.0	+11	−4.3
1955	28.8	−16	−2.5	3.2			2.0	−2	+1.3
1956	31.9	+11	−1.1	2.7		−17.2	2.4	+20	−2.5
1957	34.6	+ 8	+1.5	3.9	+37	−22.5	2.4	−0	−0.1
1958	33.8	− 2		2.8	−24	−18.2	2.5	+5	+3.6
1959	39.6	+17	+2.1	3.3	+17.8	−16.5	3.1	+26	+5.6
1960	39.6	+ 0	−.1	3.2	− 3.0	−27.2	3.9	+25	+5.1
1961	40.0	+ 1	+1.9	3.7	+15.6	−13.1	4.4	+11	+8.3
1962	46.7	+17	+.6	3.9	+ 5.4	−18.1	4.9	+13	−1.8
1963	48.1	+ 3	+1.4	3.9	0	−20.1	5.3	+ 8	−1
1964	47.2	− 1	+3.7	3.0	−23	−33.7	5.5	+ 3	−5.1
1965	46.7	− 1	−1.5	3.2	+ 6.6	− 7.6	7.1	+29	−4.4
1966	46.8	0	.2	3.2	0	− 7.0	7.9	+11	−3.5
1967	58.1	+24	+ .6	2.9	− 9	−13.3	10.4	+32	+3.7
1968	69.9	+20	− .7	2.3	−20.6	−29.4	13.2	+27	−1.3
1969	71.8	+ 3	−6.8	1.8	−21.7	−39.9	18.6	+40	−4
1970	69.9	− 3	−7.5	1.8	0	−33.1	19.7	+ 6	−0.4
1971	66.5	− 4	−3.1	1.9	+ 5.5	−11.8	19.0	− 4	+1.1
1972	70.5	+ 6	−4.1	2.2	+15.7	−27.7	21.1	+11	+4.4
1973	74.4	+ 5	−6.6	2.2	0	−28.6	28.6	+35	+4.7
1974	73.7	− 1	−5.6	1.9	−13.6	−23.4	32.9	+15	+4.4
1975	82.1	+11	−6.7	2.5	+31.6	−39.6	33.0	+ 0	−5.2
1976	93.7	+14	−6.7	3.2	+28.0	−13.4	36.7	+ 9	+2.6
1977	104.3	+11	−3.4	3.4	+ 6.3	− 7.6	56.4	+56	+2.6
1978	109.7	+ 5	−2.4	4.0	+17.6	− 2.9	60.0	+ 6	− .8

[a]In billions of dollars, excluding special appropriations

Source: See Footnote 44: Mohammed Ahrari and Andrew D. McNitt, "The Two Presidencies Reconsidered: Is There a Post-Imperial Presidency?", p. 14.

CONCLUSION

The day-to-day conduct of foreign relations remains an executive prerogative. The Congress has sought through statutes and oversight to demonstrate its determination to be involved, through consultation and appropriation, in the formulation of national security policy. Congressional support for recent Presidential proposals in national security matters does not indicate that the President's influence has significantly diminished. Despite the passage of some specific statutory restrictions, a general pattern of Congressional support for Presidential proposals in national security matters has persisted. Research examining changes in Congressional support for Presidential initiatives, budgetary requests, and vetoes in national security policy from 1954 to 1978 showed only a modest decline in support since 1973. Both houses of Congress have continued to be relatively supportive of the President in foreign and diplomatic policy. Although the level of support declined somewhat in national security matters, it still exceeded Congressional support for domestic programs. This supports the view that the President enjoys a relatively stable institutional advantage in national security policy making.[44]

The greatest area of Congressional resistance to Presidential leadership in national security policy since 1973 was in Presidential requests for appropriations. Table 9.1 shows the extent to which Congress supported administration budget requests for the Departments of Defense; Labor; Health, Education, and Welfare (HEW); and foreign aid from 1954 to 1978. Congress was most likely to vote the amount requested by the President for Defense, slightly less likely to support administration requests for Labor and HEW, and much less likely to support requests for foreign aid. Congress cut Defense requests every year from 1969 to 1978. This trend began moderating in 1977, and, in any event, these cuts never exceeded 7%. Cuts in foreign-aid requests are part of a pattern of Congressional behavior dating back to the 1950's.

In summary, rather than reversing the tradition of Presidential primacy in national security affairs, statutes recently enacted have generally acknowledged the paramount position of the executive by

44. Mohammed Ahrari and Andrew D. McNitt, "The Two Presidencies Reconsidered: Is There a Post-Imperial Presidency?" A paper presented at the annual meeting of the Midwest Political Science Association in Chicago: April 19, 1979, pp. 10–14.

seeking to promote greater consultation between the President and Congress. Congressional support for Presidential initiatives in national security policy declined somewhat during the 1970's. The precise role of the War Powers Resolution in future national security policy decisions remains to be seen.

FURTHER READING

Acheson, Dean G. *Present at the Creation: My Years in the State Department.* New York: W.W. Norton & Co., Inc., 1969. The former Secretary of State's account of the genesis of modern American national security policy.

Ambrose, Stephen E. *Rise to Globalism: American Foreign Policy, 1938–1976* (rev. ed.). New York: Penguin Books, 1976. An eminent historian assesses the development of American foreign policy, including the linkages between the American character, culture, economy, and policy.

Detzer, David. *The Brink: Cuban Missile Crisis, 1962.* New York: Thomas Y. Crowell, 1979. The latest analysis of the events which might have triggered World War III.

Halberstam, David. *The Best and the Brightest.* Greenwich, Conn.: Fawcett Publications, 1972. A comprehensive account of the national security policy makers and decisions which involved the United States in Vietnam. In the early 1960's, Halberstam received the Pulitzer Prize for his reports from Vietnam.

Head, Richard G., Short, Frisco W., and McFarlane, Robert C. *Crisis Resolution: Presidential Decision Making in the Mayaguez and Korean Confrontations.* Boulder, Col.: Westview Press, 1978. A detailed analysis of the Ford administration's handling of the *Mayaguez* incident. Included is a discussion of the implications of the War Powers Resolution and the Congressional reaction to President Ford's decisions during the confrontation.

Hoxie, R. Gordon. *Command Decision and the Presidency: A Study of National Security Policy and Organization.* New York: Reader's Digest Press, 1977. The details of the development of national security policy and machinery from Presidents Truman through Ford.

Janis, Irving L. *Victims of Groupthink: A Psychological Study of Foreign Policy Decisions and Fiascoes.* Boston, Ma.: Houghton Mifflin Co., 1972. An intriguing study which utilizes concepts from social psychology to analyze national security decision making.

Kennan, George F. *Memoirs.* Boston, Ma.: Little Brown and Co., 1967. Kennan, along with President Harry Truman, is generally regarded as the architect of the containment policy.

Kennan, George F. *The Cloud of Danger: Current Realities of American Foreign Policy.* Boston, Ma.: Little Brown and Co., 1977. Kennan discusses world politics since the breakdown of the bipolar balance of power, and offers guidelines for future American national security policy.

Kennedy, Robert F. *Thirteen Days: A Memoir of the Cuban Missile Crisis.* New York: W.W. Norton & Co., 1969. By nearly all accounts, Robert Kennedy played a crucial role in resolving the missile crisis.

275

Kissinger, Henry. *White House Years.* Boston, Ma.: Little Brown and Co., 1979.
A mammoth volume by the influential national security adviser, detailing
events and decisions in the White House during President Nixon's first
term.

Schlesinger, Arthur M., Jr. *The Imperial Presidency.* Boston, Ma.: Houghton
Mifflin Co., 1973. The Pulitzer Prize-winning historian traces the growth of
Presidential power in national-security affairs.

Spanier, John. *American Foreign Policy Since World War II* (8th ed.). New
York: Holt, Rinehart and Winston, 1980. A leading power-politics interpretation of American foreign policy, from the Cold War through the
collapse of containment.

Spanier, John, and Uslaner, Eric M. *How American Foreign Policy Is Made.*
New York: Praeger Publishers, 1974. A concise discussion of American
foreign policy decision making.

Stoessinger, John G. *Crusaders and Pragmatists: Movers of Modern American
Foreign Policy.* New York: W.W. Norton & Co., 1979. An analysis of
American foreign policy, emphasizing the importance of the personalities
of Presidents and Secretaries of State.

Chapter 10

The Presidents:
Personality and Politics

Although the Presidency is an institution, the President is an individual, and Presidential behavior has a very personal dimension. As with other individuals, the President's personality has been shaped by family upbringing and socialization. Responses to conscious and unconscious motivations, as well as the President's political ideology and world view, affect how decisions are made and the content of those decisions. Successful leadership, including the ability to adapt to changing circumstances, is related to the President's personal beliefs, skills, and traits—that is, to the President's personality.

Personality may be described by using the concepts of structure and process. Personality structure refers to a relatively stable arrangement, or pattern, of parts in the system. Personality processes refer to the functions carried out by the parts (what they do) and how they interact with the system (dynamics).[1] As the term is used here, personality refers to the relatively stable organization of the ways in which an individual deals with internal psychic conflicts and external reality.

---

1. Richard S. Lazarus, *Personality* (2nd ed.). Englewood Cliffs, N.J.: Prentice-Hall, 1971, p. 24.

PERSONALITY AND PSYCHOBIOGRAPHY

The past shapes the present just as the present encapsulates the past. Individual personality structure has its genesis in infancy and childhood. Events and relationships during childhood and adolescence profoundly affect personality development. To be useful as a concept for analyzing Presidential behavior, personality must be examined in the context of the President's life history. The art of political biography has recently been enriched by the development of psychobiography (also known as psychohistory). As defined by Betty Glad, psychobiography is "any life history which employs an explicit personality theory, that is, a perception that individual behavior has an internal locus of causation as well as some degree of structure and organization."[2]

Although there are a vast number of theories about personality development and organization, Jeanne Knutson's classification groups them into three schools of thought.[3]

Psychoanalytic Relying primarily on the work of Sigmund Freud and those who subsequently refined and elaborated his concepts, the psychoanalytic school analyzes human behavior in terms of adjustments and compromises necessitated by universal processes of personality development and socialization. The strength of this approach is that its basic concepts are widely understood and utilized, especially in the analysis of neurotic and pathological behavior. A major criticism of the approach is this emphasis on pathology and its lack of explanation of mental health and human fulfillment. Critics contend that personality development involves more than coping with anxieties and inner conflicts.

Behavioristic This approach differs radically from the other two by assuming that *all* human behavior is learned through association and reinforcement. "An association will be established between any stimulus and response when there has been gratification (reinforce-

2. Betty Glad, "Contributions of Psychobiography," in Jeanne N. Knutson (ed.), *Handbook of Political Psychology*. San Francisco, Ca.: Jossey-Bass, 1973, p. 296.

3. Jeanne N. Knutson, *The Human Basis of the Polity: A Psychological Study of Political Men*. Chicago, Ill.: Aldine Atherton, 1972, pp. 19–21.

ment) of a drive."[4]   Complex social motives such as achievement are assumed to be learned in basically the same manner as simpler ones. Freudians criticize this approach for ignoring basic instincts, while humanists attack its mechanistic assumptions. Abraham Maslow, for example, contends that this philosophy of human behavior is inadequate because man is studied "as if he were no more complicated than a white rat." [5]

Growth Actualization (or Humanistic Psychology) The essential theoretical assumption of this framework is that human contain within themselves the urge to grow and, when given the opportunity, will express the highest qualities of thought and creativity.[6] Political scientists have only recently begun to utilize this approach. Jeanne Knutson has utilized Abraham Maslow's conception of the hierarchy of needs to analyze the relationship between personality and citizen-participation in politics. In material more directly related to Presidential personality, both James David Barber and Betty Glad have incorporated some potential-for-growth assumptions into their psychobiographic approaches.[7]

Of these three approaches, the assumptions of psychoanalysis have been the most widely utilized by political scientists and historians in the analysis of Presidential personality. This is true in part because the psychoanalytical approach is more familiar and well established, and partly because personality analysts have been particularly concerned with pathology among politicians. The assumptions of learning theory are sometimes implicit in analysis of Presidential personality, but are seldom utilized as an explicit framework. The growth-actualization model has shown promise for analyzing the contribution of personality development to successful Presidential leadership. This approach does not ignore the role of inner conflicts and unmet needs, but emphasizes the contribution of the mature and rational personality in promoting adaptive, and creative, responses.

4. Lazarus, *Personality*, p. 62.

5. Cited in Knutson, *The Human Basis of the Polity*, p. 21

6. Lazarus, *Personality*, p. 78.

7. See: Knutson, *Human Basis of the Polity*, pp. 1–105; James David Barber, *The Presidential Character: Predicting Performance in the White House* (2nd ed.). Englewood Cliffs, N.J.: Prentice-Hall, 1977, pp. 1–14, 207–343; and Betty Glad, "Contributions of Psychobiography," pp. 296–321.

Analyses of the impact of personality in politics suggest two alternative hypotheses:

H_1: Self-assurance and politics. This hypothesis assumes that the relationship between personality and politics is such that *those who attain positions of leadership will, by and large, be individuals with secure, well-integrated personalities and a high level of political competence.*

This hypothesis has assumed a variety of forms, generally resting on the premise that participation in politics is significantly greater for individuals who are mentally healthy than for those who are neurotic. Most sociological and psychological variables associated with high rates of political participation also correlate positively with individuals' feelings of self-confidence and political competence. In addition, there is some evidence that psychic stress caused by unmet needs and internal conflicts reduces political participation. A variant of this hypothesis attributes to the political system the capacity for sorting out neurotic and psychopathological personalities from leadership positions. It has long been an unwarranted assumption in political science that the American political system and its institutions reject aberrant personalities because they are unable to build sufficient support to make it to the top. The behavior in office of Presidents Lyndon Johnson and Richard Nixon proved this assumption to be wishful thinking. Likewise, the argument that the structure of bureaucratic organizations sorts out unstable personalities, even if true, is not so relevant to an elective office as the Presidency, which is attained by means of campaigning.[8]

H_2: Insecurity and Politics. In opposition to the first hypothesis, this one assumes that *politics (particularly leadership positions) attracts individuals who have per-*

8. See Lester Milbrath and M. L. Goel, *Political Participation: How and Why Do People Get Involved in Politics?* (2nd ed.). Chicago: Rand McNally & Co., 1975, pp. 77–85. Robert Lane has advanced the hypothesis that among individuals suffering from intrapsychic conflict so much energy is consumed by the internal struggle that little remains for political activity. For a concise discussion of the ramifications of this hypothesis see Brent M. Rutherford, "Psychopathology, Decision Making, and Political Involvement," in Fred I. Greenstein and Michael Lerner (eds.), *A Source Book for the Study of Personality and Politics.* Chicago, Ill.: Markham, 1971, pp. 243–262. Also, see

sonality disorders. Leadership positions attract not the best and the brightest, but the devious and the neurotic, who seek power as a means of meeting their personal needs and coping with insecurities.

The genesis of this hypothesis is found in Harold Lasswell's *Psychopathology and Politics* in which he devised the formula $p \} d \} r = P$ to symbolize the sublimation of psychic energy into politics. In this formula:

p = the individual's private motives (inner conflicts, anxieties)
d = displacement onto public objects
r = rationalization in terms of the public interest
P = the Political Man
$\}$ = "transformed into"

Lasswell concludes: "The distinctive mark of the *homo politicus* is the rationalization of the displacement in terms of public interest."[9]

These two alternative hypotheses are not mutually exclusive. As James David Barber has shown, political leadership involves both types: those with high self-esteem who are able to manage their anxieties relatively easily, and those with low self-esteem who seek public office in order to improve their self-concepts.[10] Some Presidents are likely to approximate the self-assurance-and-politics model, being confident, flexible and oriented to problem solving. There have been, however, Presidents whose behavior is better described by the insecurity-and-politics model. Their personalities predisposed them to engage in inflexible and self-defeating behavior. This model of political man (as an individual motivated by inner conflicts and private needs to seek public power) has been utilized in analyzing the impact of personality on the behavior of several Presidents. There is

Betty Glad's critique of the assumption that the American political system automatically sorts out and rejects aberrant personalities from leadership positions, in Glad, "Contributions of Psychobiography," pp. 299–302. On the bureaucratic screening argument, see Rutherford, *Psychopathology, Decision Making, Political Involvement*, p. 247.

9. Harold D. Lasswell, *Psychopathology and Politics*. New York: Viking Press, 1960, p. 262. The Lasswell formula is found on pp. 261–262.

10. In addition to *The Presidential Character*, see also Barber's earlier work, *The Lawmakers*. New Haven, Conn.: Yale University Press, 1965.

considerable agreement among psychobiographers that the insecurity-and-politics thesis is most appropriate in the cases of Presidents Woodrow Wilson, Lyndon Johnson, Richard Nixon, and, perhaps, Jimmy Carter.[11]

INSECURITY AND POLITICS

Since the assumptions of the psychoanalytic personality theory have been widely utilized in psychobiographies of Presidents, it is appropriate to review briefly these assumptions. Psychoanalytic theory assumes that the ways in which an individual learns to manage inner conflicts and external frustrations shape personality development. As the ego assumes its central position in the personality structure, the individual develops various methods to cope with inevitable conflicts, anxieties, and deprivations. In the psychoanalytic framework, the development of personality rests on three concepts: identification, displacement, and ego-defense mechanisms.

Identification Incorporation of the qualities of an external object, usually those of another person, into one's personality is known in psychoanalytic theory as identification. In personality development, the most prominent objects for identification are generally the child's parents. Parental rejection, or other conflicts centering around identification with parents, have considerable impact on personality development. The following discussion will demonstrate that Lyndon Johnson, Richard Nixon, and Jimmy Carter experienced some difficulties in this area, leading to unresolved conflicts within their personality structures.

Displacement and Sublimation Psychoanalytic theory assumes that psychic energy has the property of being displaceable, and

11. On Woodrow Wilson, see Alexander L. George and Juliette L. George, *Woodrow Wilson and Colonel House: A Personality Study.* New York: Dover Publications, Inc., 1964. On Lyndon B. Johnson, see Doris Kearns, *Lyndon Johnson and the American Dream.* New York: New American Library (Signet), 1977.   On Richard Nixon, see Bruce Mazlish, *In Search of Nixon: A Psychohistorical Inquiry.* Baltimore, Md.: Penguin Books, 1973. On Jimmy Carter, see Betty Glad, *Jimmy Carter: In Search of the Great White House.* New York: W. W. Norton & Co., Inc., 1980. See also, Lloyd deMause and Henry Ebel (eds.), *Jimmy Carter and American Fantasy: Psychohistorical Explorations.* New York: Two Continents/Psychohistory Press, 1977. For more sympathetic treatments of Carter, see Bruce Mazlish and Edwin Diamond, *Jimmy Carter: An Interpretive Biography.* New York: Simon and Schuster, 1979, and Barber, *Presidential Character,* pp. 497–539. *The Presidential Character,* also contains concise psychobiographical portraits of most 20th-century Presidents.

that personality development proceeds in large part by a series of energy displacements. Various factors determine the direction the displacements will take. When the individual's means for reducing psychic tensions involve displacements of energy into culturally approved areas of endeavor, it is known as sublimation. Examples of sublimation include the deflection of psycho-sexual energy into intellectual, cultural, and artistic pursuits. Sublimation and other displacements are forms of compensatory behavior. In psychoanalytic theory, much adult behavior is regarded as an attempt to compensate for childhood deprivations and insecurities. Lasswell's conception of psychopathology and politics assumes that political behavior is partly a sublimated expression of power needs resulting from unresolved personality conflicts and insecurities.

Defense Mechanisms of the Ego A major task of the ego in personality processes is dealing with threats and conflicts that arouse anxiety. An individual whose personality is well developed will likely try to cope by adopting realistic problem-solving methods. Insecure personalities, however, attempt to alleviate anxiety by using methods that deny, falsify, or distort reality. All individuals rely on ego-defense mechanisms from time to time, but *excessive* reliance on them impedes personality development by introducing a substantial component of irrationality into the individual's decision making. Heavy reliance on ego-defense mechanisms undermines ability to manage personal conflicts by dealing realistically with the external world. The three ego-defense mechanisms most relevant to the analysis of Presidential personality are repression, projection, and reaction formation. By using these defenses, the ego copes with conflicts and insecurities subconsciously by distorting the individual's perceptions of reality and concealing, or disguising, motivations.[12]

Repression forces unacceptable impulses and threatening ideas and perceptions out of the consciousness. This is one of the primary means by which individuals distort external reality and falsify incoming information to control anxiety. People who depend excessively upon this form of defense are said to be repressed and tend to be withdrawn, guarded, and rigid. Projection relieves anxiety by attributing its causation to the external world, frequently to another individual. Denial of one's own hostility, while attributing it to

---

12. This discussion of identification, displacement, and ego-defense mechanisms is based on the analysis in Calvin S. Hall, *A Primer of Freudian Psychology*. New York: Mentor Books, 1954, pp. 74–93. Two additional ego-defense mechanisms—fixation and regression—have not been as widely utilized in psychobiographical analyses of Presidents.

someone else, is a common example, offering the defensive individual an excuse for expressing his real feelings. Projection provides a rationalization for evading personal responsibility for one's actions by blaming someone else. Reaction-formation is another unconscious form of denial by which an impulse, or fear, is hidden from awareness. In this case, the individual's feeling, or motivation, is masked by expression of its opposite. A common example is provided by men who are afraid of any sign of softness in their makeup, equating it with femininity. In an attempt to assure themselves about their sexuality, they assume an especially tough and masculine stance, becoming caricatures of masculinity in the process. Likewise, high ideals of virtue and goodness may mask baser motives.[13]

In summary, ego-defense mechanisms are irrational adjustments to anxiety, which distort, hide, or deny reality. Excessive reliance on such defenses makes the personality rigid and inflexible while introducing a significant element of irrationality into reality testing, since the defensive person's behavior is based partly on unconscious motivations. Psychobiographers contend that among recent Presidents, Woodrow Wilson, Lyndon Johnson, Richard Nixon, and Jimmy Carter each manifested extensive ego-defensive behavior, their insecurities leading them, on occasion, to adopt patterns of rigid and self-defeating behavior.

Lyndon Baines Johnson (1963-1968)

The genesis of Lyndon Johnson's insecurities can be traced to the dynamics between his parents. As a child, Lyndon was the focus of tensions between his combative and somewhat incompatible parents. The President's most intimate biographer describes Johnson's mother as "a drastically unhappy woman."[14] Rebekah Baines had married beneath her station, and, for much of his childhood, Lyndon paid a price for her bad judgment. From a proper family, rich in money and culture, Rebekah surrendered her respectability by marrying a small-time Texas cattle trader and local politico, Sam Ealy Johnson, a rowdy, hard-drinking Texas good 'ole boy. Exactly why Rebekah married Sam remains a mystery, but this union of opposites occurred only eight months after the death of Rebekah's beloved father, Joseph Wilson Baines. Trapped in near poverty in rural Texas,

13. *Ibid.*, pp. 85-93.

14. Kearns, *Lyndon Johnson*, p. 25.

(Reproduced from the Collections of the Library of Congress)

Rebekah continually conveyed to her son the contrast between her cultured past and the grimness of her existence with Sam. This was apparently one of the sources of Lyndon Johnson's feelings of cultural deprivation and inferiority.

Rebekah's decision to live her life vicariously through her son left an indelible imprint on his personality. Lyndon did not experience his mother's love as a steady and reliable force, but as a conditional reward. This constitutes a basic source of insecurity, which affected his political behavior throughout his career. Determined to make Lyndon into a gentleman, Rebekah lavished him with love when he was responsive, but withdrew her affection for prolonged periods when he resisted. The withdrawal of approval in retaliation for non-cooperation subsequently proved to be a pattern of behavior that Johnson followed throughout much of his political life. A search for unconditional affection became an integral part of his personality, a prime motive for seeking political power.

Her own ambitions throttled, Rebekah directed her energy toward fostering an achievement-oriented environment that would shape Lyndon into a gentleman of refinement. This world of books, poetry recitation, dance, and violin lessons contrasted starkly with the style and values of the significant male figures in Lyndon Johnson's life. Lyndon's grandfather, who was an authentic Texas cowboy, conveyed to Lyndon the heritage and rituals of manhood in rural Texas. History and tall tales intertwined as Lyndon absorbed his grandfather's stories about roundups, cattle drives, and the lusty life of the cowboy. From the men in the family Lyndon was indoctrinated into the virtues of manliness and the practical, active life. The world of books, refinement, beauty, and intellect in contrast with manly courage, toughness, and action created a tension that contributed to a dualism characteristic of Lyndon Johnson's personality and behavior all his life.[15]

Outwardly, at least, Sam triumphed over Rebekah. Caught between the cowboy and the lady, Lyndon emulated his father, adopting the crude patterns of behavior Rebekah despised—wheeling and dealing, vulgarity, and life-long distrust of impractical intellectuals. Rebekah's manipulations had, however, made a lasting imprint on her son's personality, contributing to the insecurities that Lyndon Johnson brought with him into the Oval Office.

Hurricane Lyndon It is not altogether surprising that Lyndon Johnson became a politician. His father was politically active, and after being elected to the Texas state legislature, would occasionally let Lyndon accompany him to the state capitol in Austin. It is interesting, however, to ponder Lyndon's retrospective account of his decision to become a professional politician:

> "I still believed my mother the most beautiful, sexy, intelligent woman I'd ever met and I was determined to recapture her wonderful love, but not at the price of my daddy's respect. Finally, I saw it all before me. I would become a political figure. Daddy would like that. He would consider it a manly thing to be. But that would be just the beginning. I was going to reach beyond my father. I would finish college; I would build great power and gain high office. Mother would like that. I would go to the Capitol and talk about big ideas. She would never be disappointed in me again."[16]

15. *Ibid.*, pp. 21–45.

16. *Ibid.*, p. 47. Used with permission of the publisher.

For Lyndon Johnson, this sublimation involved a tremendous amount of psychic energy, representing a total commitment. Johnson developed an energetic political style based on his ability to overwhelm others by the force of his personality. Even as a freshman in college, he demonstrated a grasp of campus politics and power relationships. He began his social climbing near the bottom of the ladder, starting out in a part-time janitorial position. Within a short time, by using his high-energy formula of hard work, attention to detail, and persistence, he advanced from assistant to the janitor to special assistant to the college president's personal secretary. He succeeded in transforming this position into that of a *de facto* appointments secretary, bringing much of the president's business into his purview. According to one of Lyndon's college chums: "He once said to me, 'Boody, the way you get ahead in this world, you get close to those that are the heads of things. Like President Evans, for example.' . . . And before long he was working as a clerk in Prexy's office."[17]

Lyndon Johnson's style of dominating social relationships through personal energy and persuasion would later be refined into a systematic treatment, tailored to the individual needs of his target. In this aspect of his style Johnson's boundless energy merged with his personal insecurities and affection needs to produce a domineering personality—an individual for whom all social interactions had a purpose. He wanted to be liked by everyone he met, but he defined friendship in terms of willingness to accommodate his objectives.[18]

No matter how persuasive, politicians seldom dominate others solely by the force of personality. Flattery, cajolery, backslapping, and rational argument have their limits. Equally important in Johnson's personal style was an extensive network of obligations. From the way his career developed, it is evident that early on Johnson appreciated the importance of building political connections for the future. Sensing which way the political winds were blowing, he entered politics by casting his lot with the New Deal Democrats. His initial entree into Washington politics was as assistant to Texas Congressman Richard Kleberg, a position conferred on the basis of a recommendation by a Texas state senator.

17. Merle Miller. *Lyndon: An Oral Biography.* New York: G.P. Putnam's Sons, 1980, p. 28.

18. Kearns, *Lyndon Johnson,* p. 83.

Once in Washington, diligence and persistence were rewarded. In 1935, on the recommendation of Texas Congressman Sam Rayburn, President Franklin Roosevelt named Johnson the Texas Director of the National Youth Administration, a New Deal agency awarding hundreds of loans and part-time jobs in Texas. As director of the NYA, Johnson began building a political base in Texas by providing services and favors to constituents. With his wife's assistance, Johnson was elected to Congress in 1937. Lady Bird provided not only funds to finance the campaign; equally important, she helped Johnson organize and focus his tremendous energy.

A strong supporter of New Deal programs as a congressman, Johnson gradually began moving to the right politically. After losing a Democratic primary election for the Senate in 1941, Johnson realized that he would have to come to terms with Texas' conservative oil and financial interests.   Likewise, Johnson discerned that to win a state wide election in Texas, he could not permit himself to be portrayed as a liberal on civil rights matters.   By 1948, he was ready to risk his Congressional seat by running against arch-conservative Democrat Coke Stevenson in the primary election for United States Senate.   Amidst charges of vote fraud by both sides, Johnson defeated Stevenson by the incredible margin of 87 votes, beginning the remarkable Senate career of "Landslide Lyndon" Johnson.   The freshman class of 1948 was one of the most distinguished in Senate history, including Senators Hubert Humphrey, Estes Kefauver, Paul Douglas, Robert Kerr, and Russell Long.[19] Within a short time, however, it was Lyndon Johnson who led the Senate.

In the Senate, as elsewhere, Johnson displayed boundless energy, perceptive personal skills, and flair for leadership. As his route of advancement he chose party leadership, being elected whip in 1951 (the youngest ever), and Democratic leader in 1953 at age 44. The Republicans controlled the Senate in 1953, and, as minority leader, Johnson displayed a spirit of bipartisanship, helping President Eisenhower by generating support for parts of his legislative program.

When the Democrats regained control of the Senate in 1955, Johnson began to flourish as majority leader, earning a reputation as a master of accommodation. Combining his personal forcefulness (the treatment) with the network of obligations he cultivated as party leader, Johnson perfected his persuasive style. In an intimate setting

19. *Ibid.,* pp. 88–106.

even veteran Senators sometimes found it diffucult to resist his tactics. "He could flatter men with sentiments of love and touch their bodies with gestures. The intimacy was all the more excusable because it seemed genuine and without menace. Yet it was also the product of meticulous calculation. And it worked."[20]   Through his extensive efforts and with President Eisenhower's support, Johnson managed to guide a civil rights bill through the Senate in 1957, the first one in 87 years. On one side he counseled Senate liberals to help him make sure this "long overdue bill" was passed. To prevent a Southern filibuster, he used different persuasive tactics with his Southern colleagues: "These Negroes, they're getting pretty uppity these days . . . we've got to give them a little something, just enough to quiet them down, not enough to make any difference. For if we don't move at all . . . it'll be Reconstruction all over again."[21]   Johnson's style of accommodation through intimate persuasion and compromise served him well in the Senate, and as President he compiled a remarkable legislative record. Yet, as President he was destined to encounter problems fueled by forces beyond the reach of his persuasive skills.

Exactly why Lyndon Johnson accepted the Kennedys' offer of the Vice Presidential nomination is not certain. Perhaps he really believed he would be able to make the Vice Presidency into something more than it is. Or, perhaps he perceived the Vice Presidency as the best, or only, route a Southerner could follow to the Presidential nomination. Uncomfortable with the cultured Kennedy crowd, he endured nearly three years of anonymity and frustration. During this period, he dreamed repeatedly of being powerless, physically incapacitated, and unable to move.[22]

It was a different matter when fate intervened and he was unexpectedly elevated to the Presidency. Johnson moved immediately to assume control of the office and its powers. Within six months the President and a bipartisan coalition had broken the Southern dominance of the Senate. After bypassing the Judiciary Committee by parliamentary maneuver, they shut off a Southern filibuster and passed the 1964 Civil Rights Act which, among other things, integrated public accommodations nationwide. Also signed into law

20. *Ibid.*, p. 131.

21. *Ibid.*, p. 155.

22. *Ibid.*, pp. 173–174.

were a tax cut and the Economic Opportunity Act, an expression of the President's genuine concern for the disadvantaged. In each case the President's legislative strategy involved careful consultation with key Congressmen and interest-group representatives. Johnson was now ready to seek reelection on his own. As the votes were counted and his 1964 victory shaped up as one of the greatest Presidential election landslides in history, Johnson told his confidant Doris Kearns, "For the first time in all my life I truly felt loved by the American people."[23]

The Great Society and Vietnam   Scholars analyzing the personalities of Presidents continually emphasize that personality is only one variable, not the total explanation of Presidential behavior. According to James David Barber, at least two other factors must be considered in analyzing the President's successes and difficulties in office. Presidential personality interacts with the power situation and the climate of expectations confronting the President. The power situation refers to the support or resistance the President will likely encounter from other institutions, including the Congress and the Supreme Court. The national climate of expectations is more elusive, but refers to the needs and expectations of the public (presumably the more activist and organized components).[24]

As Lyndon Johnson began his first full term as President, his exceptional legislative skills combined with heavy Democratic dominance of Congress and increasing public acceptance to produce a major emphasis on social legislation. All of his life Lyndon Johnson had enjoyed bestowing gifts and was well aware of the reciprocity implied by acceptance of his gifts. In Johnson's mind, this ritual created a bond of dependence, or at least appreciation, on the part of recipients.[25] The President, by virtue of the very favorable power situation, was now in a position to lavish gifts upon the American people. He was determined to go beyond even the New Deal, to win the war on poverty, and build the Great Society.

So began the culmination of postwar liberalism. In addition to the 1965 Voting Rights Act, the Congress had passed, under the President's personal supervision, a package of poverty programs which were subsequently expanded. Included were the Job Corps for

23. *Ibid.*, p. 219.

24. Barber, *Presidential Character*, pp. 8–9.

25. Kearns, *Lyndon Johnson*, pp. 10–11.

training unemployed youth, Community Action Programs offering a variety of neighborhood services, legal aid for the poor, and Head Start to begin the education of preschool children. The first year $800 million was appropriated, $1.5 billion the next, then $1.6 billion, and by 1968, nearly $2 billion.[26] In 1966, these programs were extended and supplemented by Medical Care for the aged (nearly $1 billion the first year alone), increased Federal aid to education, model-cities programs, increases in the minimum wage and unemployment benefits, subsidies for farmers, and, in 1967, a day-care program. The President and his legislative liaison team were especially effective during the 89th Congress. Of the 115 legislative recommendations Johnson sent to the Hill in 1965, he later signed 90 into law.[27]

Characteristically, many of these new programs were housed not in the existing bureaucracy but in the Office of Economic Opportunity, located in the Executive Office of the President. Although this more easily enabled the President's staff to monitor these programs, it also made it easier for President Richard Nixon to dismantle some of them.

In retrospect, it appears that under Johnson's leadership the Federal government may have bitten off more than it could chew. These programs assumed that the government had the duty, and the capability, not just to end discrimination, but to raise the standard of living of poor people, integrate the races, and revise long-standing social patterns. By shifting the emphasis of government action from political equality to social and economic equality, these programs made the government responsible for problems that it could not solve. "This inequality was impervious, unaffected by the economy's cycles, and irremediable short of drastic action—the redistribution of income [and] large-scale integration of the races .... These solutions, the liberals found, were beyond their reach."[28]

Aside from philosophical questions about the proper scope of government, solutions to these pervasive problems proved beyond

26. John Fredrick Martin, *Civil Rights and the Crisis of Liberalism: The Democratic Party 1945-1976.* Boulder, Col.: Westview Press, 1979, p. 183.

27. Miller, *Lyndon,* p. 443.

28. Martin, *Civil Rights and the Crisis of Liberalism,* p. 191. For a detailed critique of the administration of the Community Action Programs of the Great Society's war on poverty, see Daniel Moynihan, *Maximum Feasible Misunderstanding: Community Action in the War on Poverty.* New York: The Free Press, 1969, especially pp. 75-164.

the reach of government for two additional reasons. First was the technical failure of some of the programs resulting from poor planning.   The second was President Johnson's decision to escalate America's Vietnam commitment into a large-scale war.   Both of these factors were related to President Johnson's personality.

Johnson's personal impatience produced a politics of haste in the construction of Great Society programs.   The President shaped his legislative program in response to its political feasibility and urgencies of the moment, giving little consideration to the long-term consequences that the programs might have.   Legislative solutions were enacted before the problems were understood or objectives clearly defined.   Johnson's standard of success was the *passage* of the law, which became an end in itself.   "There is but one way for a President to deal with Congress, and that is continuously, incessantly, and without interruption . . . he's got to build a system that stretches from the cradle to the *grave,* from the moment a bill is introduced to the moment it is officially enrolled as the law of the land."[29] From Johnson's perspective, once the law passed, the process ended, implementation of the program becoming, at best, a secondary priority.

Even if the Great Society had been carefully planned and implemented, it is difficult to believe that these programs could have functioned effectively as the Vietnam conflict heated up.   As the President escalated the war, it consumed an increasingly larger share of the government's resources—an average of $30 billion per year.[30] Like two of his Democratic predecessors—Woodrow Wilson and Franklin Roosevelt—Lyndon Johnson was destined to oversee the sacrifice of progressive social programs to the demands of a large-scale military conflict.   The irony in Johnson's case is that it was a war of his own making, a self-defeating commitment shaped in large measure by his Cold War world view, and reinforced by his personal insecurities.

There is abundant evidence that Lyndon Johnson regarded the Cold War as permanent and Communism as a monolithic enemy. Shortly after Johnson became President, a Senate colleague gave this assessment of him: "Lyndon's ideas were set in thick concrete by World War II.   Every big action he takes will be determined

---

29. Kearns, *Lyndon Johnson,* pp. 236–237.

30. The $30 billion per year figure is cited in Barber, *The Presidential Character,* p. 33.

primarily on the basis of whether he thinks any other action will look like a Munich appeasement. . . . And he will not change course even when he knows he is wrong, because he has a preposterous idea he is bound to lose face if he does."[31]

In the area of foreign relations, Johnson lacked detailed command of realities, relying on a simplistic world view which attributed great strategic significance to Vietnam: "If we quit in Vietnam, tomorrow we'll be fighting in Hawaii and the next week we'll have to fight in San Francisco."[32] In Johnson's mind, falling dominoes intertwined with personal insecurities: "We could tuck our tails between our legs and run for cover. That would just whet the enemy's appetite for greater aggression and more territory, and solve nothing,"[33] and "then I would be seen as a coward and my nation would be seen as an appeaser."[34] Saving Vietnam from the Communists became a very personal struggle for President Johnson. Failure was unthinkable because it would mean that "I had let a democracy fall into the hands of the Communists. That I was a coward. An unmanly man. A man without a spine."[35]

Unwilling to write off Vietnam, but hoping to avoid the appearance of a massive commitment, Johnson initiated a policy of gradual escalation of the conflict. The publicly stated objectives of the policy shifted as the nature of the American commitment grew from a small number of advisers, to American bombing and war by remote control, and, finally, massive involvement of American ground combat forces. The more ineffective American policy appeared, the more stubborn Johnson became. Eventually, more than half a million United States' military personnel were unable to pacify the Vietnamese countryside.

In the end, Johnson's Presidency was a shambles, the President becoming virtually a prisoner under siege in the White House. The foundations of the Great Society nearly within his grasp, he had squandered it on military adventurism, disuniting the nation in the process. He finally withdrew from it all. "Why do these things happen to me?" he moaned in exasperation. "How is it possible that

31. Alfred Steinberg, *Sam Johnson's Boy*. New York: Macmillan Publishing Co., 1968, p. 724. Cited in Barber, *The Presidential Character*, p. 89.

32. Barber, *Presidential Character*, p. 54.

33. Miller, *Lyndon* p. 462.

34. Kearns, *Lyndon Johnson*, p. 263.

35. *Ibid.*, p. 264.

all these people [meaning the American people] could be so un-
grateful to me after I had given them so much?"[36]

Summary Psychobiographical analyses suggest that Lyndon
Johnson experienced at least two major unresolved conflicts which
influenced his personality development. The first involved difficulties
centering around parental identification. Insecurities about his
parents' acceptance and love for him, and the constant tension
between his parents, motivated Johnson throughout his adult life
to seek the unconditional affection he was denied as a child. In addition, Johnson's political behavior was motivated by his fear of
being rendered powerless. A recurring theme in his dreams, this
fear was explicitly manifested as a reaction formation against any
appearance of being unmanly, or not tough enough.

For Johnson, political power was partly a means for dealing with
these insecurities. His need for affection contributed to a humanitarian element in his character that helped to produce the Great
Society programs. This same insecurity caused him to demand positive
responses from his environment. As President, he continually de-
graded his subordinates, demanding constant reassurance, affection,
and total loyalty. This behavior contributed significantly to the
development of a distorted image of reality within the White House.
His fear of being perceived as weak and unmanly, when reinforced
by his Cold War world view, led him to assume a tough militaristic
stance in international affairs, culminating in the tragic escalation in
Vietnam. As the casualties mounted and the antiwar movement
gained strength, Johnson's political world began to come apart.
He withdrew into the White House, blamed his enemies for his
problems, and clung stubbornly to his Vietnam policy. Eventually,
the evidence became overwhelming that the policy was not achieving
its objectives, and President Johnson withdrew from politics, providing Richard Nixon with yet another crisis to resolve.

Richard Milhous Nixon (1969–1974)

On the surface, Lyndon Johnson and Richard Nixon were very different men. Johnson was a dynamic, raucous, and socially gregarious
man who disliked being alone. Nixon was somber, brooding, and
reclusive, sometimes to the point of becoming isolated. Johnson

36. *Ibid.*, p. 11.

(Reproduced from the Collections of the Library of Congress)

was a New Dealer, a dedicated social liberal convinced that there was no limit to the good works that government could accomplish. Nixon, particularly after his experience inside the government bureaucracy, was a conservative, believing in the wisdom of limitations on the scope and direction of governmental social policy. Yet in many ways, these two men were more alike than different. They had in common the childhood experiences of economic deprivation and inconsistent parental affection which contributed to emotional insecurities and compensatory striving on the part of both men. As was the case with Lyndon Johnson, the peculiar construction of Richard Nixon's personality eventually played a significant role in the destruction of his Presidency.

Hard Times Richard Nixon did not have an easy life as a child, and this was reflected in his personality development. In addition to insecurities about parental identification and affection, Nixon experienced the childhood trauma of the death of two of his brothers. He emerged from this series of childhood difficulties as a somewhat pessimistic, suspicious, and defensive person.

That Richard Nixon might have some difficulties with aspects of parental identification is easily understandable. His father, Frank Nixon, had a sixth-grade education and is described as a man with "a fierce temper—a loud, argumentative, opinionated person."[37] Frank Nixon loved the excitement and battles of political life, enjoyed arguing about politics, and, incidentally, was very mistrustful of the news media. Belligerent and unpredictable, he had difficulty holding a steady job. The family struggled economically, existing on the edge of poverty even after Frank settled into a marginally successful small business.

Hannah Milhous, Richard's mother, was long suffering and hard working, a stabilizing force in the family. A devout Quaker, she was apparently the model of stoical repression, able to endure hardship and tragedy with an even temperament. Slow to anger and display emotion, rigid self-control was integral to her character.[38] She cared deeply for Richard, and apparently the feeling was mutual. President Nixon spoke fondly of her (declaring her to be a saint) the day he resigned.

As a child, Richard's one reliable source of affection was disrupted by his mother's absence for an extended period.   First Harold, Richard's older brother, and then Arthur, a younger one, contracted tuberculosis. In an effort to improve Harold's chances for survival, Hannah took him to Arizona for recuperation. Richard was 10 at the time, and Hannah was gone for nearly two years. Meanwhile, Arthur's condition unexpectedly worsened, and he died a short time later. To make matters worse, Harold returned from Arizona uncured and eventually succumbed to the disease.[39]

Any attempt to assess the impact of these hardships and traumatic experiences is, of course, partly guesswork. Psychohistorian Bruce Mazlish suggests that Richard Nixon is likely to have experienced subconscious feelings of guilt as well as remorse over his brothers' deaths.   Survivor guilt is a commonplace phenomenon in similar circumstances.[40]   At the very least, Richard Nixon emerged from these experiences somewhat fatalistic and more than a little insecure.

37. Barber, *Presidential Character,* p. 396.

38. Mazlish, *In Search of Nixon,* pp. 19–22.

39. There seems to be some uncertainty about the exact sequence of these events. See Mazlish, *In Search of Nixon,* pp. 20–21, and Barber, *Presidential Character,* pp. 397–398.

40. Mazlish, *In Search of Nixon,* pp. 22–26.

His outlook and expectations reflected a personality that had been shaped by hardship and tragedy. The inevitable hostility of his environment became an assumption structuring Richard Nixon's personality. Life was less an experience to be enjoyed than an ordeal to be overcome by hard work and personal diligence.

In his traits of hard work, persistence, and repressed anger, Richard Nixon resembled his mother. During her prolonged absence, he began increasingly to identify with his father. This was manifested by growing competitiveness and compensatory striving, a strong determination to succeed against the odds. As Nixon explains it, there were two major reasons for his competitive drive. One was economic, the other personal. "The personal factor was contributed by my father. My biggest thrill was to see the light in his eyes when I brought home a good report card. I was determined not to let him down."[41]

Although Hannah wanted him to be a preacher, by the time Richard was 13 he had decided differently. In an incident laden with irony, Richard announced his decision, declaring to his mother: "I will be an old-fashioned lawyer, a lawyer who can't be bought."[42]

The Political Nixon   Richard Nixon was recruited by a group of California businessmen to run for Congress in 1946. Prior to that time, he had attended Whittier College, where he distinguished himself as an enthusiastic debater, and Duke University Law School, where he earned the nickname "Gloomy Gus." During World War II, he served in the Navy and worked in Washington, D.C., in the Office of Price Administration. As a result of his experiences in the OPA, he became disillusioned with bureaucracy, shifting from a self-described liberal to a conservative.

Shortly after being released from the Navy, he was contacted by a representative of some conservative southern California businessmen interested in sponsoring a Republican candidate to run against liberal Democratic Congressman Jerry Voorhis. Nixon accepted and, in a Republican year, swept the incumbent out of office. This unexpected victory, and his subsequent defeat of Congresswoman Helen G. Douglas, rested on a campaign style that became a Nixon trademark. His emphasis was on detailed preparation, aggressive rhetoric, personal attack, and innuendo.

41. *Ibid.*, p. 29.

42. *Ibid.*, p. 28.

After six years of service in Congress, Nixon's career took another upward swing when he became the Republican nominee for Vice President, sharing the ticket with General Dwight Eisenhower. As Vice President, Nixon worked hard in service to the party, laying the foundation for his three Presidential campaigns. By then the pattern was set: "In the presidency Nixon would return again to a style stressing intensive preparation, fighting rhetoric, and single-handed decision making."[43]

Two distinctive patterns of behavior characterized Richard Nixon's political career. The first was repressed anger displaced onto his opponents, sometimes in an impulsive manner. The second was a syndrome of crisis-oriented behavior. Aspects of Nixon's behavior conformed closely to a pattern of repression, involving both denial and aggression. He projected his own repressed impulses onto others who became not merely critics and opponents but "enemies" and "bums." According to James Barber, "A good deal of Nixon's emotional energy is taken up with resisting the 'temptation' to lash out at his enemies. The work and pain of repression confirms its moral rightness."[44]

As often as not, it was Nixon who smeared his opponents while accusing them of low motives. Nixon seems to have had ambivalent feelings about the release of his hostile emotions, which contributed to the impulsive manner in which he would occasionally vent his anger. Despite his efforts at self-control, the aggression came to the surface sooner or later. One of his favorite targets was the "hostile liberal press." His press conference after he lost the race for Governor of California in 1962 remains one of his better sour grapes performances. "Now that all the members of the press are so delighted that I have lost. . . . Just think how much you're going to be missing. You won't have Nixon to kick around any more. . . ."[45]

As Mazlish interprets this pattern of behavior, it reflected Nixon's *need* for an enemy onto whom he could project his aggressive feelings.[46] For an individual who perceives his environment as threaten-

43. Barber, *Presidential Character,* p. 416.

44. *Ibid.,* p. 362.

45. This is an excerpt from Nixon's famous "last press conference," cited in Earl Mazo and Stephen Hess, *Nixon: A Political Portrait.* New York: Popular Library, 1968, p. 294.

46. Mazlish, *In Search of Nixon,* p. 85.

ing, and people as untrustworthy, his is perhaps an understandable need. It took on a more ominous dimension as Nixon and his White House assistants began compiling their enemies' list. Throughout his career, Nixon left no doubt that, when the chips were down, he played hardball. When your enemies are out to get you, it makes sense to get them first.

One of the more intriguing insights into Richard Nixon's character is the notion, shared by several psychobiographers, that crises have a positive value for Nixon. Crises were essential to Nixon's conception of leadership, providing him with a means to test himself and raise his self-esteem by successfully surmounting the crisis. In the introduction to his first book, *Six Crises*, Nixon states: "No one really knows what he is capable of until he is tested to the full by events over which he may have no control."[47] A leader is one able to act in a crisis, and the successful handling of a crisis enhances the leader's status. Yet crises were for Nixon more than a test of leadership; they constituted an exhilarating experience, a method of coping, and a way of life. Crises were functional for Richard Nixon's personality structure, an integral part of his political outlook. Upon closer examination, Nixon's six crises prove not to be decisions of worldwide significance, but mostly events which constituted a threat, or challenge, for Nixon personally.[48]

> The Hiss case which launched Nixon's career in Congress
> The controversy over the slush fund, which nearly cost him the Vice Presidential nomination
> President Eisenhower's heart attack, which might have thrust Nixon into the Presidency
> Nixon's trip to Caracas, Venezuela, involving a confrontation with an unruly mob
> Nixon's debate with Khrushchev
> Nixon's defeat in the 1960 Presidential election

It may well be that crises for Nixon constituted a method of functioning in a hostile environment. He expected to confront crises and, perhaps, even needed crises to continually test himself. Seen in this light, some of his behavior becomes more comprehensible.

47. Richard Nixon, *Six Crises*. New York: Doubleday & Co., Inc., 1968, p. XXVI.

48. *Ibid.*, for Nixon's analysis.

"Nixon is like a daredevil who, to prove himself, must constantly and unnecessarily risk failure."[49]   Life may have been difficult for Richard Nixon, but he repeatedly took actions which made it more so.   His insecurities prompted him to choose events which opened up probabilities for confrontation and crisis, frequently unnecessarily. Examples abound: As a law student at Duke University, his anxiety about grades was so great that he and several other students broke into the dean's office to sneak a look at their grades.   Apparently his apprehension about failure motivated him to risk possible expulsion.[50] On other occasions during his political career, from the slush fund to the Watergate activities, Nixon authorized or sanctioned unnecessarily risky activities on the borderline of legality.   His behavior during the Senate fight over the Carswell nomination to the Supreme Court, his decision to order an American invasion of Cambodia, and his handling of the Watergate affair are regarded by psychobiographers as instances in which Nixon's personality traits of repressed anger, anxiety, and seclusion significantly affected his behavior.

In the Supreme Court nomination struggle, Nixon opted for a confrontation with the United States Senate, with the result that the President had two consecutive Supreme Court nominees rejected.   In line with his Southern strategy, Nixon had decided to nominate a Southern strict constructionist to the Court.   He delegated the task of finding one to Attorney General John Mitchell.   As a result of poor staff work by Mitchell and his aides, the President was embarrassed.   The nominee suggested, a Federal Circuit Court judge named Clement Haynsworth, proved unacceptable to the Senate.   In addition to a possible conflict of interest (Haynsworth had heard a case involving a company in which he owned stock), was his even more troublesome record of pro-segregation judicial decisions. With his civil rights voting record being the reason, and the conflict of interest providing the excuse, Haynsworth was rejected by the Senate as a nominee for the Supreme Court.

Incensed, Nixon lashed out at Haynsworth's critics, denouncing them as character assassins.   Even though he had not consulted with Senate leaders about the nomination and had accepted Mitchell's sloppy staff work, the President blamed his enemies in the Senate for this defeat.   After condemning those Republican Senators who

49. Mazlish, *In Search of Nixon*, p. xii.

50. Robert E. DiClerico, *The American President*.   Englewood Cliffs, N.J.: Prentice-Hall Inc., 1979, pp. 276–277.

"betrayed their President," he decided to stand fast and apply the same criteria to the next Supreme Court nominee. Incredibly, the next nominee suggested by Mitchell's staff proved to be even less satisfactory than Haynsworth. In addition to having a record favoring white supremacy, Judge G. Harold Carswell's judicial credentials bordered on incompetence, in the opinion of Senate liberals and civil rights spokesmen. Nixon's response was that the issue was not Carswell's competence, but the President's right to *choose* Supreme Court justices.[51] This challenge to the Senate's prerogative of advice and consent was an indication of the President's intransigence. Take it or leave it, he would not withdraw the nomination. One week later, the President's second consecutive Supreme Court nominee was rejected by the Senate.

Several of President Nixon's biographers have been intrigued by a possible connection between the President's highly emotional reaction to the Haynsworth–Carswell debacle and the subsequent American invasion of Cambodia, initiated by the President less than three weeks later. Various military options had been under consideration during Nixon's Presidency, but the juxtaposition in time of these events, along with the fiery Presidential rhetoric accompanying them, has been interpreted as displaced aggression on the part of the President. In March 1970, Prince Sihanouk's government in Cambodia had been overthrown by a military regime more sympathetic to the United States. On 23 April 1970, only two weeks after Carswell's rejection by the Senate, the President instructed his national security advisers to develop more aggressive options for coping with Communist advances in Cambodia. Close advisers to the President cautioned him that a move into Cambodia by American ground forces would provoke massive unrest by American antiwar activists while producing little in the way of concrete military gains. The President withdrew to Camp David to think it over. Three days later he announced to his aides his decision to use American ground forces for an attack into Cambodia. In his address of 30 April 1970, the President stated: "It is not our power but our will and character that is being tested tonight . . . . If we fail to meet the challenge, all other nations will be on notice that despite its overwhelming power, the United States, when a real crisis comes, will be found wanting. . . ."[52]   Characteristically, President Nixon

51. Barber, *Presidential Character*, pp. 427–429.

52. *Ibid.*, pp. 435–436.

justified his decision by contending that it was the North Vietnamese, and not the Americans, who were violating Cambodian neutrality. Mazlish's analysis concludes: "Coming shortly after the Carswell episode—a real defeat—Nixon's incursion into Cambodia and attack on his 'peacenik' critics must have been very satisfying emotionally."[53]

From the perspective of Richard Nixon's personality needs, the events of Watergate become somewhat understandable. Risk taking, aggressive confrontation, and crisis management were integral to Nixon's conception of leadership. Seen in this light, some of the events of Watergate become part of a larger pattern linked to his personality structure and motivated by personal needs and insecurities. What distinguishes Watergate was that Nixon obliged his enemies by electronically recording his role in the episode, thereby laying the foundation for the destruction of his Presidency. Writing *before* Watergate, James Barber warned that the danger of Nixon's Presidency was that crisis might be transformed into tragedy if the President risked public exposure of inadequacy by confronting a crisis from which he could not escape by moving on to some alternative crisis. "The loss of power to forces beyond his control would constitute a severe threat. That would be the time to go down, if go down one must, in flames."[54]

53. Mazlish, *In Search of Nixon*, p. 132.

54. Barber, *Presidential Character*, p. 442.

Summary Richard Nixon had his share of difficulties during his childhood. In addition to real economic deprivation, he also experienced uncertainties about parental affection and lost two of his brothers. He emerged from this series of childhood difficulties as a somewhat pessimistic, suspicious, and defensive individual. Throughout his political career, he frequently denied his own motives, projecting them onto others while behaving in an impulsive and crisis-prone manner. Crises were functional for Nixon's personality structure, providing him with a means to test himself. By surmounting crises, he reassured himself that he was a strong leader who was in control. He had a marked preference for handling crises in seclusion, sometimes making decisions single-handedly.

Before his Presidency was discredited by the Watergate scandal, Richard Nixon established several policies that left a lasting imprint on American politics, particularly in the area of international affairs. Domestic politics was not a consuming interest of the President, but he did successfully sponsor the revenue-sharing program, an innovative approach to Federal aid to the states. International affairs were his forte. In addition to eventually extricating the nation from involvement in the divisive Vietnam War, he initiated new American relationships with the Soviet Union and the People's Republic of China. This policy of detente contributed to a lessening of international tensions during his administration.

Unnecessarily risky and illegal actions on the part of the President and his subordinates eventually led to his downfall. In the words of one observer, "When Nixon had come on stage in January 1969, asking Americans to lower their voices, they were shouting at one another. Now they were shouting at him."[55]

James Earl Carter, Jr. (1977–1980)

Jimmy Carter is proving to be one of the more difficult Presidents to analyze. Only the second Democratic President since Franklin Roosevelt to be elected with an absolute majority of the vote, he subsequently became the only Democratic incumbent to be defeated in this century. With an effective, folksy style of campaigning, and a seemingly positive personality, a few commentators found him somewhat reminiscent of John Kennedy as he assumed the Presi-

55. R. Gordon Hoxie, *Command Decision and the Presidency: A Study of National Security Policy and Organization.* New York: Reader's Digest Press, 1977, p. 305.

dency. But there was to be no Camelot South. As President Carter left office four years later, his stilted and uninspiring style of public address, defensive campaign tactics, and ineffectiveness in economic affairs seemed more reminiscent of Herbert Hoover. Self-assured as a candidate, he appeared uncertain as President, a man without clear direction who was in over his head.

The passage of time may provide a clearer perspective; but at present, psychobiographers, perplexed by the complexities of his personality, do not seem to know what to make of Jimmy Carter. Mazlish and Diamond, and James Barber (in his preliminary assessment), regard Carter as having a relatively positive personality, high self-esteem, and the capacity for growth in office. Presumably many of his difficulties as President would be attributable to his lack of experience in Washington.   Others are more skeptical, viewing Carter's apparent self-confidence as a surface trait.   Betty Glad, Lloyd deMause, and Paul Elovitz have concluded that Jimmy Carter is an insecure and defensive person whose political difficulties are related to his personality.[56]   Both Elovitz and Glad analyze Jimmy Carter as a narcissistic personality. The most distinctive personality trait associated with this type of individual is the projection of a highly idealized, i.e. unrealistic, self-image.   There is a noticeable contrast between the individual's claims to virtual perfection and the reality of his performance. The narcissist displays a seeming abundance of self-confidence and may, in fact, be somewhat gifted, but he tends to overrate his capabilities while discounting his shortcomings.   The unrealistic self-image creates difficulties in dealing with the real world because the idealized self-concept is so perfect that it is beyond human realization.   The narcissistic individual, however, has convinced himself that this ideal is, in fact, attainable and that he has attained it. This leads him to dismiss his own shortcomings and failures and to react defensively to criticism.   An air of seeming self-assurance and confidence is maintained only in the absence of serious criticism.

The narcissistic individual becomes the victim of a self-imposed pride system, which has an inevitable inferiority complex built into it.   Unrealistic perfectionist standards are internalized and, when they subsequently cannot be met, evoke feelings of inferiority for not

56. See Glad, *JC: In Search;* Lloyd deMause, *"JC and American Fantasy,"* and Paul H. Elovitz, "Three Days in Plains," both in deMause and Ebel eds., *J.C: and American Fantasy: Psychohistorical Explorations,* pp. 9–58.

(Photo by Bill Fitz-Patrick)

measuring up. The individual has defined his self-worth in terms of being something he is not. This ideal self can be maintained and protected only by distorting reality, especially by refusal to permit internal or external questioning. Thoughts not in accord with the ideal image are repressed, erecting a barrier between the individual and some kinds of external reality.[57]

This complex personality pattern of surface self-confidence, in conflict with more deeply rooted insecurities, develops early in life as a defense against underlying feelings of vulnerability. In Jimmy Carter's case, it may be attributed to the necessity of dealing with perfectionist standards imposed by his parents, stern demands for obedience to authority, and insecurities associated with conditional parental affection.

Why Not the Best? The Carter family's economic circumstances during Jimmy's childhood can best be described as ranging from modest to comfortable. After a few years as a somewhat successful

57. Glad, *In Search*, pp. 489–495.

small businessman, Earl Carter, Sr., acquired some farmland a few miles outside of Plains, Georgia. The family enterprises entailed hard work.on everyone's part, including the children who had their farm chores to do. Economic deprivation was not really a problem, however. According to Miss Lillian, as Jimmy Carter's mother prefers to be known, "We didn't feel poor and we always had a car. We had the first radio in Plains. We had the first TV set."[58] From relatively modest beginnings the Carter family prospered, building the family businesses into an enterprise worth several million dollars. At one point, there were more than 200 black men and women working for Mr. Earl as field hands and sharecroppers.[59]

The President's mother is a vibrant, independent, and compassionate individual. A number of observers have concluded, however, that in her relationships with her children she was a distant mother. As a nurse, she was gone much of the time, ministering to the sick 10 to 12 hours a day. After Jimmy Carter was nominated for President, Paul Elovitz visited Plains and interviewed Miss Lillian. Finding her a charming but very ambivalent woman, he was intrigued by the prospect of what a consistent dosage of such ambivalence would do to a person psychologically.[60] According to Betty Glad's analysis, Miss Lillian tends to see herself in perfectionist terms, as an outspoken proponent of virtue and tolerance, giving and receiving perfect love: "I would like to be remembered as a person who loves everybody and everything." In another interview, Miss Lillian said, "I'm sure I'm not bragging when I say that I never had anybody work for me who didn't love me. . . . Nowadays, I am supposed to be, and I think I am, the most liberal woman in the county, maybe the state."[61]

Jimmy's father, James Earl, Sr., was perhaps the most influential figure in his life. Jimmy often described him in highly idealized terms.

58. Barber, *Presidential Character*, p. 502.

59. Although the President would later portray himself and some of his family as liberals on racial matters, it appears that the Carters assumed a relatively traditional stance in relationships with blacks, both races following a strict social etiquette which recognized the superior position of whites. The Carter family is perhaps better described as genteel white patrons with a humanitarian concern for black people than as courageous progressives who challenged the dominant Southern caste system. See Glad, *JC: In Search*, pp. 40–42.

60. Elovitz, "Three Days in Plains," in deMause and Ebel, *JC and American Fantasy: Psychohistorical Explorations*, pp. 34–46.

61. Glad, JC: *In Search*, pp. 31–32.

Earl, Sr., communicated two indisputable lessons in life to his first-born son: obedience to authority and a striving for perfection. Their relationship appears to have been such that the father set very high standards, and Jimmy Carter was expected to meet them. Success was seldom rewarded or praised—it was simply expected. Anything less than the best was unacceptable. Likewise, misbehavior was equally unacceptable and punishment was swift, being personally administered by Earl Carter with the aid of his peach tree switch.

There is every reason to believe that Jimmy Carter internalized his father's lessons in obedience and upward striving. He tried to earn his father's love, but meeting his perfectionist standards proved difficult. According to Jimmy's sister Gloria, "No matter how well Jimmy did, Daddy always said he could do better."[62] Not surprisingly, Jimmy Carter developed into a very competitive and somewhat anxious person, having grown up with the belief that being less than perfect is essentially the same as failure. The title Jimmy Carter chose for his autobiography, *Why Not the Best?*, is indicative of the major assumption structuring his personality.

Being very achievement oriented, Jimmy Carter set challenging goals for himself. Having graduated from high school at 16, he attended junior college in preparation for attending a university. In 1943, he was admitted to the United States Naval Academy in Annapolis. After completing his education and a tour at sea, he applied for duty aboard the Navy's new atomic submarine. By his own account he seems to have liked the Navy and quite possibly would have made a career of it. His goal was to be Chief of Naval Operations. His father's death in 1953 changed things. Jimmy Carter made a difficult career decision and, over his wife Rosalynn's objections, returned to Plains to manage the family businesses. Having assumed his father's role as head of the family, Jimmy proved to be an astute entrepreneur.

As a successful businessman and community leader, Jimmy Carter was only peripherally involved in politics, confining his service to the Sumter County school board. Yet, in the back of his mind was the notion that some day he would like to be governor of Georgia. In the fall of 1962, he made his first move for state office, announcing his candidacy for a seat in the Georgia Senate. Because of the corrupt practices of a local county political boss, Carter lost the Democratic primary. Unwilling to be beaten by vote fraud, Carter launched a

62. Mazlish and Diamond, *JC: Interpretive Biography*, p. 82.

battle in the courts and within the Democratic party. In a fight that went down to the wire, requiring voters in several counties to write in Carter's name, he eventually triumphed in the general election.

Jimmy Carter took his seat in the Georgia Senate 10 years after Earl Carter had served a term in Georgia's House of Representatives. One of the bills Jimmy Carter helped get passed was a new election code. In the Georgia legislature, Carter earned a reputation as a hard worker with a command of detail. A weakness that emerged was his tendency to try to do too much by himself. Not a team player, he displayed little flair for collegiality. His reluctance to participate in the give and take of political compromise and bargaining was a trait that would come back to haunt his Presidency.

After his early political successes, Jimmy Carter began to think big. When a fellow legislator advised him to run for lieutenant governor, Carter responded "Why *lieutenant* governor?"[63] In 1966, Carter's determination to reach the top and his confidence in his ability to win prompted him to try the first in a series of long-shot candidacies. Passing up a relatively sure Congressional seat, he decided to risk the crowded Democratic primary for governor. It was a bold move for a relatively unknown state senator, but he had overestimated his chances. The voters of Georgia awarded the Democratic gubernatorial nomination to fried-chicken restauranteur Lester Maddox. This defeat was a wrenching emotional experience for Carter, but he came back to win the governorship in 1970. As governor, he began building the personal and financial organization that would be the basis for his Presidential nomination in 1976.

As both Governor and President, Jimmy Carter manifested personality-related behavior patterns which affected the quality of his leadership. Because of his highly idealized self-concept, he frequently overrated his capabilities.[64] His analysis of the problems facing American government tended to be simplistic, and he seemed unaware, or unconcerned, about the formidable power of other national political institutions.

Nowhere was Carter's failure to grasp the complexities of national politics more evident than in his relationship with Congress. Despite large Democratic majorities in both houses, the President and his disorganized liaison staff spun their wheels for much of their

63. Barber, *Presidential Character,* p. 526.

64. Glad, *In Search,* pp. 476–493.

first two years in office. A conversation between the President and Speaker of the House, Thomas P. O'Neill, is instructive. When Carter told O'Neill how he had handled the Georgia legislators by going over their heads directly to the people, the Speaker said: "Hey, wait a minute, you have 289 guys up there (the House Democrats) who know their districts pretty well. They ran against the Administration (Ford), and they wouldn't hesitate to run against you." The President, apparently surprised, replied "Oh, really?"[65]

The clash between Jimmy Carter's expectations of himself and the reality of his performance caused him to react defensively to criticism, perhaps making it difficult for him to learn from his mistakes. This guarded and defensive posture may be one reason why Carter did not enjoy the wheeling and dealing of politics. He needed to be right, or at least to *feel* that he was right. In a meeting between the President and George Meany, the labor leader explained why organized labor could not support the President's wage guidelines. Carter's response was, "If you can't support me, I'd rather not talk," and then he walked out of the room.[66] Former White House Chief of Staff Hamilton Jordan was perhaps hinting at the same problem when he described Carter this way: "He doesn't understand the personal element in politics, though nobody is better at campaigning."[67]

When Carter was comfortably ahead of his opponents, his campaign style seemed warm, relaxed, and self-assured. In a less-secure position, particularly when running behind in the polls, Carter's warm and folksy style gave way to more strident and aggressive tactics, including personal attacks on his opponents. When threatened, Carter relied increasingly on a campaign style employing thinly veiled aggression and innuendo. In the 1970 gubernatorial campaign in Georgia, Carter disparaged the integrity of former Governor Carl Sanders. In his campaigns for the Democratic Presidential nominations in 1976 and 1980, there were innuendos about Morris Udall's health, Hubert Humphrey's age, and Edward Kennedy's character. His campaign for reelection in 1980 relied heavily on personal attacks on Ronald Reagan, employing scare tactics such as portraying Reagan as a warmonger and a racist. When Secretary of State Cyrus Vance left the Carter administration the President rewarded Vance's three

65. Mazlish and Diamond, *JC: Interpretive Biography*, p. 235.

66. Glad, *In Search*, p. 496.

67. Barber, *Presidential Character*, p. 533.

and a half years of service by giving him a kick in the pants, saying that he hoped his new secretary, Edmund Muskie, would be "much stronger" and "more statesmanlike."[68]

In addition to the overestimation of his capabilities, and the defensive posture which resulted, Carter as President tended to emphasize form over substance. The *appearance* of doing well was more important than the contents of his policies and the quality of his accomplishments. This emphasis on style and appearances at the expense of substance had two consequences. One was a heavy emphasis on symbols and public relations techniques. Early in the Carter Presidency, the public was treated to a barrage of cardigan sweaters, town meetings, and even a fireside chat. As things began to go sour, different gimmicks were employed, culminating in July 1979, with his retreat to Camp David to reevaluate his Presidency. The President had concluded that something was wrong, not with his performance, but with the way his Presidency was being presented to the country. After his retreat, the President reshuffled his cabinet (accepting five resignations), proclaimed that the problem lay elsewhere (in the "crisis of the American spirit"), and proposed a new energy program. These face-saving antics prompted the editors of *The New Republic* to draft an editorial entitled, "Ennui the People":

> Two weeks into the official crisis of spirit, President Carter's search for "bold" actions that will excite all of us without offending any of us grows more desperate by the hour. What next? Will he have the White House torn down and rebuilt facing in the opposite direction? Will he order all his Cabinet members to wear funny hats? Will he stage ritual bonfires across the country? Since the beginning of July, Carter and his advisers have been putting on a circus. It is a farcical and insulting attempt to distract us all from the fact that our standard of living has begun to decline, and they don't have a clue what to do about it.[69]

Describing Carter's energy program as a "public relations gambit" designed to give the electorate the impression that he had taken bold and decisive action, *The New Republic* concluded that "President Carter, even at his most serious, is concerned only with the appear-

68. Richard Reeves, "Carter Employs Humiliation When Threatened by Enemies," *Dayton Daily News,* May 26, 1980, p. 12.

69. "Ennui the People," *The New Republic,* August 4 and 11, 1979, p. 5.

ance of things. . . . This administration will take no action that helps us all in the long run but hurts anyone in particular."[70]

A second consequence of Carter's concern with appearances was that, as President, he never clarified the priorities of his administration. As described by one of his speech writers, Jimmy Carter holds explicit opinions on a wide variety of issues, "but he has no large view of the relations between them, no line indicating which goals (reducing unemployment? human rights?) will take precedence over which (inflation control? a SALT treaty?) when the goals conflict."[71]

In her assessment of President Jimmy Carter, Betty Glad concludes:

> Rather than acting as the moral and political leader of the nation, he has used his position and his ability to command attention to promote a further trivialization of political dialogue in America and obfuscation of the political alternatives before the nation. . . . The agenda for the nation has been compiled out of a random list of promises he had made on the campaign trail and his *ad hoc* reaction to events in terms of his political interests.[72]

Summary Preliminary assessments of Jimmy Carter's potential as President tended to be relatively positive. After four years of disappointing performance, a reassessment is underway. Speculation about Jimmy Carter's difficulties as President have focused on his inexperience and on his personality, both reasonable causes for concern.

Jimmy Carter may prove to be the prototype of a new kind of Presidential candidate—the inexperienced outsider running against the Washington establishment. Prospects for electoral success by this type of candidate have been enhanced by recent developments in the Presidential nominating process. As President, such individuals are likely to find themselves somewhat disconnected from Washington politics, having neither the national power base and connections, nor the political experience necessary to manipulate the Presidential system. In Carter's case, by the time he figured out how the system worked, he had lost much of his Congressional and public support.

70. *Ibid.*, p. 6.

71. Glad, *In Search,* p. 485.

72. *Ibid.*, p. 506.

Beyond these difficulties, but related to them, is the question of Jimmy Carter's personality. Psychobiographers are by no means unanimous in their analyses, and it is too early for a definitive assessment. Betty Glad's psychobiographical profile is the most successful, thus far, in linking Carter's personality attributes to his behavior as President. Regarding Jimmy Carter's personality development as having been heavily influenced by his parents' perfectionist standards, Glad concludes that because of his highly idealized self-concept, the President tended to overrate his capabilities. The resulting gap between this ideal and the reality of performance caused him to react defensively. Concerned especially with the appearance of success, the President frequently emphasized form over substance.

SELF-ASSURANCE AND LEADERSHIP

The insecurity-and-politics model of political leadership rests on the assumption that individuals are motivated to seek political power primarily by the need to compensate for personal insecurities. Politics and power become a means for raising self-esteem. This model is most appropriate when an individual's personality development results in heavy reliance on mechanisms of ego defense as a means of coping with threats and insecurities. Psychobiographical analyses suggest that significant aspects of the Johnson and Nixon Presidencies may be understood by this approach. Likewise, this approach has contributed considerable insights into the behavior of Presidents Jimmy Carter and Woodrow Wilson, President Wilson being portrayed as insecure and highly moralistic. These personality traits are attributed primarily to Wilson's relationship with his domineering father, a Presbyterian minister. Wilson's political behavior was, on occasion, characterized by inflexibility, particularly toward the end of his Presidency. Although instrumental in creating the League of Nations, Wilson also possessed the messianic zeal and moral absolutism to destroy it rather than compromise with Senate opponents of the League of Nations Covenant. Likewise, President Theodore Roosevelt's militarism has been analyzed as a response to his personal needs to assume a manly and courageous posture.[73]

73. On President Wilson, see George and George, *Woodrow Wilson and Colonel House,* pp. 219–315; and Barber, *Presidential Character,* pp. 58–68. On Theodore Roosevelt, see Henry F. Pringle, *Theodore Roosevelt.* New York: Harcourt Brace, 1931.

The psychoanalytic model analyzes behavior in terms of personal insecurities. Yet it is possible that highly insecure individuals are the exception rather than the rule among Presidents. If the majority of political leaders is reasonably well adjusted, then another approach may be appropriate for assessing the impact of personality on political behavior. An alternative school of thought, known as growth-actualization, has suggested a different model of personality development. Although retaining the notion of biologically based needs (and the potential for personality insecurities associated with unmet needs), this approach contends that once basic needs are met, they *cease* to be a primary motive for behavior. The human personality may grow beyond the point of simply striving to meet basic needs and reach a new level of creativity. Human existence can be more than a constant struggle with personal insecurities. An individual whose basic needs have been met is likely to develop a secure personality and the self-assurance which permits creative growth. Conversely, those whose needs have not been met will continue to struggle with personal insecurities associated with meeting those needs. The behavior of such psychically deprived individuals resembles that of the insecure, defensive individual in the psychoanalytic model. Psychically deprived persons may use politics as a vehicle for meeting their needs for affection and esteem. However, pursuit of power may also be based on healthy personality drives. All those seeking power are not neurotics; individuals do, on occasion, seek power for more noble purposes.[74]

The growth-actualization model assumes .that basic needs are arranged in a hierarchy and that, as each need is met, the individual becomes free to pursue higher needs. The order of needs in Abraham Maslow's hierarchy is:

5. Self-actualization—the need for creative growth
4. Esteem—including self-esteem and external recognition
3. Affection
2. Safety and security
1. Physiological—basic drives, including hunger, sex, and shelter

74. This discussion is based on Jeanne Knutson's application of Maslow's hierarchy of needs. See Knutson, *Human Basis of the Polity*, pp. 27–48.

Self-actualization is defined as a state of growth, or creativity, which begins to unfold when an individual's basic personality needs have been met. In contrast to the insecurity-and-politics hypothesis, Jeanne Knutson has suggested an alternative: "Individuals who achieve leadership roles tend to have self-actualizing personalities."[75] Such self-assured individuals would bring considerable creative potential to positions of political leadership. They are likely to be relatively tolerant, secure and undogmatic, and low in anxiety and hostility. Being growth-motivated, they are less focused on ego defense and more free to focus on competent problem solving. They are better able to assess the external world in realistic terms because they are less threatened by it. In addition, Knutson suggests that self-assured politicians are likely to retain commitment to democratic values despite strong counter pressures.

In summary, leadership by self-assured individuals allows more problems to be solved because of the lack of rigidity, more realistic assessments of reality, and the inclusion of more people with differing opinions into the decision making process. There are likely to be substantial differences in both the style and quality of leadership provided by psychically secure individuals relatively free from anxieties, as opposed to psychically insecure individuals whose unfulfilled needs encourage rigidity and inflexibility.

The self-assured, adaptable, growth-oriented politician as President should be regarded as an ideal type which may be approximated in varying degrees. Even the most self-assured individual does not approach all problems systematically and rationally, nor does the insecure, defensive person behave in a totally pathological fashion. Among modern Presidents, Franklin Roosevelt is perhaps the most likely candidate as a self-actualizing personality.

Franklin Delano Roosevelt (1933-1945)

Franklin Roosevelt's childhood home environment was characterized by emotional warmth and economic abundance. His father, James Roosevelt, was vice president of several corporations. In his spare time, he enjoyed the good life at his Hyde Park estate, distracting himself with a stable of horses and occasionally dabbling in Democratic politics. Sara Delano, James' second wife and Franklin's mother, was likewise accustomed to the benefits of economic privilege.

75. *Ibid.*, p. 102.

(National Archives 306. PS–49. 1935)

Her father owned copper, iron, and coal mines and a fleet of clipper ships.

Franklin was their only child and was reared with unusual indulgence. He had governesses, tutors, ponies, and his own sailboat. Trips to Europe were commonplace. At 14, he entered the Rev. Endicott Peabody's Groton School to be educated with his peers. The Groton boys, about 90% of whom were from social register families, lived in an atmosphere of paternal kindness and solicitude.[76]   As was the custom for young men of his class, Franklin completed his education in the Ivy League, first at Harvard and then at Columbia Law School. Bored with the tedious study of law, he left Columbia without a degree, although he absorbed enough to pass the bar. With a touch of understatement, Sara summed up his youth this way: "After all, he had many advantages that other boys did not have."[77]

76. Richard Hofstadter, *The American Political Tradition.* New York: Vintage Books, 1954, pp. 318–319.

77. *Ibid.,* p. 319.

Having grown up in an environment that nurtured his self-esteem, Franklin Roosevelt was blessed with a strong sense of social and personal identification. This self-assurance contributed to his easy going tolerance and genuine liking for people, including his willingness to learn from others. The family tradition of involvement in progressive Democratic politics reinforced his penchant for public service.

Franklin's enthusiasm and social skills, along with his father's political connections, made it easy for him to enter politics. Democratic nominations were relatively easy to obtain in Republican upstate New York, so in 1910, Roosevelt was nominated for a state Senate seat. He campaigned vigorously, running well ahead of the Democratic ticket. After two years of service to the progressive cause in Albany, he was selected by President Woodrow Wilson to be Assistant Secretary of the Navy. He was 31. In 1920, he added his prestigious family name to the national Democratic ticket as Vice Presidential nominee in a losing cause.

In August 1921, he contracted polio and it appeared that his promising career was finished. It would have been easy for Roosevelt to surrender his political aspirations by retiring as a semi-invalid to the comfortable privacy of Hyde Park. Franklin Roosevelt would have none of it, and, with his wife Eleanor's help and support, he launched an amazing comeback. By spring of 1922, he was walking on crutches and steadily gaining strength. He never regained full use of his legs, relying instead on his inner strength to carry him to the most spectacular political career in American history. He served first as Governor of New York from 1929 to 1933, and then 12 consecutive years as President of the United States.

President Roosevelt There is little doubt that Franklin Roosevelt's personality traits, especially his openness and receptivity to other people's opinions, and his personal warmth and charm, contributed to his successful Presidential leadership. It should be remembered, however, that FDR confronted a very favorable power situation and climate of expectations. The problems he faced were enormous, but so were his opportunities to experiment. Swept into office by a landslide, the Democrats controlled both houses of Congress by two-to-one majorities. As they expanded the Federal bureaucracy with new programs, President Roosevelt was able to appoint sympathetic administrators. Only the Supreme Court was beyond his control.

The economic catastrophe of the Great Depression had stunned the nation, nearly totally disrupting the economy. Historian Richard Hofstadter describes the national climate of expectations as Roosevelt assumed the Presidency: "When he came to power, the people had seen stagnation go dangerously far. They wanted experiment, activity, trial and error, anything that would convey a sense of movement and novelty."[78] With the possible exception of the first two years of Lyndon Johnson's second term (1965–66), no modern President has enjoyed so favorable a power situation in combination with highly supportive public expectations. President Roosevelt and the New Deal Democrats had won nearly total control of the government. They had been given virtually carte blanche and proceeded to make the most of it.

President Roosevelt's style of leadership relied on his personal charm and persuasiveness in intimate settings, and on inspirational rhetoric for communicating with the public. His extroverted personality and warmth, along with his party's near-total control of the government, combined to make him very persuasive. The stage was set. A skillful politician controlled the Presidency, and his party's loyalists dominated the Congress. The crisis atmosphere assured that action would be forthcoming. It remained for Franklin Roosevelt to influence the pace and direction of government policy.

Under Roosevelt's leadership, the Democrats launched the New Deal, a series of innovative and pragmatic social and economic programs aimed at alleviating the economic chaos by stabilizing the banking system, regulating the stock market, and putting people back to work. A series of programs was implemented making credit available to farmers and businessmen, providing direct relief for the unemployed, and creating jobs through public-works projects. Given the abundance of problems and the shortage of solutions, the New Deal was inevitably experimental in nature. According to Hofstadter: "(Herbert) Hoover lacked motion. Roosevelt lacked direction. But his capacity for growth, or at least for change, was enormous."[79]

Determined to learn from others, Roosevelt organized his administration in a way that would maximize ideas, information, and alternatives. In the interest of "creative competition," his selections of advisers and Cabinet personnel reflected a variety of political outlooks. He frequently delegated similar responsibilities to more than one assistant, encouraging the clash of ideas and philosophies to

78. *Ibid.*, p. 316.

79. *Ibid.*

provide himself with competing alternatives. In this manner, he retained the prerogative of final decision in matters he considered important, while encouraging diversity of input from his subordinates.

As legislative leader, he worked through the Congressional leadership, carefully defining priorities while reserving his personal persuasive efforts for "must" legislation. He was interested in determining legislative goals but was flexible about means.[80] The President's sensitivity to consultation and compromise, his personal energy and persuasiveness, and the exigencies of the crisis situation produced an immense outpouring of legislation. The symbolism of the New Deal programs was, perhaps, as significant as their substance. Action and, equally important, the impression of action, had been successfully initiated. Restoration of public confidence in the economic and governmental system rested partly upon this impression, and partly on Franklin Roosevelt's ability to inspire the public with his eloquent rhetoric. President Roosevelt's Inaugural Address is one of the classics of American political rhetoric:

> First of all, let me assert my firm belief that the only thing we have to fear is fear itself—nameless, unreasoning, unjustified terror. . . . We are stricken by no plague of locusts. . . . Plenty is at our doorstep, but a generous use of it languishes in the very sight of supply. Primarily this is because rulers of the exchange of mankind's goods have failed, through their own stubbornness and their own incompetence, have admitted their failure, and have abdicated. . . . The money changers have fled from their high seats in the temple of our civilization. We may now restore that temple to the ancient truths.[81]

Franklin Roosevelt's rare gift was the ability to communicate effectively with the public. Contrasting Roosevelt's skill at public address with that of his predecessor, Hofstadter states: "When Hoover bumbled that it was necessary only to restore confidence, the nation laughed bitterly. When Roosevelt said 'the only thing we have to fear is fear itself,' essentially the same threadbare half-truth, the nation

---

80. Erwin C. Hargrove, *The Power of the Modern Presidency.* New York: Alfred A. Knopf, Inc., 1974, p. 53.

81. Cited in William E. Leuchtenburg, *Franklin D. Roosevelt and the New Deal.* New York: Harper & Row, 1963, p. 41.

was thrilled."[82]   Audiences in excess of 60 million Americans tuned in on radio to hear the President's fireside chats as he called for sacrifice, discipline, and action. He had created the impression of a man who knew how to lead and had faith in the future.[83] Time and again he was able to appeal successfully for public support as he led the nation from depression to recovery and from peace into world war.

There were miscalculations, of course, resulting as much from overconfidence as from arrogance. His first major Congressional defeat came after his overwhelming reelection victory in 1936. Frustrated by the Supreme Court's unfavorable rulings about the constitutionality of some New Deal programs, Roosevelt devised a thinly disguised plan to pack the Court with liberals. To promote greater judicial efficiency, the President proposed legislation expanding the size of the Court by permitting him to make an additional appointment for every Justice 70 years old. Although this proposal failed to pass the Congress, commentators noted a subsequent change in the attitude of the Court—"the switch in time that saved nine."

Roosevelt's boundless self-confidence and his control of American foreign policy during World War II led him to pursue a highly personalized brand of diplomacy, sometimes with mixed results. The President's belief in his personal charisma and charm caused him, on occasion, to overestimate his ability to manipulate other world leaders, notably Joseph Stalin. At the Yalta conference in February, 1945, "Roosevelt, Churchill, and Stalin sat down to remake a good part of the world map and reshape the structure of world power."[84] The President, by now a sick man with only two months to live, found Joseph Stalin an extremely tough negotiator who was not to be disarmed by pleasantries and personal charm. Roosevelt focused on three major issues: Soviet membership in the United Nations, the future of Poland, and Soviet participation in the war against Japan. Stalin demanded 16 votes in the U.N. General Assembly, one for each republic in the Soviet Union. Roosevelt bargained him down to 3. The President was concerned about the question of Poland's sovereign independence. Stalin, whose army occupied Poland, replied

---

82. Hofstadter, *American Political Tradition*, p. 316.

83. Leuchtenburg, *FDR and the New Deal*, p. 42.

84. John G. Stoessinger, *Crusaders and Pragmatists: Movers of Modern American Foreign Policy*. New York: W. W. Norton & Co., Inc., 1979, p. 49.

that he would consider reorganizing the existing government on a "broader democratic basis." Roosevelt's belief in his personal charm and manipulative skill confronted the reality of Stalin's hardened attitude, based on Soviet military control of Eastern Europe. The President probably fared about as well as he could have under the circumstances.[85]

CONCLUSION

Presidential biographers have become increasingly sensitive to the impact of Presidential personality on the style and substance of decision making in the White House. Presidential personality may contribute to successful political leadership by promoting a realistic assessment of the capabilities and limitations of the Presidential office and its occupant. Franklin D. Roosevelt perhaps epitomizes the self-assured leader as President. His buoyant and confident personality encouraged an openness and diversity within his administration which functioned to maximize his information sources and political alternatives.

Psychobiographical analyses suggest that, to varying degrees, several postwar Presidents, including Truman, Eisenhower, Kennedy, and Ford have approximated the self-assured leader model.[86] Having had reasonably secure childhoods, these individuals developed the self-confidence which contributed to a generally positive outlook and a capacity for growth in office during their Presidencies. Analysis of Presidents Kennedy and Ford is complicated somewhat by their brief tenure in office, each having served less than three years.

Having for years been regarded by many historians and political scientists as a conservative and mediocre President, Eisenhower is currently the focus of a reevaluation. A more balanced image of Eisenhower is emerging, which portrays the President as a self-confident leader committed to systematic decision making through staff organization and teamwork. A man of broad military experience, President Eisenhower was committed to peace and refused to be

---

85. *Ibid.*, pp. 50–52.

86. In addition to Barber, *Presidential Character,* see also Merle Miller, *Plain Speaking: An Oral Biography of Harry S Truman,* New York: Berkley/ Putnam's, 1973; and J. F. terHorst, *Gerald Ford and the Future of the Presidency,* New York: The Third Press, 1974.

stampeded into hasty decisions. Although significantly different from Franklin Roosevelt in politics and style, Eisenhower, like Roosevelt, was able to sense the kind of political leadership called for by the times. President Eisenhower chose to lead with restraint and dignity, demonstrating a keen awareness of both the potential and the limitations of Presidential power.[87]

Events since Eisenhower's Presidency have served to emphasize the importance of Presidential personality in national politics. The personality of the President is an important factor influencing which alternatives are considered and which policies are promoted by the White House. Despite its postwar institutional expansion, the Presidency retains a very personal dimension. The modern Presidency has exhibited a high level of potential for reflecting, or perhaps magnifying, the personal insecurities of its occupants.

87. See, for example, R. Gordon Hoxie's evaluation of Eisenhower in Hoxie, *Command Decision and the Presidency,* pp. 244–259; see also Stephen E. Ambrose, "The Ike Age," *The New Republic,* May 9, 1981, pp. 26–34.

FURTHER READING

Barber, James David. *The Presidential Character: Predicting Performance in the White House* (2nd ed.). Englewood Cliffs, N.J.: Prentice-Hall Inc., 1977. A comparative analysis of the personalities, styles, and world views of 13 20th-century Presidents.

Burns, James McGregor. *Roosevelt: The Lion and the Fox*. New York: Harcourt Brace, 1956. An analysis of the personality and character of the only man to be elected President four times.

Carter, Jimmy. *Why Not the Best?* Nashville, Tenn.: Broadman Press, 1975. Jimmy Carter's autobiography, written prior to the 1976 election.

Clinch, Nancy Gager. *The Kennedy Neurosis*. New York: Grosset & Dunlap, Inc., 1973. A very unflattering psychobiographical analysis of the Kennedy clan.

Daniels, Jonathan. *The Man of Independence*. Philadelphia, Pa.: Lippincott, 1950. A detailed account of Harry S Truman's early life and entry into politics.

deMause, Lloyd, and Ebel, Henry (eds.). *Jimmy Carter and American Fantasy*. New York: Two Continents/Psychohistory Press, 1977. Five research associates of The Institute for Psychohistory analyze the character and politics of Jimmy Carter.

Eisenhower, Dwight D. *Mandate for Change*. New York: New American Library, 1963. The President's memoir of the White House years.

Evans, Rowland, and Novak, Robert. *Lyndon B. Johnson: The Exercise of Power*. New York: New American Library, 1966. A detailed account of Johnson's Presidency by two well-known Washington journalists.

Ford, Gerald. *A Time to Heal: The Autobiography of Gerald R. Ford*. New York: Harper and Row, 1979. The President's account of his political career and Presidency.

George, Alexander L., and George, Juliette L. *Woodrow Wilson and Colonel House: A Personality Study*. New York: Dover Publications, Inc., 1964. A highly regarded and thorough psychobiographical analysis of the character of Woodrow Wilson.

Glad, Betty *Jimmy Carter: In Search of the Great White House*. New York: W. W. Norton & Co., Inc., 1980. A detailed and penetrating analysis of the complex character of the man from Plains.

Hall, Calvin S. *A Primer of Freudian Psychology*. New York: Mentor Books, 1954. A concise summary of the assumptions of psychoanalytic theory.

Johnson, Lyndon B. *The Vantage Point: Perspectives of the Presidency, 1963–1969*. New York: Holt, Rinehart & Winston, 1971. The President's version of events during the tumultuous era of his administration.

Kearns, Doris. *Lyndon Johnson and The American Dream.* New York: New American Library (Signet), 1977. A fascinating psychobiographical portrait, remarkable for its insights and clarity of analysis.

Lasswell, Harold D. *Psychopathology and Politics.* New York: Viking Press, 1960. This pioneering work was originally published by the University of Chicago in 1930.

Leuchtenburg, William E. *Franklin Roosevelt and the New Deal, 1932-1940.* New York: Harper and Row, 1963. An historical treatment rich in detail.

Mazlish, Bruce, *In Search of Nixon: A Psychohistorical Inquiry.* Baltimore, Md.: Penguin Books, 1973. A character analysis of Richard Nixon's complex and puzzling personality.

Mazlish, Bruce, and Diamond, Edwin. *Jimmy Carter: An Interpretive Biography.* New York: Simon & Schuster, Inc., 1979. A relatively sympathetic analysis of Carter's character.

Miller, Merle. *Plain Speaking: An Oral Biography of Harry S Truman.* New York: Berkley/Putnam's, 1973. A series of interviews containing the President's retrospective reflections on his childhood, career, and Presidency.

Miller, Merle. *Lyndon: An Oral Biography.* New York: G. P. Putnam's Sons, 1980. Nearly 200 interviews are used to construct a portrait of Lyndon B. Johnson as he was seen by his family, friends, and enemies.

Murphy, John F. *The Pinnacle: The Contemporary American Presidency.* Philadelphia, Pa.: Lippincott, 1974. A concise and somewhat conservative historical analysis of Presidential administrations from Hoover through Nixon.

Nixon, Richard M. *Six Crises.* New York: Pyramid Books, 1968. Nixon's account of six significant events in his political career.

O'Donnell, Kenneth P., and Powers, David F., with Joe McCarthy. *Johnny We Hardly Knew Ye: Memories of John Fitzgerald Kennedy.* New York. Pocket Books, Div. of Simon & Schuster, Inc., 1973. The view from inside the White House during the Kennedy Presidency. O'Donnell and Powers were advisers to the President.

Phillips, Cabell. *The Truman Presidency.* New York: Macmillan Publishing Co., Inc., 1966. Regarded as one of the leading historical analyses of Harry Truman and his Presidency.

Smith, Hedrich, et al. *Reagan the Man, the President.* New York: Macmillan Publishing Co., Inc., 1981. Five *New York Times* correspondents attempt to assess the kind of President Ronald Reagan will be. The book includes background on the President's childhood, family, career, and service as Governor of California.

Sorenson, Theodore C. *Kennedy.* New York: Harper & Row Publishers, Inc., 1965. A sympathetic account by the President's friend, adviser, and speechwriter.

Stoessinger, John G. *Crusaders and Pragmatists: Movers of Modern American Foreign Policy.* New York: W. W. Norton & Co., Inc., 1979. American foreign policy analyzed in terms of the personalities of modern Presidents and key advisers.

terHorst, J. F. *Gerald Ford and the Future of the Presidency*. New York: The Third Press, 1974. Gerald Ford's life and political career as described by the President's former press secretary.

Truman, Harry S *Memoirs* (2 vols.). Vol. 1: *Year of Decisions*. Vol. 2: *Years of Trial*. Garden City, N.Y.: Doubleday & Co., Inc., 1955. President Truman's account of the events and decisions he made during the difficult period from 1945 through 1952.

Wicker, Tom. *JFK and LBJ: The Influence of Personality Upon Politics*. Baltimore, Md.: Penguin Books, 1969. Tom Wicker was chief Washington correspondent for *The New York Times* from 1964 through 1968 before becoming associate editor. This book is a comparative analysis of the Kennedy and Johnson administrations.

Chapter 11

Conclusion

The American Presidency must function within the constraints of a fragmented governmental structure and constitutional limitations on executive power. Traditional limitations on Presidential power have been augmented by several recent developments.

Growth of the Presidency as an Institution   The creation of the Executive Office of the President and the staff system was intended as a means of insuring an adequate flow of competent advice to the President, as well as of providing the President with necessary staff assistance. As the Executive Office has expanded, the Presidency has assumed some of the characteristics of a bureaucracy. Key members of the White House staff have become increasingly important as Presidential advisers. Frequently, senior staff positions have been filled by persons from the President's campaign organization, rather than by individuals with expertise in an area of policy. Relations within the White House staff have tended to be secretive, frequently emphasizing loyalty at the expense of critical analysis. In addition to potential for isolation and information distortion, the institutionalized Presidency has demonstrated a propensity for magnifying the President's personal insecurities.

Decline of Public Confidence and Trust in the President   Among the most dramatic of recent developments relating to the Presidency has been the systematic erosion of the long-standing reservoir of public trust and approval of the President. The causes of this phenomenon are complex, and include public disillusionment about the Vietnam War, revelations of government misconduct and deception, and growing public mistrust of institutions in general. These trends have been accompanied by decreasing public interest and involvement in Presidential elections. The mobilization of public opinion into effective political support has never been an easy task for Presidents. It has been made more difficult partly because of the public's response to the behavior and policies of recent Presidents.

Changes in the Presidential Nominating Process   The proliferation of Presidential primary elections has effectively removed the nomination of Presidents from the hands of government officials and party leaders. By heavily emphasizing organizational and campaigning skills, the new nominating system does not effectively test other skills which are essential to Presidential leadership, including the nominee's abilities at bargaining and persuasion. In addition, the primary system does not automatically assure support for the nominee among the party's leading politicians and public officials. In brief, requisite skills and political support that would contribute to effective Presidential leadership have become secondary criteria in the Presidential selection process.

Changes in the President's Powers   In response to abuse of power, excessive secrecy, and deception on the part of Presidents, the Congress enacted a number of statutory restrictions on executive power. These have ranged from relatively innocuous provisions for clarifying the President's emergency powers and requiring greater accountability in the area of executive agreements, to concrete limitations on the President's power to impound appropriated funds, and the ambiguous and controversial War Powers Resolution. Although these provisions have left the powers of the Presidency basically intact, they are perhaps indicative of a greater willingness of the Congress to challenge Presidential prerogatives.

The post-Vietnam era has been a difficult one for the nation and its Presidents. The Lyndon Johnson administration began with great promise and then floundered in the quagmire of an unpopular Presidential war. Having been elected by a landslide in 1964, President

Johnson gave up his office under fire four years later. Despite some significant accomplishments in the area of foreign relations, President Richard Nixon was eventually forced to resign in disgrace. Gerald Ford, Nixon's appointed successor, was defeated for reelection, and President Jimmy Carter was subsequently repudiated by the voters.

In his analysis of the post-imperial Presidency, columnist Joseph Kraft concludes that the difficulties of recent Presidents cannot be attributed only to bad fortune or idiosyncratic quirks of personality. The last four Presidents have been disparate in personality, politics, regional base, and religion. "The nature of the trouble lies in a mismatch between responsibilities and resources, promise and performance, expectations and abilities."[1]

Political science literature is replete with proposals for strengthening the President's hand vis-a-vis the Congress or the bureaucracy.[2] Few of these are likely to be enacted, given the post-Watergate climate of expectations. A more realistic alternative may be the redefinition of the responsibilities of the Presidency and the expectations we have regarding the office. The scope of this task is not confined to paradoxical and inconsistent popular expectations about the Presidency. Politicians, opinion leaders, and media analysts must assume a more realistic stance regarding the responsibilities and limitations of Presidential power.

In his discussion of the Ultimate Modern Presidency, Stephen Hess, Brookings Institution scholar, has proposed redefining the tasks of Presidents to include only those activities that they must perform and that cannot be performed by others. In this role as Chief Political Officer of the United States, the President's primary responsibilities are "to make a relatively small number of highly significant political decisions each year, such as setting national priorities, which he does through the budget and his legislative proposals, and devising policy to insure the security of the country, with special attention to those situations that could involve the nation in war."[3] Less important functions, particularly the details of implementing policy

1. Joseph Kraft, "The Post-Imperial Presidency," *New York Times Magazine*, November 2, 1980, p. 31.

2. For an authoritative discussion of various proposals for reforming the Presidency, see Thomas E. Cronin, *The State of the Presidency* (2nd ed.). Boston: Little Brown and Company, 1980, pp. 340–366.

3. Stephen Hess, "The Ultimate Modern Presidency," in John C. Hoy and Melvin H. Bernstein (eds.), *The Effective President*. Pacific Palisades, Ca.: Palisades Publishers, 1976, p. 125.

and managing the bureaucracy, can be delegated to department heads. While this is a more modest definition of the Presidency than our leaders and some scholars have led us to expect, it has the advantage of not overloading the institution beyond its capacity to effect change and deliver services.

Likewise, Thomas E. Cronin, has concluded that the President cannot act as a serious initiator of reform in more than a few areas at a time. "If a President is forced to respond to all the major issues of the day, he doubtless will be forced to respond mainly on the plane of symbolic and superficial politics."[4]

An assessment of the role of the modern Presidency in providing national political leadership must consider the limitations, as well as the responsibilities, of the office. The appropriate Presidential leadership strategy is to use the visibility and powers of the office to clarify and emphasize a small number of national priorities, and to focus the energy and resources of the Presidency on these essential areas. The most basic of these is national security policy, and the Presidency is reasonably will equipped to provide leadership in this area. Presidential leadership in the definition of national economic priorities will be increasingly important in the foreseeable future. Effective leadership in this area constitutes a formidable challenge for the President. Inflation, steady growth in Federal budget deficits, soaring energy costs, and declining capital investment and productivity are problems that will not be remedied easily. The uncoordinated and highly political nature of government economic policy making will not make the President's task any easier. Nonetheless, the President must concentrate budgetary, legislative, and persuasive energies to address the nation's economic difficulties.

THE REAGAN ADMINISTRATION
AND SUPPLY-SIDE ECONOMICS

Since the early 1970's, a condition of gradually worsening inflation has plagued the economies of the United States and numerous other Western industrialized nations. Specifically, in the American case, after a surge of inflation immediately following World War II, prices

---

4. Cronin, *State of the Presidency*, p. 375.

stabilized and the economy entered a period of expansion. From 1955 to 1965, the rate of inflation was only 2.5% a year. With the additional fiscal stimulus of government spending for the Vietnam War and the Great Society programs, the inflation rate climbed to nearly 6% a year between 1965 and 1972. Fueled by increasingly large Federal deficits and skyrocketing energy costs after the Organization of Petroleum Exporting Countries (OPEC) quadrupled the price of oil, inflation reached a double-digit rate by 1979.[5]   Projections by economists indicate that if this kind of inflation continues until the year 2050, a loaf of bread will cost $37.50, a medium-sized car will sell for around $281,000, and a modest home will cost about $3.4 million.[6]

Causes and Solutions

Economists are by no means in agreement about the causes or solutions for these economic problems. Analyses frequently focus upon several interrelated factors, including indiscriminate deficit spending by the Federal government, spiraling energy costs, and declining productivity in American industry.   Most significant for purposes of this discussion, the Presidential election of 1980 swept into power executive officials and Presidential advisers committed to testing a different set of assumptions about the proper role of government economic policy.

Deficit Spending President Ronald Reagan and his economic advisers have approached economic management by emphasizing invigoration of the supply-side of the American business system. While by no means an unorthodox approach to government-business relations, supply-side economics is a departure from the manner in which government economic policy has been implemented by recent Democratic and Republican administrations. Since the early 1960's, the United States and many other Western industrialized societies have employed government economic policy, especially fiscal policy,

5. Albert T. Sommers, "The Challenge of Inflation in the 1980s", in Walter E. Hoadley (ed.), *The Economy and the President: 1980 and Beyond.* Englewood Cliffs, N.J.: Prentice-Hall, Inc., 1980, p. 35.

6. Reported by United Press International in *The Dayton Daily News,* November 22, 1979, p. 6.

in a manner that stimulated aggregate demand. Pursuit of full-emloy-
ment policies and expansion of social outlays has led to changes
in the pattern of Federal spending and to dependence on deficit
financing. The spending side of the budget has been swollen by
transfers to individuals and to state and local governments. (See
Table 7.2.)

The pattern of persistent deficit spending by the Federal government is shown in Table 11.1. It is apparent from the data in this
table that the Federal government has begun to rely regularly on
deficit financing, and that this has been true of both Republican and
Democratic administrations. Since 1960, the Federal government
has operated at a deficit every year but one (1969). The notion of
using deficit spending to stimulate the economy during a recession
has been supplanted by the use of deficit financing simply to enable
the government to meet its budgetary obligations. The really large
deficits began during the Lyndon Johnson administration when the
President opted for a policy known as "guns and butter." This
policy operated on the questionable assumption that it was possible
to pay for a war in Vietnam and progressive social programs without
raising taxes. The deficits have grown increasingly larger since then
because of inevitable increases in payments for social programs in
which benefits rise automatically with the cost of living. Payments

for indexed programs and entitlements now constitute almost half of Federal budget outlays.

Causes of Inflation These increasing budget deficits are considered by President Reagan and his advisers to be an essential contributor to the inflation rate. According to the assumptions of supply-side economics, the fiscal stimulus provided by Federal deficit spending, in conjunction with easily available consumer credit, spurs the economy in an inflationary manner. This situation is aggravated when, in response to demand-inspired inflation, the government imposes severe monetary constraints by driving up interest rates and making

Table 11.1 Federal Budget Receipts, Outlays, and Debt: ars.
1960 to 1981, in billions of dollars.

Year	Receipts	Outlays	Surplus or Deficit (−)	Outstanding National Debt
1960	92.5	92.2	.3	290.9
1961	94.4	97.8	− 3.4	292.9
1962	99.7	106.8	− 7.1	303.3
1963	106.6	111.3	− 4.8	310.8
1964	112.7	118.6	− 5.9	316.8
1965	116.8	118.4	− 1.6	323.2
1966	130.9	134.7	− 3.8	329.5
1967	149.6	158.3	− 8.7	341.3
1968	153.7	178.8	−25.2	369.8
1969	187.8	184.5	3.2	367.1
1970	193.7	196.6	− 2.8	382.6
1971	188.4	211.4	−23.0	409.5
1972	208.6	232.0	−23.4	437.3
1973	232.2	247.1	−14.8	468.4
1974	264.9	269.6	− 4.7	486.2
1975	281.0	326.1	−45.1	544.1
1976	300.0	366.4	−66.4	631.9
1976, TQ*	81.7	94.7	−13.0	646.4
1977	357.8	402.7	−45.0	709.1
1978	402.0	450.8	−48.8	780.4
1979	456.0	493.4	−37.4	839.2
1980, est.	523.8	563.6	−39.8	892.8
1981, est.	610.0	662.0	−52.0	939.4

*TQ = Transition Quarter (See Table 7.1)

Source: *Statistical Abstract of the United States* (100th ed.), 1979 U.S. Department of Commerce, Bureau of the Census. Table No. 427, p. 256. Updated by the author, using estimates reported by the N.Y. Times Service in the *Dayton Daily News,* December 13, 1980, p. 1.

credit less available and more expensive for business. The effect of government policy has been to stimulate consumption while shrinking investment. The period between 1965 and 1981 was characterized by increasingly powerful cycles of fiscal stimulus (deficit spending) followed by monetary restraint during the late stages of expansion. The severe applications of monetary restraint in response to inflation acted to truncate investment and capital expansion. At precisely the time when business investment was most appropriate, the credit was not available. These cyclical interruptions of investment have contributed to inadequate and aged capital stock and physical plant, resulting in a decline in productivity and deterioration of the competitive position of American industry.[7]

In summary, the emphasis of government economic policy has, for years, been to stimulate demand while taking supply pretty much for granted except during defense emergencies. A shift in government policy to emphasize supply management would focus on increasing investment, productivity, research and development, and savings. The goal of such a policy shift would be the generation of a level of investment that is adequate to maintain capital stock in a condition of growth. Supply-side economics emphasizes real economic growth and rising productivity as the best hedge against inflation. Consequently, in addition to budgetary restraint by the government, supply-side economists advocate changes in policy that would encourage citizens to save money, and businesses to invest in capital modernization. In the absence of real economic growth, continued increases in wages and government spending are bound to be inflationary. Investment and capital expansion are regarded as the keys to returning the dollar to a sound and stable basis.

Prescriptions for strengthening the nation's economy are complicated considerably by the growing dependence of the United States on foreign sources of energy. In 1980, the United States imported more than 40% of its petroleum needs, as compared to about 25% 10 years earlier. In 1978, imported oil cost the United States $43 billion. It is estimated that the cost of imported oil will be at least $112 billion in 1982, and will approach $170 billion by 1985. Aside from the political implications for American national security policy, increasing energy dependence is a major contributor to inflation.

---

7. Sommers, *"Challenge of Inflation in the 1980's,"* pp. 45–51. Sommers' analysis includes a thorough discussion of the assumptions of supply-side economics. See, also, Felix G. Rohatyn, "Our Economic Crisis and What to Do About It," *New York,* June 16, 1980, pp. 12 ff.

Authoritative estimates are that the cost of oil imported into the United States accounted for about one-fourth of the rate of inflation in 1980.[8] Since the Arab oil embargo of 1973, the President and the Congress have been unable to agree on an energy policy to reduce American dependence on foreign oil, or to manage the balance-of-trade deficits associated with it.

Presidential Impact Of the various areas of government economic policy, including taxes, spending, and interest rates, the President can have the greatest impact on government spending. The authority to initiate the Federal budget is one of the President's most effective economic tools. President Reagan chose to begin the reordering of government economic priorities by recommending significant cuts in government spending. While it is doubtful that all of the President's recommended cuts will be enacted by the Congress, it is likely that many of them will.

Beyond the power to initiate cuts in the budget, significant economic innovations will require the President to concentrate legislative and persuasive efforts to secure the cooperation of the Congress, business, labor, and consumers. A significant portion of the public and the Congress tends to regard increased tax incentives for business investment and proposals to accelerate the rate at which capital costs are recovered (depreciation allowances) as little more than government giveaways to big business. Selling these ideas as essential for the reindustrialization of America may be a difficult persuasive task.

It is apparent from this brief discussion that leadership in the area of government economic policies will be a priority for Presidents in the foreseeable future. The means for shaping effective economic policy do not rest solely in the President's hands. The President is incapable, by himself, of requiring the nation to adopt sensible oil-import policies, to save more money, and to increase the rates of capital investment and research and development. It is the President, however, who possesses the leverage to begin moving the Federal budget in the direction of less inflationary fiscal policies. Likewise, it is the President who possesses the visibility and the budgetary and legislative initiative to become the catalyst for inspiring new directions in government economic policy. Not since the New Deal era has the executive leadership of the United States been

8. Otto Eckstein, "Choices for the 1980's: Core Inflation, Productivity, Capital Supply and Demand Management," in Hoadley, *Economy and the President,* pp. 95–96.

so willing to reconsider assumptions about the appropriate relationship between government and business. The United States may be
on the verge of a new economic experiment with significant implications for us all.

FURTHER READING

Heineman, Ben W., and Hessler, Curtis A. *Memorandum for the President: A Strategic Approach to Domestic Affairs in the 1980's.* New York: 1980. A realistic assessment of modern Presidential government, written by two Carter administration assistant secretaries.

Hoadley, Walter E. (ed.). *The Economy and the President: 1980 and Beyond.* Englewood Cliffs, N.J., Prentice-Hall, Inc., 1980. An assortment of economists and financiers analyze the relationship between government and the economy.

Hoy, John C., and Bernstein, Melvin H. (eds.). *The Effective President.* Pacific Palisades, Ca.: Palisades Publishers, 1976. A symposium on the state of the American President, including contributions by scholars, journalists, and politicians.

Smith, Hedrick, et al. *Reagan The Man, The President.* New York: The MacMillan Co., 1981. Five *New York Times* correspondents attempt to assess Ronald Reagan's potential and likely performance as President.

Appendix

Table A.   Popular and Electoral College Vote for President: 1948-1980.

Year	Candidates	Party	Popular Votes (in thousands)	%	Electoral Votes	%
1948	Harry S. Truman	Democrat	24,179	49.6	303	57
	Thomas E. Dewey	Republican	21,991	45.1	189	36
	J. Strom Thurmond	States' Rights Democrat	1,169	2.4	39	7
	Henry A. Wallace	Progressive	1,157	2.4	—	—
	Others		290	.6	—	—
1952	Dwight D. Eisenhower	Republican	33,936	55.1	442	83
	Adlai E. Stevenson	Democrat	27,315	44.4	89	17
	Others		300	.5	—	—
1956	Dwight D. Eisenhower	Republican	35,590	57.4	457	86
	Adlai E. Stevenson	Democrat	26,023	42.0	73	14
	Others		410	.6	1	—
1960	John F. Kennedy	Democrat	34,227	49.7	303	56
	Richard M. Nixon	Republican	34,108	49.5	219	41
	Harry F. Byrd	Independent	—	—	15	3
	Unpledged Electors	Democrat	116	.2	—	—
	Others		385	.5	—	—
1964	Lyndon B. Johnson	Democrat	43,130	61.1	486	90
	Barry M. Goldwater	Republican	27,178	38.5	52	10
	Others		337	.5	—	—

Table A. Popular and Electoral College Vote for President: 1948–1980. *(continued)*

Year	Candidates	Party	Popular Votes (in thousands)	%	Electoral Votes	%
1968	Richard M. Nixon	Republican	31,785	43.4	301	56
	Hubert H. Humphrey	Democrat	31,275	42.7	191	35.5
	George C. Wallace	American	9,906	13.5	46	8.5
	Others	Independent	243	.3	—	—
1972	Richard M. Nixon	Republican	47,170	60.7	520	96.6
	George S. McGovern	Democrat	29,170	37.5	17	3.2
	John G. Schmitz	American	1,091	1.4	—	—
	Others		295	.4	1	—
1976	James E. Carter, Jr.	Democrat	40,831	50.1	297	55
	Gerald R. Ford	Republican	39,148	48.0	240	45
	Eugene J. McCarthy	Independent	757	.9	—	—
	Others		721	.9	1	—
1980	Ronald W. Reagan	Republican	42,951	51.0	489	91
	James E. Carter, Jr.	Democrat	34,663	41.1	49	9
	John Anderson	Independent	5,551	6.7	—	—

Source: Figures for 1948–1976 Compiled from the *Statistical Abstract of the United States* (100th ed.), 1979. United States Department of Commerce, Bureau of the Census, Table No. 809, p. 496. Figures for 1980 are from the *Statistical Abstract of the United States* (101st ed.), 1980, p. 498.

Index